CIDER

Making, Using & Enjoying
Sweet & Hard Cider

Annie Proulx & Lew Nichols

A Storey Publishing Book

STOREY COMMUNICATIONS, INC.
SCHOOLHOUSE ROAD
POWNAL, VERMONT 05261

This book is dedicated to cider apples
and amateur cidermakers everywhere

The mission of Storey Communications is to serve our customers by publishing practical information that encourages personal independence in harmony with the environment.

Edited by Mary Grace Butler and Pamela Lappies
Cover design by Eugenie Seidenberg Delaney
Front cover photograph by Kevin Kennefick, back cover photograph by Cindy McFarland
Text design by Cindy McFarland
Text production by Eugenie Seidenberg Delaney
Line drawings on pages 5, 6, 17, 140, 141 (top drawing) by Beverly Duncan, and by Judy Elaison on page 141 (bottom)
Indexed by Susan Olason, Indexes and Knowledge Maps

Printed in the United States by R. R. Donnelley
10 9 8 7 6 5 4 3 2 1

Library of Congress Cataloging-in-Publication Data

Proulx, Annie.
    Cider : making, using & enjoying sweet & hard cider / Annie Proulx & Lew Nichols.— 2nd ed.
          p.   cm.
    Rev. ed of: Sweet & hard cider. c 1980.
    "A Storey Publishing Book"
    Includes index.
    1. Cider.   2. Apples.   I. Nichols, Lew.   II. Proulx, Annie. Sweet & hard cider.
    III. Title.
TP563.P76   1997
641.2'6—dc21
                                                 97-12169
                                                  CIP

CONTENTS

ACKNOWLEDGMENTS

Scores of people — amateur and commercial cidermakers, professional cider researchers, librarians, curators, tax authorities, nutritionists, chemists, pomologists, nurserymen and -women, apple growers, and many others — have given us suggestions, explanations, tours, rulings, services, opinions, their time, and an occasional sample of the subject.

Our sincerest thanks go to: R. L. La Belle, Jerome Van Buren, and Roger Way of the N.Y. State Agricultural Experiment Station, Geneva; F. W. Williams of the Long Ashton Research Station, Long Ashton, Bristol, England; J.-F. Drilleau of the Station de recherches cidricole, Le Rheu, France; W. P. Mohr of the Agriculture Canada Smithfield Experimental Farm, Ontario; J. A. Kitson of the Agriculture Canada Research Station, Summerland, B.C.; R. L. Granger of Agriculture Canada Station de recherches, Saint-Jean, Québec; R. J. Traverse, Newfoundland Dept. of Forestry and Agriculture, St. Johns; C. G. Embree, Nova Scotia Dept. of Agriculture and Marketing, Kentiville; E. N. Estabrooks, New Brunswick Dept. of Agriculture and Rural Development, Fredericton; E. J. Hogue, Canadian Society for Horticultural Science.

Also, F. P. Corey of the International Apple Institute, Washington, D.C.; L. D. Tukey of the Dept. of Horticulture, Pennsylvania State University; R. E. Daugherty, chief, Rulings Branch, U.S. Dept. of the Treasury; Claude Bourgeois and Luc Désautels of the Société des Alcools du Québec; Normand Cormier and Marie-Andrée Beaupré of the Bibliothèque Nationale du Québec; the McLennan Library of McGill University, Montreal; library staff at MacDonald College, Ste. Anne de Bellevue, Québec; Library of the Jardin Botanique, Montreal; Bailey Library at the University of Vermont, Burlington; Ms. I. Peggy Keeton of the Long Ashton Research Station Library, Long Ashton, Bristol, England; the Northeast Regional Library, St. Johnsbury, Vt.; the libraries of the University of Massachusetts, Amherst; Dr. G. S. Carlson of Palo Alto, Ca.; C. D. Osborne of H. P. Bulmer Ltd., Hereford, England; Alain Lecours of La Cidrerie du Québec, Ltd.; and Ms. Gail Hyde of the Geneva Station Library.

The help of nurserymen and apple growers Lewis Hill of Greensboro, Vt.; K. E. Parr of East Burke, Vt.; Hertel Gagnon of Compton; Paul Gadbois of Rougemont, and Marc Bieler of Frelighsburg, all in Québec, is also appreciated. And thanks to cidermakers S. Thatcher of Sandford, Somerset, and Robert and Hartley Williams of Backwell, Bristol, England; Maurice Lemoine of Janzé, Brittany, France, and Herbert Ogden of Windsor, Vt.

INTRODUCTION

Interest in cidermaking and cider drinking has had an explosive resurgence in this country in recent years. Hard cider is the fastest-growing segment of the liquor industry, riding on the coattails of the microbrew surge, and is considered by many to be the drink of the future. What many people may not know is that cider, both sweet and hard, was the drink of America's past.

Cider drinking has been an American tradition since the days of the Mayflower, whose passengers brought it with them from Europe. By 1638, barrels of cider could be found in the cellars of virtually every farmhouse and city home in New England. Cider, truly the outstanding American beverage, was regularly enjoyed by many notable historical figures. John Adams, second president of the United States, drank a tankard of cider every morning before breakfast, and lived to the age of 91. In 1840, the Whig Party nominated William Henry Harrison as its candidate for president, and the campaign symbol was a barrel of cider. This "Cider Campaign," in which the Whigs served free cider to all who could or would vote, brought Harrison to a landslide victory. Obviously, the voters knew the true meaning of the American spirit! Between 1870 and 1892, cider consumption rose a healthy 200 percent to become the most popular drink in America.

Early in the twentieth century, poet Robert Frost wrote "In A Glass of Cider," a loving tribute to the effects of drinking cider. And on hot African nights, while on rugged lion safaris, Ernest Hemingway's favorite drink was — you guessed it — cider.

The cultural phenomenon in the United States during the late 1980s and early 1990s of home brewing and microbrew beers has enticed the American palate to try varied styles of old-time recipes. The relative ease with which one can make cider has contributed to this growing popularity. Although there are technical aspects and personal preferences involved, essentially all you need is the apple — nothing added, nothing taken away — to make a delicious sweet cider that when allowed to ferment will create a sparkling hard cider that rivals the finest of champagnes.

Until about 1990 there were very few domestic ciders commercially available. For the most part, the only imported ciders available commercially in the United States were from the United Kingdom and France, two regions that have been producing cider for many centuries. Apples specifically grown and harvested for European cider are selected for their sugar, acidity, and tannin contents and are not commonly produced in the United States. These bittersweet and bittersharp apples, as they are called, produce a cider tannic and somewhat bitter in taste. Although these imported ciders are tremendously popular in Europe, they were not to the American taste and were unable to make a strong impact in the American market.

The current cider market consists of dozens of commercially produced domestic ciders with more popping up every day. Unlike the imported ciders, most American ciders are not made from bittersweet and bittersharp varieties. In general, American ciders are made from sweeter, less tannic apples commonly grown in this country. The ciders from these varieties produce a fruity, somewhat sweeter, less tannic flavor than the European ciders and have been extremely successful in the United States. Current marketing data estimate that the annual American consumption of 3.7 million gallons of hard cider may more than triple by the end of the century to more than 11 million gallons.

This surge of interest in cider has created new opportunities for traditional apple growers as well as for entrepreneurs. The wonderful book you are holding now contains all the information necessary to make whatever style cider you choose, either sweet or hard. Enjoy your work and its results and remember, cidermaking is not an exact science — it's an art.

— John Vittori
Berkshire Cider Company and
Johnny Mash Original American Cider
Richmond, Massachusetts

CIDERMAKING:
What You Need and How to Do It

*H*undreds of variables affect cidermaking — the acidity of the juice, the weather, the varieties of apples used, the bacteria in and around the juice and the conditions for their growth, the size of the cidermaking operation itself and the nature of the equipment, the use of sweeteners or chemical additives, different procedures in the making proscribed by law or custom, and, finally, the regional tastes and preferences of the cider drinkers. Yet all cider goes through three simple stages. In autumn, the ripe fruit is crushed; then the juice is pressed out. The juice may be fermented for weeks or months, but usually by late winter the finished cider is bottled.

CIDERMAKING, STEP BY STEP

Here is the basic 12-step sequence of events in cidermaking, followed by a discussion of cidermaking machinery and equipment, instruments, chemicals and additives, and then the when, why, and how of using them.

Step 1: The Harvest

Cidermaking begins in the late summer or fall when the apples are ripe. Ripe apples have brown seeds, which are a good test for ripeness. Green, immature apples make poor cider. Use sound, ripe apples of several varieties to make a balanced cider blend. Don't use windfalls, for they usually harbor *acetobacter* (the active bacteria in vinegar making) and may have developed the toxin patulin if they have been lying on damp ground for several days. A few worms won't hurt the cider, and scabby apples are fine, but no rotten apples should get in with your good cider fruits.

Step 2: "Sweating"

Store your apples in a clean, odor-free area. Don't heap the fruit directly on the ground, but keep it on a tarp or concrete or a wooden platform. When the apples have mellowed and softened to the point where a good firm squeeze leaves finger impressions in the fruit — about a week to ten days — they are ready for grinding. This *"sweating"* makes the apples easier to grind, increases the sugar in the juice, and allows good flavor to develop. Some North American apple varieties do not benefit from this mellowing period, notably Jonathan, Newtown, and Rome Beauty; they should be pressed ripe and freshly picked.

Step 3: Washing

Before milling, wash the apples to remove leaves, twigs, harmful bacteria, insects, and any spray residues. Throw out any rotten or moldy fruits, and cut brown spots out of otherwise sound apples. Any clean tub or vat will do for apple washing, though the job is best done outdoors. Fill the tank halfway with clean water and tip the apples in. A powerful stream of water from a garden hose played over the fruit will finish the job. The clean, ripe, mellow fruit is now ready for grinding.

Step 4: Grinding

It is important to grind, crush, or mill the apples to a fine pulp to extract the maximum amount of juice. This pulpy mass of ground-up apples is called the *pomace*. A motor-driven hammer mill will produce a very fine pomace, while an antique hand grinder may produce only coarse, chunky particles. As a general rule, the finer the consistency of the pomace, the greater the yield of juice. True European cider apples, crab and wild apples, grind into a drier, more granular mass than dessert varieties, which reduce to a soupy applesauce.

Grinding can be done with a hand- or power-driven home mill, at a commercial cider mill, or, with very small quantities of apples, in a kitchen blender. Most apple-crushing machinery takes the whole fruit, but if you use a kitchen blender, core and quarter but do not peel the fruit before blending it.

North American machinery built to crush soft dessert apples may jam and balk when small, hard crab or wild apples are fed in. Owners of some cider mills that custom press are unwilling to "break" these hard little apples. The recommended method with such fruits is to mill them in a hand grinder, grinding the pulp twice since the apples often escape.

If you plan to blend the different juices or the finished varietal ciders, of course you must keep the different varieties of apples separate while you grind and press.

Grind the apples to a pulp to make the pomace. Apples may be ground whole, including cores and skin.

Unless you are making French cider (see *Chapter 2*), the freshly ground pomace should be pressed soon if not immediately after milling. Letting the pomace stand unpressed attracts wasps and vinegar flies, greatly increasing the chances of acetobacter contamination, while oxidation turns both pulp and juice dark brown. Your equipment largely dictates your procedures. With some home grinder/press cider mills it is possible for two people to grind and press simultaneously. With smaller rigs it's more convenient to grind all of one variety or the whole apple pile, and then proceed to the pressing operation. You may wish to grind and then press a small portion of your apples every day until you are through, or to have a marathon grinding-pressing day. If you are fermenting the juice of varieties of apples that ripen at different times, you will mill and press several times as each variety comes into maturity.

Step 5: Pressing

The cider press (or "wring," as it was called many years ago) exerts pressure on the milled apple pulp until all the juice has flowed from the ruptured fruit cells.

In the old days, the pulp was wrapped in "cheeses" of twisted straw. Today, press cloths and bags are used to hold the milled pulp. These are

usually made of nylon — easy to clean and sturdy enough to withstand many pressings. According to the type of press used, the pulp may be dumped onto press cloths, which are folded over and built up in many layers within a series of racks, or poured into a bag that fits inside the slatted pomace container of a "tub press." As pressure is applied, the juice flows out. As the flow of liquid lessens, more pressure is exerted until the last reluctant dribbles of juice are squeezed out.

A pressing takes about half an hour in most cider mills and with most home presses, but some cidermakers like to keep pressure on the pulp overnight or at least for several hours. Juice yields are greater, and

As the cidermaker presses the juice from the pulp, the "must" flows out below into a plastic or stainless-steel container.

the liquid is finer and clearer. The effect of air on the juice gives it a rich brown color, but the risk of acetobacter contamination is greater.

As the juice pours from the press, a trough or funnel channels it into a plastic or stainless-steel collecting vessel. Do not use copper, aluminum, iron, galvanized metal, or chipped enamel containers for holding apple juice. The acid in the juice will react with the metal, giving the cider off-flavor and -colors. An easy way to ruin good cider is to collect the fresh juice in an old milk can or a chipped canning kettle.

The fresh, unstrained juice, now called *"must,"* is poured into fermentation vats. These can be as small as a gallon jug or as large as a huge commercial tank. Don't expose the juice to air and insects but funnel it into fermentation containers as soon as the pressing is over.

Step 6: Blending

Different varieties of apples are blended for well-balanced finished cider; juices of aromatic, astringent, and acid-tart apples are added to a neutral or bland juice base until the mixture tastes right to the maker.

Popular proportions are:

Juice Type	Percent of Juice Total
Neutral base	30–60
Tart	10–20
Aromatic	10–20
Astringent	5–20

The more common North American varieties in these classifications are listed in the directions for *Basic Still Blended Cider from North American Varieties* on page 61.

BLENDING STAGES

Blending different varieties of apples will help you produce a well-balanced cider. The blending may be done at any of the following stages:

→ **Before grinding.** It is easiest to blend the apples before they are ground into pomace, but the cidermaker can only guess at the results. Most commercial cider mills grind mixed apples.

→ **Before fermentation.** The fresh juices are blended after pressing. Use your nose to judge the most aromatic juice, a hydrometer to measure the sugar content, an acid tester to gauge the level of acid, and your taste buds to test for the astringency that gives cider good flavor and body. The hydrometer measures the sugar and the potential alcohol that can be made from the amount of sugar in the juice. Using the hydrometer and acid-testing equipment is explained in the next section.

→ **After fermentation.** The different varieties of juice may be fermented separately to "dryness" (the near-complete conversion of sugar to alcohol that occurs during fermentation) and blended after fermentation but just before bottling. Blending at this time gives the greatest control over the quality of the finished cider. If you make cider from varieties that mature at different times, this is the stage at which to blend.

Step 7: Testing

It is important to know the sugar and acid levels in the fresh juice. The sugar will be converted into alcohol during fermentation, and

knowing the amount of sugar in the fresh juice gives the maker information on the alcoholic strength of the finished product. You may have to add honey or sugar to get a higher level of alcohol. As the fermentation proceeds, the acid level should drop *unless* the cider has been contaminated by acetobacter and the acetic acid of vinegar is being manufactured. Checking with acid-testing equipment before and after fermentation can be more reassuring to an amateur cidermaker than suspicious tasting. Write the measurements down in a notebook.

Step 8: Fermentation

Alcoholic fermentation is the process in which simple sugars are converted into alcohol and carbon dioxide through the growth of certain yeasts when conditions are right. The basic, natural fermentation of cider is often in two stages.

The first stage is one in which the yeast flora in the juice are nourished by the natural hexose sugars, converting them into alcohol and carbon dioxide. The cider may "boil over" in the violence of early fermentation before it settles down to a steady hissing, bubbling ferment that can last for weeks or even months, depending on the temperature and the juice constituents. When no more sugar is available to the yeasts for conversion into alcohol, the fermentation slows, then stops. The yeast cells eventually die off for lack of nourishment. At this point the cider is said to have fermented to dryness. Now it is usually drawn off its lees (dregs) into another vessel for the second stage of fermentation.

The second fermentation occurs when lactic acid bacteria in the cider ferment the natural malic acid into carbon dioxide and lactic acid. Lactic acid is more subdued and mellow than malic acid, so a malo-lactic fermentation gives a smoother, gentler cider and is very desirable if the cider is harsh and acidic at the end of the first fermentation. A malo-lactic fermentation usually occurs spontaneously after the first fermentation when the cider has been drained off its dregs into a storage container. If the cider, at the end of the first fermentation, is still very acidic it is often allowed to *stand on its lees* for a month to encourage the malo-lactic fermentation. Low-acid ciders never stand on their lees, but are racked off, or drained from their lees, as soon as fermentation ceases. The importance of testing for acid is clear.

The cidermaker's role in the fermentation process calls for pouring the freshly pressed, tested juice into the fermenting vessel, and adjusting

What To Do with the Pomace?

After the juice has been pressed from the apple pulp, you are left with cakes or sheets of nearly dry, compacted pomace, the skins and solids of the apples that are loaded with seeds and still contain plenty of sugar, tannins, flavor, and pectin. The dry pomace can be used in many ways.

→ **Livestock feed:** Dry or wet apple pomace, mixed one-to-four with other forage, may be fed to livestock such as cows and pigs. According to Dr. James Wadsworth of the University of Vermont Extension Service, apple pomace aids the animals' digestions, and they relish the flavor. Do not feed the pomace straight and unadulterated to livestock, for it can cause diarrhea. Commercial cider mills often sell their pomace to dairy farmers.

→ **Seedling stock:** If you want to grow your own seedling stock for hardy grafting stock, spread the seedy pomace in a clearing or unused field, or pick out the seeds and start them in a seedling bed. In England, the practice of spreading pomace directly on the fields as a fertilizer in the old days produced many wild apple-crab trees.

→ **Weed killer and brush reducer:** Pomace, spread directly on the ground, discourages the growth of noxious weeds and brush due to its high acid content.

→ **Compost:** Pomace may be added to the compost heap — a layer of pomace, a sprinkling of lime, a layer of soil — until the heap is well built up. Let it mature two years before using it on your garden. Never spread fresh apple pomace directly on your garden; it is too acidic. You could also end up with innumerable apple seedlings in your potato patch.

the chemical composition of the juice to be certain of a good ferment. Since nature does not always distribute good sugar levels, the best yeasts, the right amounts of acids, nitrogen, tannins, and other important elements in the juice, nor provide precisely the right conditions for a perfect fermentation, the crafty hand of the cidermaker may have to rearrange things. With experience comes skill. Here are the most common additions to the must. How much and how to use these additives is discussed in detail in the next section.

SO$_2$, or sulfur dioxide. This "sterilizer" is added to the freshly pressed juice before fermentation begins — right after the juice is poured from the collecting vessel into the fermenting tank. The sulfited juice is allowed to stand for twenty-four hours, during which time most of the sickness-causing bacteria and undesirable yeasts in the must will be killed. Enough of the "good" fermenting yeasts will survive and flourish when the competition is knocked out.

Yeasts. Many cidermakers prefer not to rely on natural yeasts, but add a commercial white wine yeast to the cider for a strong, dependable fermentation and for the different nuances of flavor that a champagne, sauterne, or Tokay yeast can give their cider. The yeast, either dry or liquid, is added after the sulfited juice has stood for twenty-four hours.

Yeast nutrients. Both ammonium sulfate and thiamine are "nutrients" that encourage yeast growth. Many cidermakers add them at the same time they add commercial yeast, to be on the safe side; others use them only when they have a "stuck" fermentation — one that has slowed or stopped because of too-low nitrogen levels in the cider.

Sugars. White sugar, honey, or other sweeteners are frequently added to the unfermented juice to increase the amount of alcohol in the finished cider. First, the amount of natural sugar in the must is measured with a hydrometer, the instrument calibrated to measure the specific gravity of the soluble solids (mostly sugar) in the juice, and the percentage of alcohol in the final cider that will result from that amount of sugar when fermented to dryness. See page 47 for a table showing how much sugar to add to arrive at a specific percentage of alcohol. Many cidermakers add the sweetener to their cider when they add yeast and

yeast nutrients, after the sulfited juice has stood twenty-four hours. Others wait a few days or a week until the natural fermentation has settled into a steady rate before adding sugar.

Tannins and acids. The experienced cidermaker may want to experiment with additions of tannic, malic, or other acids to give the cider more character. Standard and experimental sources of these substances are discussed in the next section. If you are just beginning to make cider, don't worry about adding these.

If you are making a natural, organic cider, you will take your chances with acetobacter and add none of the above, simply pouring the juice into a fermenting vessel and letting the natural yeasts convert the natural sugars into cider.

In the fermenting tank the cider will soon (within days) work up into a roiling, overflowing ferment that carries away many impurities. If possible, during this stage the sides of the container should be wiped clean daily until the ferment subsides to an even bubbling. The tank remains open during this period, for the vigorous eruptions of gases and liquid protect the young cider from airborne bacterial contamination.

As soon as the ferment subsides, the cider is topped off with a jug of fresh cider that has been put aside awaiting this moment, and a *water seal* is attached. The water seal keeps bacteria-laden air away from the cider while allowing the cider gases to escape.

The slower the cider ferments, the finer it is, claim many aficionados. The temperature of the room in which the cider ferments is largely responsible for the rate of fermentation, and there is considerable disagreement in the various cider regions over the proper temperature. A constant temperature anywhere between 55°F and 65°F (12.7°C and 18.3°C) in a clean, dark area is a safe cider fermentation range.

The cider is now left alone to ferment to the desired stage. Most cider is fermented to "dry," then sweetened to taste, but some skillful cidermakers interrupt the fermentation process *before* all the sugar is converted into alcohol to make a naturally sweet cider.

Depending on the temperature, the cider may be dry in a few weeks, or a few months. It is now ready to be *racked off* into another container to undergo malo-lactic fermentation or to be stored. It may even be bottled now, either as dry cider, or with a little sweetening added.

Step 9: Racking off

The cider is siphoned off its lees — the thick sediment that has settled at the bottom of the fermenting vessel — with a clean plastic tube into the second fermenting tank, into storage containers, or directly into bottles. Acid levels and alcohol content should be tested and compared to preformentation readings.

Step 10: Filtering or fining

Some people like the natural slight haze in cider; others prefer it crystal clear. Racking off clears the cider considerably, but filtering and fining will clarify it still further.

Filtering involves running the cider through muslin bags or diatomaceous earth, mediums that entrap or catch the suspended particles that make the cider hazy. Filtering, in any but a closed filter system, exposes the cider to air with the risk of acetic bacteria contamination.

Fining involves mixing any of several substances — gelatin, bentonite, and pectic enzyme are the most popular — into the cider and allowing the affected particles to drop to the bottom of the vessel. The cleared, or "fined," liquid is then racked off and bottled.

Step 11: Bottling

The finished cider is siphoned out of the fermentation or storage tank into strong, sterile bottles. Small amounts of sugar may be added to each bottle for a further in-bottle fermentation into sparkling cider. Those who prefer a sweet, still cider add sugar now, cap or cork the bottles, and then pasteurize the cider to prevent a further fermentation.

Step 12: Storage

The bottled cider is put to sleep in a cool, dark storage place for several months.

EQUIPMENT AND MATERIALS: HOW TO USE THEM

It is possible to make cider with a very simple if clumsy homemade grinder and press, and to ferment the juice naturally in a clean vessel without the aid of hydrometers, titration equipment, or various yeasts and chemicals, using judicious taste as your only guide. Cider made this

way can be very good — or dreadful. Without measuring and testing equipment it may be difficult to duplicate good results or to avoid a repetition of bad ones the next year. A few inexpensive measuring instruments, a sturdy, efficient grinder and a small press, and a cider notebook or log can replace guessing and seat-of-the-pants attempts with knowledge built on experience, which makes consistently fine cider. You may never use all the equipment discussed here. After all, in the final analysis your senses are the best testing equipment of all.

The Grinder

Most important of the preliminary cidermaking processes is the grinding or "breaking" of the apples, for they must be well pulverized for the press to extract the maximum juice from the pulp.

The most primitive and ancient way of crushing apples is by hand.

The "horse-mill" crushed large quantities of apples very fine. This was a large, circular trough of stone with a large stone wheel set in it that a horse, harnessed to a sweep, turned round and round. In North America, where timber was plentiful, these mills were sometimes made of hewn logs with heavy wooden wheels to do the crushing. The grinding process was also called "stamping the apples." The apples were dumped into the trough, and a boy kept mixing in the apples and crushed pulp with a "stirrer." When the apples were reduced to a more or less uniform mush, the pomace was scraped together with a "reefer" or pomace rake, then shoveled out of the trough with a wooden shovel. Many old cidermaker's manuals warn against using an iron shovel, which was acted upon by the strong acid and often gave the cider a dark brown color and objectionable flavor. The wheel smashed apples, seeds, stems, and skin to a fine texture. Some cider lovers protested that the seeds gave a bitter taste to the cider, while others praised it. Often rotten or near-rotten apples were used because they were so much easier to crush or press.

From the Elizabethan period on, numbers of ingenious hand- and horse-operated grinders were invented. But beginning in the late eighteenth century, the Industrial Revolution saw a proliferation of fierce-looking rollers set with iron teeth, arms, and knives, described as "tooth mills," "chewer mills," "scratcher mills," and "crusher mills." The "continental mill" featured wrought-iron knives that sliced the fruit into strips before pressing. The donkey steam engine took the place of man

and horse, and was itself replaced by the gas engine. Today, the most common commercial crusher is the electrically powered hammer mill.

The home cidermaker has a choice of several different manual or electrically powered grinders. Most of them have bushel-sized hoppers and do a good to excellent job of turning hard apples into soft mush.

If you have an antique grinder, the teeth (usually cast iron) may be so worn that you will have to put all pomace through twice or else replace the mill mechanism. It is also possible to have new "teeth" welded or brazed onto the roller. Since iron reacts with the apple juice, you might prefer to buy a new grinding mechanism of stainless steel.

The grinder may be separate from your press, or attached. If the grinder is unattached, simply mount it on top of a barrel open at one end. The process is simple. Just feed the fruit into the hopper of the grinder and turn on the power. If the power is your right arm, most hand grinders are comfortably enough geared so that only a little elbow grease can convert a lot of apples into a satisfactory pomace.

The ancient stone horse-mill outside the cider house
at the Long Ashton Research Station, Bristol, England.

Types of Apple Presses

The earliest presses wrung the juice from the pomace by means of heavy weights or leverage and wedges. By the eighteenth century, screw presses — the larger ones with massive wooden screws that preceded the iron screws of the next century — were popular. The lever-and-screw combination press, operated by water- or machine power, was widely used in cider regions in the last century. Around the time of the Civil War, an Ohio orchard owner, Augustus Q. Tucker, who had a penchant for mechanical engineering, began a series of experiments that ended in 1877 with the first working hy-

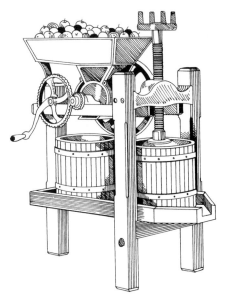

An old-fashioned grinder press like the one shown here is heavy, but dependable and efficient.

draulic cider press. In his efforts to promote the newfangled machine, Tucker loaded the press onto a horse-drawn wagon and drove around the countryside "squeezing and crushing pine sticks" to illustrate the vast power of his invention. Eventually a manufacturer adopted the design and made hydraulic cider presses in Mount Gilead, Ohio — which, until the Depression years of the 1930s, was the hydraulic press center of the world. Many old cider presses are stamped MOUNT GILEAD.

Modern presses are awesome giants. The Swiss Bücher-Guyer cider press uses a hydraulic ram in a repeated batch process. The spiral screw press, developed in the United States but only built in Europe, is a true continuous press.

Hand cider presses, usually of the screw type and of many different designs, were made through the nineteenth century and are still made today. Modern hand cider presses are of the screw type or the single- or double-ratchet type, or have small hydraulic jacks that exert the necessary pressure. The screw presses usually have single or double baskets. The ratchet presses are single tub, and the hydraulic presses feature racks and cheesecloths.

Operating the screw press. Manual operation of these presses requires some muscle power and, with the double tub, a certain degree of teamwork.

Single tub: A plastic or stainless-steel collecting vessel is placed under the press to catch the juice. The hand screw is raised to its highest point. A cloth bag is fitted into the basket or tub, and the freshly milled pulp is shoveled in until the tub is full. The bag top is folded over and a sturdy pressing plate placed on top. The screw is turned manually as far as it will go to begin the pressing process. When the gush of juice has slowed, more pressure is applied. When no more juice flows — which may be as much as half an hour after the first turn of the screw — the screw is reversed, the dry pomace is emptied from the cloth, and the process is repeated.

Double tub: The double-tub screw press usually has the grinder affixed at the rear, and with two or three people working together, something like a leisurely continuous press operation is possible. One person dumps apples into the hopper while another grinds the pomace, which falls into one of the waiting tubs below. When a tub is full, the third person slides it forward to its place under the pressing mechanism, then slips the second (and empty) tub under the grinder to catch the continuing stream of pomace. While the first two people continue to grind pomace, the third works the screw down onto the pressing tub. A two-by-four inserted in the screw handle will give welcome leverage to exert further pressure. When all the juice is expressed, the front tub is emptied and placed under the grinder as the filled pomace tub slides forward into position under the pressing screw, and so on until all the apples are squeezed. After their use, the grinder, press, and cloths must be rinsed with scalding water.

Operating the ratchet press. The tub is loaded just as in the screw press, the collecting vessel placed beneath the juice outlet, and the pressing mechanism raised. The ratchet handle is inserted, then worked up and down like a ratchet auto-jack until maximum pressure is reached. Let the press stand until the juice stops flowing freely, and apply more pressure until the pomace is pressed dry. Reverse the pressure, empty the tub, and repeat the process.

Operating the hydraulic press. Small hydraulic cider presses are miniature versions of large commercial presses. Instead of tubs, these presses take a number of drainage racks. A press cloth is spread onto each rack. The milled pulp is dumped onto the cloth until it's a few inches thick. The corners of the cloth are folded into the center, enveloping the pulp. On top another rack is placed, another cloth, more pulp, and so on, until five to ten layers are built up. The pressure plate creeps up as the hydraulic jack goes into operation. Small presses are usually operated by a foot pedal. When full pressure is on, the apparatus stands for some time, until the juice stops flowing. A waiting cart, wheelbarrow, or portable bin is needed for the dry pomace.

A small hydraulic press in operation. Note the stacked drainage racks, which take the place of tubs to catch the apple juice.

Custom pressing. If you don't have a cider press, and you do have a lot of apples, find out whether nearby cider mills do custom pressing. Call first, because there may be only special days or hours for custom work, or you may have to have an appointment.

Some mills charge a straight per-gallon rate, others will barter the pressing service for apples, and still others will take *your* apples and give you *their* juice. Naturally you will prefer to know what kinds of apples the mill is pressing before you drag home fifty gallons of insipid McIntosh juice.

If you take your own special varieties, be sure the mill will accept them. We know of one mill that refuses to press dessert apples, and another that will not let crab apples near the grinder, for they jam up the mechanism. Some cider mills have small hand mills and presses for the use of customers with only a bushel or two of apples to press.

Before you have your apples custom pressed, take a good slow look around the cider mill. Check to see where the vinegar vats are, and how clean the works look. Are there heaps of pomace thickly clustered with fruit flies in the vicinity of the press room? Is the place sparkling white tile and stainless steel vats, or ancient wood, iron, and stone? In a very clean operation you may not get as much of the microflora in your cider as you would in the harder-to-clean wooden cider mill. You can go home from the latter not only with accumulated natural yeasts from the mill machinery, but also with acetic bacteria and worse.

When you are taking home your apple juice, carry it in wood, stainless steel, plastic, or glass containers. An old milk can may be a handy container, but if you use it, kiss your cider goodbye. Enough of the metal will be dissolved into the acid cider to wreck the flavor.

Other juice sources. If you have no apples and no handy cider mill, the game is still not over. City dwellers in apartments can make cider, too, in small amounts. Check your local supermarket for pasteurized sweet apple cider *without preservatives.* It is preferable to use a juice that is a blend of several different varieties, but most manufacturers are not obliging enough to list them, largely because the varieties change with the seasons, and so do the bottled ciders. You can guess by noting where the main factory is located and knowing what apples are grown in the region. Better, buy a small container of each of several brands and taste them all judiciously before settling on one for cider experiments.

If you make cider this way you have one advantage: You don't need to wait for the harvest, but can make it any time of year.

Choosing the right barrels

Cider was traditionally fermented in barrels, and some still believe you cannot make good cider without an oak barrel. However, most modern commercial operations use less temperamental containers: lined concrete tanks, high-density polyethylene tanks, and glass-lined stainless steel vats. Many farm cidermakers still use barrels and you, the home cidermaker, may want to use wooden containers — because they are easily obtainable in your area, or because you already have some on hand, or simply because of their traditional association with cider.

If you choose barrels, recognize that they are cranky vessels whose cellular pores often absorb unwanted flavors, harbor harmful bacteria,

and expand and contract to a surprising degree. Barrel care will be an ongoing part of your cidermaking. You may also want to buy a bung starter and a hoop driver, the one to "start" your bungs, and the other to drive the hoops up tight.

Secondhand barrels. If you buy used barrels or find some old barrels up in the hay loft of your newly acquired farm, see if they are stout oak barrels with thick staves and strong iron hoops. There should be no holes in them except for the bunghole. With a stout stick, give each barrel a whack. A dull *thunk* is the sign of a barrel with loose hoops and spread staves. A tight barrel, which is what you want, will give off a sharp, competent ring.

Don't be shy. Put your nose right up to the bunghole. Sniff for odors of vinegar, mold, mustiness, or foulness. If the barrel doesn't smell sweet and healthy, you don't want it. Avoid barrels that have contained liquid, except for cider, whiskey, applejack, sherry, brandy, rum, or port.

New barrels. New barrels will give an unpleasant "woody" taste to the cider unless treated by steam cleaning or chemical cleaning (see box, page 20).

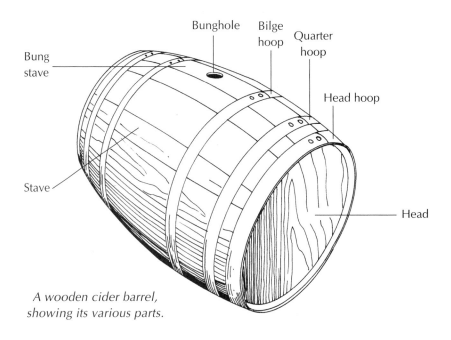

A wooden cider barrel, showing its various parts.

TREATING NEW BARRELS

New barrels can be cleaned with steam or chemicals to remove their "woody" taste. Here are the two methods:

↪ **Steam cleaning.** *Some garages have steam cleaners and will let you steam out an occasional barrel. Some cider mills will steam the barrels for you for a slight charge.*

A steam cleaner can be improvised by fitting one end of a section of garden hose to a capacious tea kettle and heating the water in the kettle over an outside fire until a gentle stream of steam can be fed into the barrel. If the barrel is a small one, you can manage the process in the sink. Put the barrel on its side, bunghole down. Feed the steam into the bunghole. The steam will reach every niche and crevice inside the barrel and, in condensing, carry away the raw new-oak flavor in a trickle of reddish brown water. When the water runs clear, stop steaming and rinse the barrel with clean water.

↪ **Chemical cleaning.** *Fill the barrel with clean water and let it stand several days until the wood fibers are soaked and swollen. Empty it and refill with a hot solution of sodium carbonate (also called "washing soda" or "soda ash") and hot water, using two ounces of soda for every five gallons of water. Let the barrel stand another day or so, then empty it and rinse once more with clear water. Neutralize any traces of soda by rinsing with a solution of five ounces of citric acid dissolved in six gallons of water. Swill this solution vigorously about in the barrel, drain, and rinse once more.*

Wine supply stores carry premixed commercial preparations to remove the woody taste from new barrels. Follow the directions.

Sterilizing barrels. Used barrels or your own freshly emptied cider barrels should be sterilized at bottling time. First, rinse out the barrel thoroughly. Then sterilize by one of the following methods:

↪ If the barrel is fairly clean, burn sulfur strips or a sulfur candle inside the barrel with the bunghole closed until all the oxygen is

Blown glass fermentation locks. A row of glittering, full glass carboys, each topped with a delicate, old-fashioned glass fermentation lock, is a beautiful sight. Alas, the glass locks are expensive, fragile, and not the best closures, since they are inserted in corks or rubber stoppers that have to be worked into the mouth of the carboy. Often the closure is not complete and air can get at the cider.

Plastic fermentation locks. These water traps have a lot going for them. They are inexpensive and will last for quite a long time if they are not put into boiling water at any point.

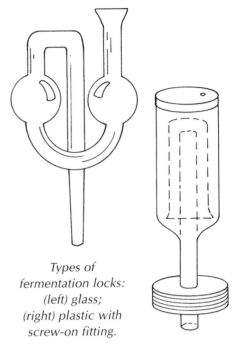

Types of fermentation locks:
(left) glass;
(right) plastic with
screw-on fitting.

Plastic fermentation locks are available with thirty-eight-millimeter screw caps that fit gallon jugs and many five-gallon polyethylene carboys. They can also be fitted into drilled corks or rubber stoppers. Wine supply catalogs inevitably describe them as "foolproof," but we've experienced a situation where they failed. If you keep fermenting vessels on the floor in a wood-heated house, a sharp drop in temperature at night can temporarily stop the fermentation; the cooling (and shrinking) liquid will create a partial vacuum in the vessel, sucking the water out of the water lock and down into the cider, bringing with it airborne bacteria.

Homemade water seal. Gather a cork or rubber stopper, a section of plastic tubing or bent glass tube (available from your local pharmacist), and a small jar such as a baby-food jar, along with a couple of stout rubber bands, and you can make a water lock. It may not be as aesthetically pleasing or as convenient as the store-bought model, but it is inexpensive and will work just as well.

If you are fermenting cider in a barrel, you'll need a long section of tubing to reach from bunghole to a jar or pail of water on the floor.

but this thermometer has a handy little ring on the top, allowing you to attach a string and lower it into a barrel or carboy. You also need a thermometer to use with your hydrometer to get an accurate reading.

Titration Equipment

The cidermaker uses titration equipment to measure the amount of acid in the cider, to check for any increase in acid that means acidification (vinegar manufacture) is occurring, and to monitor the desirable malo-lactic fermentation. Apple juice, of course, is acidic, but the amount of acid varies considerably from cultivar to cultivar. North American dessert apples are often high in acid, and if you are using crab apples to bring up the tannin level in your cider, you will also be increasing the acidity of the juice — sometimes too much.

It is helpful to take acid readings from time to time as fermentation proceeds. Acid readings will usually decline during fermentation, but if acetobacter begin to grow, acetic acid will develop and the acid reading will increase. If you catch the acidification process early enough you can still save your cider. A malo-lactic fermentation, desirable in high-acid juices, may cause the acid level to drop considerably at the end of fermentation. There are several ways of testing the acid in your juice.

Titration with a burette. Laboratory-quality titration kits are available with full instructions from most wine supply stores.

Acid test strips and pH papers. Dip sensitized litmus papers into the cider, and compare the resulting color to a color chart. This is a fast, inexpensive, but not very accurate way of determining acid content.

Direct reading acid tester. This sophisticated home acid tester is calibrated to give an immediate acid reading as tartaric acid. A few minutes with pencil and paper and the conversion tables gives values for citric, lactic, malic, acetic, and sulfuric acid.

Fermentation Locks, Water Seals, Valves, and Air Locks

Fermentation locks keep bacteria-laden air from contact with the cider and at the same time allow the carbon dioxide gas produced by fermentation to escape.

blunt chisel and mallet. Now steam the barrel gently for several minutes. Fill the barrel with water. It will probably still leak, so keep filling it until the fibers have swollen enough so it is watertight.

If the barrel has been allowed to dry with lees or other deposits or residues in it, it may be impossible to clean it. You can try, though. A scouring chain is helpful in this job — a length of galvanized chain with a rope on one end. You drop the chain into the barrel with some hot water, then roll the barrel about vigorously. The chain breaks up the deposits — you hope.

If, after soaking, driving the hoops tight, gentle steaming, and constant filling with water, the barrel still leaks, it needs a cooper's attention or should be discarded.

Other Suitable Containers for Cider

Never use any containers for cider except wood, glass, some plastic and fiberglass, stainless steel, or earthenware. Avoid iron, copper, and galvanized containers, for they discolor the juice and give it unpleasant flavors. Even enamel should be avoided if possible because of the probability of tiny chips exposing the underlying metal, which will react with the acid juice. Do not use aluminum vessels, especially if SO_2 (sulfur dioxide) is used in the process.

Glass carboys. These big jugs hold four and a half Imperial gallons or five U.S. gallons. They are the perfect fermentation vessels, in conjunction with a number of one-gallon jugs, for the home cidermaker. A number of these big fellows lets you ferment several varieties of juice separately and blend them later. It's fascinating to watch your cider working, to note the different colors according to the varieties, and to see the haze or clearing in the liquid or the early formation of some cider problems. Glass carboys can be bought at wine supply houses and chemical supply stores. Sometimes you find them at auctions or antiques shops. They are easy to clean and do not retain odors. They do have a few disadvantages: You must fit your fermentation locks into large, bored-out corks or rubber stoppers, and the big jugs are breakable and heavy.

Glass gallon jugs. Save your old gallon jugs that came full of wine or fruit juice. They are perfect for fermenting small batches of scarce varieties or crab apple juice, and are useful in the cidery in a dozen ways.

Inveterate cider drinkers may prefer to bottle off in gallon jugs rather than puny bottles.

Collapsible polyethylene containers. These are cheap and light-weight and come in several sizes, from one to five gallons. They have several disadvantages: They can be inadvertently punctured; when picked up carelessly their nonrigid construction can cause the water in the water trap to be sucked into the must; and they are opaque enough to rob the fermenting cider of some of its visual individuality. If you don't care about watching your cider ferment, place these collapsible containers in a cardboard box to protect them from puncture and water-trap mishaps.

Rigid polyethylene containers. The five-gallon and ten-gallon heavy-duty polyethylene carboys — some with handles, some without — are the wave of the future in home cider-making. Unbreakable, lightweight, relatively inexpensive, easily cleaned, and with fitted, screw-on fermentation locks, these containers have one disadvantage: They are opaque.

Hydrometer

Invented in the early eighteenth century, the *hydrometer* is a floating instrument calibrated to measure the specific gravity of liquids. Different models have different names, reflecting what they measure — alcoholmeter, lactometer, sucrometer — and the arbitrary scales of their inventors — Baumé, Gay-Lussac, Sikes, Twaddel.

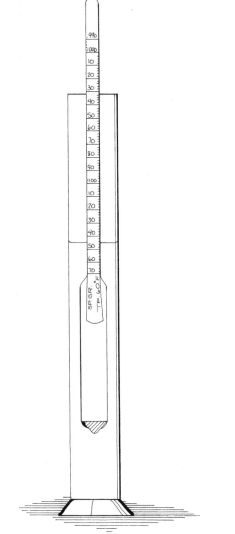

The correct reading from this hydrometer is 1.045.

The cidermaker is interested in the hydrometer — sold as a wine maker's or brewer's hydrometer — that measures the sugar and other soluble solids in a liquid. This instrument is a slender, sealed, hand-blown glass tube weighted on one end with lead shot. It has from one to three scales printed on paper in the upper stem. Used with a testing jar or chemist's graduate, the hydrometer is accurate at 60°F (15°C) when calibrated for specific gravity and the Balling Scale. If the Brix scale is used, it may be calibrated to a temperature reading of either 17.5°C or 20°C. The third scale measures the potential alcohol of the liquid.

When the testing jar is filled with juice and the hydrometer inserted, it will sink to a level determined by the density of the soluble solids (mostly sugar) contained in the juice. The specific gravity, the Balling or Brix scale, and the potential alcohol scale will climb if sugar is added to the juice. Because the acids in the juice can complicate these hydrometer readings somewhat, there may be an error of as much as 1 percent in the Brix and Balling readings. If you are using either of these scales, subtract 1 percent from the reading for greater accuracy.

Hydrometer scales. The scales help the cidermaker determine the sweetness of the apple juice, the amount of sugar in it, and the potential alcohol level.

Specific gravity: Water, on the specific gravity scale, is expressed by the weight of 1.000 — that figure being the weight of distilled water (1.000 grams per liter). When sugar and minor soluble solids are present in the apple juice, or sugar is added, the soluble solids increase. This density is reflected in increasing decimal points (1.005, 1.015, 1.050, etc.) read directly off the calibrated stem floating in the liquid. The sweeter the juice, the more shallow the hydrometer, with 1.000 to 1.170 the range.

The Balling or Brix scales: These are popular in North America, and express sugar in terms of grams per 100 grams of solution.

Potential alcohol: The unfermented apple juice can be measured to learn the probability of alcoholic content by volume, based on the assumption that all the soluble sugars will be fermented into alcohol. To compute the alcohol level of your finished cider, take a hydrometer reading *after* fermentation as well as before, subtract, and you have the percentage of alcohol in the cider. More often you will use the hydrometer to measure the level of an apple juice deficient in sugars needed to make a strong cider, adding sugar until the desired potential strength is reached.

Using the hydrometer. Fill the test jar three-quarters full and insert the hydrometer, spinning it in the liquid to dislodge any air bubbles clinging to the glass, which could cause an error. Sight across the jar, taking a reading at eye level where the surface of the liquid cuts across the hydrometer's stem and *not* where the liquid clings to the sides of the test jar. The reading will give you the specific gravity, the Balling or Brix reading, or the amount of potential alcohol — or all three.

Compensation for temperature: Most of the hydrometers in North American home cideries are accurate when read at a temperature of 60°F (15°C), but if the temperature of the cider is higher or lower, you will have to make corrections.

Correction for Specific Gravity

TEMPERATURE		CORRECTION
°F	°C	
50	10	$-\frac{1}{2}$
60	15.5	1.0000
70	21	Add 1
77	25	Add 2
84	28.8	Add 3
96	35.5	Add 5
105	40.5	Add 7

On an Indian summer day when the temperature is 95°F (35°C), and your apple juice reads 1.056 on the specific gravity scale, correct the reading:

$$\begin{array}{ll} 1.056 & \text{Specific Gravity Reading} \\ +\quad 5 & \text{Correction} \\ \hline 1.061 & \text{Correct Specific Gravity} \end{array}$$

Thermometer

A *winemaker's thermometer* is a valuable piece of equipment. Not only can you check the air temperature of your fermentation room with it,

French cidermakers say. This means inspecting the interior of the barrel. Fasten a birthday-cake candle to a stiff wire and carefully insert the burning candle into the barrel. It will cast enough light to let you see if any patches of white or yellow mold desecrate the interior. If there is widespread moldiness, abandon the barrel for cidermaking; knock the head out and use it to store nails, ore samples, or glass beads. If there are only a few moldy patches, you *may* be able to save the barrel by sending it to an experienced cooper (if you can find one!) to be shaved and charred inside. When it comes home to you after its internal rejuvenation, sterilize it as discussed with a laundry bleach and water solution.

Acetic barrels: This is a common problem, especially when cider barrels are not rinsed and sterilized after they've been emptied, or when cider is drawn directly from a spigot in the barrelhead for leisurely consumption. The cider, vulnerable to contact with air that sets acetobacter to multiplying, turns to vinegar and the very pores of the wood are impregnated with it. Rinse the barrel well; then sterilize it with a doubly strong solution of sodium carbonate and boiling water — six ounces of the sodium carbonate per gallon of water — following the third procedure in *Sterilizing Barrels.* Most cidermakers, ourselves included, prefer not to use a vinegar-tainted barrel for cider under any conditions.

"Foul" barrels: If you have ever had the unpleasant experience of smelling a newly opened barrel in which water has been standing stagnant for a long time, you understand that there is *no way* to sweeten that barrel again. It cannot be used for cidermaking. Knock the head out and use it for storage of nonedible items. The old books on cider list dozens of amazing ways to restore foul, musty, or moldy barrels, but one writer reported an old fellow who said that he "found it a better plan to burn up the cask altogether, and use a new one instead." Amen.

Dry barrels: If you have the bad luck to acquire a dried-out barrel, you may have a maddening time making it tight again. A small barrel can be submerged in a tub or pool of water. If you have a large barrel and nothing big enough in which to soak it, swath it in wet burlap bags in a shady place and drench it often with the garden hose. Let dry barrels soak for two or three days. The hoops will probably have slipped when the barrel was in its dry condition, so drive the hoops up tight with a used up. The burning process creates sulfur dioxide gas, which kills bacteria and mold.

→ Fill the barrel with a solution of laundry bleach and water — four ounces of bleach to ten gallons of water — and let the barrel stand a day or so. Empty and rinse thoroughly.

→ Mix a solution of sodium carbonate (soda ash or washing soda) and boiling hot water — three ounces of soda per gallon of water — and fill the barrel half full with it. Bung the barrel tightly and roll it around energetically every now and then for forty-five minutes. Let the barrel stand until the water is cool; then drain and rinse thoroughly.

To neutralize any chemical residues after sterilization by bleach or sodium carbonate, dissolve a quarter ounce of sulfite crystals (potassium metabisulfite or bulk Campden tablets sold by wine supply stores) and a quarter ounce of citric acid in a gallon of water. Slosh this thoroughly around in the rinsed barrel for a few minutes, then empty and rinse the barrel with clear water once more.

Barrel storage. Barrels should never be stored empty or allowed to dry out. After they have been cleaned and sterilized, pour two gallons of the following mixture into a fifty-gallon barrel, a quart into a five-gallon barrel:

½ **ounce sulfite crystals**
½ **ounce citric acid**
1 **gallon water**

Store the barrels, tightly bunged, in a cool cellar. Roll the barrels over every few weeks to prevent the upper portions from drying out. If you store them more than two months, drain, rinse, and add fresh storage solution. This will keep your barrels sweet. When you're ready to use one of your stored barrels, drain it, rinse it thoroughly, and sterilize it before pouring in new cider.

Barrel problems. Because wooden barrels are made of organic material, they are subject to a variety of potential problems of use and aging. Some problems are less serious than others.

Moldy barrels: If you notice a musty smell at the bunghole, or see moldy, musty patches around the bung, you must "visit" your barrel, as

Laboratory Scales

When yeasts, nutrients, pectic enzymes, sulfur dioxide, and other cider-making supplies are purchased in bulk to save money, a laboratory scale will help you divide the supplies into usable quantities. A packet of yeast, for example, is usually enough to start five gallons of cider fermenting. Just add the whole thing to your carboy and you're off. But suppose you want to start five separate gallon jugs for blending experiments using one packet of yeast. You *can* count the minute grains with tweezers and divide by five, or you can weigh out the proportions to within a fraction. Good lab scales, compact and easy to store, cost under ten dollars.

Filtering, Fining, and Racking

When fermentation ends, most cider is not crystal clear. Many cidermakers don't mind a slight pectin haze, but balk at thick sediment and visible particles swirling about in the glass. Filtering, racking, and fining are all ways of getting clear cider.

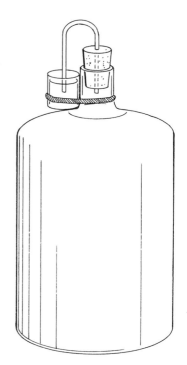

A homemade water lock consists of a tube that extends up through the cork and then down into a small cup of water, permitting gas to flow out of the container but preventing air from being drawn into the container.

To some extent all these processes slow down fermentation by removing some of the yeast cells from the cider. Very fine filtration can remove so many that fermentation virtually halts. This is a useful way of stopping fermentation before all the sugar in the cider has been converted to alcohol and is a standard commercial way to make a natural semisweet cider. Commercial cidermakers use large continuous filter systems and massive centrifuges to clarify and halt fermentation in their ciders; both of these systems are closed to air. The home cidermaker can also buy, for around twenty-five dollars, a closed-system filter that will filter one thousand gallons before the filter plate needs replacing. If you filter your cider with *any* method that allows it to come into contact with air, you are running the very real risk of contaminating the cider with acetobacter. The most frequent result is a nice clear vinegar. If you can avoid air-contact filtering, do so.

Racking, filtering, and fining should all be done on cold days when suspensions tend to settle a little.

Racking off. This is a basic clarification method in which the drinkable — the cider — is separated from the nondrinkable — the lees — by siphon or pump. For small amounts of cider the siphon is more practical and economical. You'll need a racking stick and a section of plastic tubing with a half-inch inside diameter, long enough to reach from the fermenting vessel to the storage container. The siphon tubing can be kept below the liquid surface and above the lees by fastening it

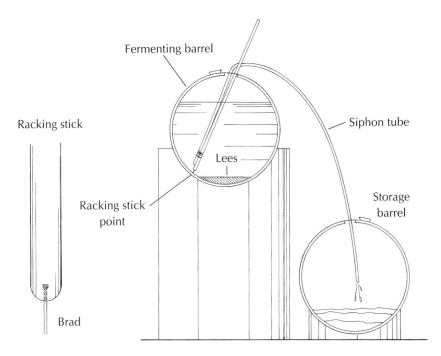

When racking off from an opaque container,
be sure to leave at least three inches for the lees when
positioning the racking stick and siphon.

with a rubber band to the racking stick. Drive a wire brad into the bottom of your racking stick, then stab this into the bottom of the barrel to hold the stick steady when you are draining the barrel.

Measure the depth of the barrel or other opaque container and allow a good three to five inches for the lees, affix the tubing to the racking stick, and insert into the barrel. Mouth suction primes the siphon. A tube this large really moves the cider, about three gallons per minute. If you are racking off directly into bottles, you will want to use a smaller-diameter tube. Glass and translucent containers are easier to rack off, since the lees are visible.

Funnel and filter paper. This is a simple and risky filtration method. A large funnel is lined with filter paper, available from wine supply stores and some pharmacies, then inserted into the clean vessel, and the cider is siphoned in slowly. In a short time the filter paper will clog with detritus and must be discarded for a fresh one. The process is slow, and the cider is exposed to the air during the operation.

The fast-flow filter: An expensive item especially designed for home wine makers, but effective and safe. A resin filter element is good for up to one thousand gallons of filtering. The filter has tubing and fittings made for the thirty-eight-millimeter openings of fermenting jugs and carboys, so that the cider is never exposed to air during the filtering process. This rig filters up to two gallons a minute.

Diatomaceous earth or kieselguhr or Filter-Aid: This material is composed of billions of microscopic diatom fossil skeletons. The structure of the tiny forms — hollow and sharply spined — catches yeast cells and solid particles while the liquid cider passes through. Diatomaceous earth can be mixed with small batches of cider, then poured into a funnel fitted with a filter pad; the kieselguhr will build up a thicker filter on top of the pad. If you want to use it you can order it through your pharmacist.

If you have only a few gallons to filter, use a funnel. For twenty-five to fifty gallons, or more, you may want to make the homemade muslin filter developed especially for cider filtration by the Michigan Agricultural Experiment Station in 1932, by R. B. Hickok and Roy E. Marshall. See page 33 for a modified diagram of their plan.

The homemade muslin tube filter: This system has three parts: the mixing/supply tank; a V-shaped wooden trough; and the filter tube.

The mixing/supply tank is simply a barrel with one head knocked out, and a brass spigot to take a five-eighth-inch-diameter garden hose connection fitted at the bottom. The barrel is mounted six feet above the filter tube. A length of plastic garden hose connects the barrel tank with the filter tube.

The filter tube is made of a piece of unbleached muslin about eleven by thirty-six inches, cut and sewn into a long tube three inches in diameter and thirty-six inches long. The mixing tank hose is inserted into the muslin tube, which is tied tightly to it with cord. The "dead" end of the tube is folded back on itself three or four inches, carefully gathered, and tightly tied with a miller's knot. (A miller's knot is a simple three- or four-turn wraparound, with the last turn tucked beneath the previous turn and pulled tight.) A miller's knot is essential if you're using cotton or nylon twine, but with other materials, any knot will do.

The tube is laid in the V-shaped wooden trough that has been fitted with a bed of plastic screening to support the tube. This trough is lower at the dead end than the head.

The cider is placed in the mixing barrel, and Filter-Aid is added at the rate of one pound per thirty gallons of cider, well mixed in. As the cider flows into the muslin tube a filter cake is built up on the inside of the cloth. The first two or three gallons of cider filtered will contain some of the filter compound, so dump it back into the mixing tank and run it through again. At somewhere between twenty and fifty gallons the tube will be too clogged to allow a free flow of cider. Turn off the hose spigot, remove the tube, shake it out, rinse it in running water, then replace the tube and continue filtering. This system will filter 1.4 gallons per minute.

If you use kieselguhr with a muslin filter, you may want to experiment a bit to find the right amount to use with your cider. Start with the minimum suggested by the manufacturer. The amount may range from one pound per twenty gallons to one pound per forty gallons. Stir the cider in the mixing tank from time to time to prevent settling.

Fining agents. Fining is much more popular with home cidermakers than filtering and does not expose the cider to the air as does filtering.

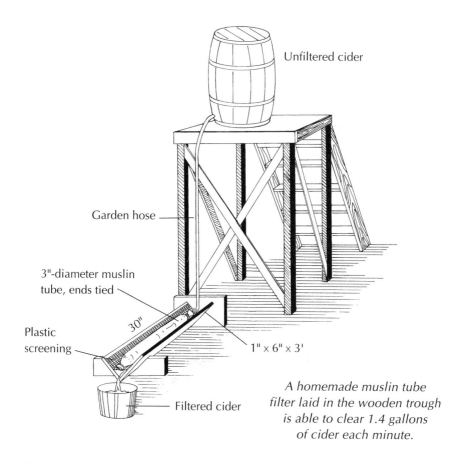

Unfiltered cider

Garden hose

3"-diameter muslin
tube, ends tied

Plastic
screening

30"

1" x 6" x 3'

Filtered cider

*A homemade muslin tube
filter laid in the wooden trough
is able to clear 1.4 gallons
of cider each minute.*

Fining is always followed by racking off. Crystal-clear cider is an aesthetic preference. Fining or clearing a cider that retains a slight natural haze after it's been racked off at post-fermentation storage improves the cider in only one way — cosmetically. The pectins that cause the haze can also aid digestion and are considered by some food authorities to be beneficial. Removing pectins can be a headache unless you have a centrifuge. However, if you like a brilliantly clear cider, and many home connoisseurs of this noble beverage do, there are several things you can try.

Gelatin: Sometimes sold under the brand name "Sparkolloid," this combination of gelatin and diatomaceous earth is mixed with warm water and added to the cider. A quarter teaspoon treats one gallon of cider. Unfortunately, gelatin reacts with the tannin in the cider at the same time as it entrains the haze-causing particles, so you get rid of the best tannins as well as the haze. The final product is a clear but emasculated

cider. If you prefer to mix your own clearing agent with gelatin from the kitchen cupboard, you should include some tannic acid so that the mixture can work efficiently and your cider will retain some tannin for body.

TO CLEAR FIFTY GALLONS OF CIDER

2 ounces U.S.P.-quality tannic acid
1 gallon warm water

1. *Mix well, stir into the cider, and mix well.*
2. *Soak 2 ounces gelatin in 1 cup cold water for ½ hour. Dissolve thoroughly in 3 cups boiling water. Add 3 quarts cool water. Mix well.*
3. *Add the gelatin mixture to the cider-tannin mixture. Mix all together well. Let the mixture stand until the gelatin-tannin carries the haze particles to the bottom of the vessel. This may take an hour, or the mixture may have to stand overnight.*
4. *Rack off the clear cider.*

Bentonite: This is a soft, porous, moisture-absorbing rock of clayey minerals, usually volcanic in origin, that absorbs and settles the particles in the cider. Bentonite was once used widely in commercial wineries. It can impart a harsh, earthy flavor to the cider. About one teaspoon per gallon of cider will clear it.

Pectic enzyme: The apple fibers are held together by a substance known as pectin — the material that puts the gel into your jelly and in cider appears as a haze. In the arsenal of clearing agents, one, an enzyme (sold under different brand names), can be used to break down the pectin bonds in the cider either at the start of the cidermaking or at the finish.

When the apples are sprinkled with a pectic enzyme solution several hours before they are pressed, the enzymes dissolve the pectin bonds that hold millions of particles of vegetable matter together. As a result, there is less fibrous resistance during milling and pressing, giving faster press runs and greater yields of juice as well as clearer cider.

The enzyme is available in tablet or powdered form; it is mixed and applied to the unmilled fruit with a watering can or to the finished cider by the tablet or teaspoon. Pectic enzymes work best at a temperature of 80°F to 100°F (26.6°C to 37.7°C); at lower temperatures they take longer to work.

Long Ashton Research Station studies how the ciders and apple juices clarified by the use of pectic enzymes are higher in methanol, the result of the demethylation of juice pectins; the methanol content has run from ten to four hundred parts per million in those observations.

Isinglass, egg white, and so on: Many old cidermaking manuals call for the addition of isinglass, fish bladders, glue, fresh blood, milk, or egg whites to clear hazy ciders. All these depend on interaction with the tannins in the cider for salification. Then these particles, being heavier than the liquid, sink slowly to the bottom of the tank, taking suspended matter with them. Since North American apples are low in tannins, frequently the reaction is not complete and some foreign material is left floating in the cider. Use of these is not recommended.

Wine Thief

This important piece of equipment is a syringe with a two-foot length of slender plastic tubing for taking samples from barrels and vats without disturbing the contents. A simple homemade wine thief is nothing more than a length of plastic tube that is inserted into the cider. Clamp your finger tightly over the opening of the tube and withdraw the tube from the cider — voilà! — a cider sample.

Vinometer

The vinometer measures the percentage of alcohol in the finished cider. A small calibrated glass capillary tube

A homemade wine thief made of plastic tubing can be used to sample cider from a vat or barrel.

topped with a tiny funnel, the vinometer works on the principle that the surface tension of various concentrations of alcohol differs. Six or seven drops of cider drip from the gauge, then the instrument is inverted. The cider creeps down the capillary tube and finally stops at a point on the calibrated scale marking the percentage of alcohol in the sample. The vinometer does not work with effervescent or particle-filled cider; the liquid must be clear.

Using Yeasts in Cidermaking

More than eight thousand strains of the vegetable microorganisms called yeast have been classified, but only a few are relevant to cider- or winemaking. Of the natural yeasts found on the skins of apples, those of the genus *Saccharomyces* are important to the fermentation process, but they are sparsely scattered. For a vigorous fermentation to occur naturally, these yeasts have to build up, which they did in old-time cidermaking on the press cloths, on the press itself, on the grinder, on the walls, in the barrels — in fact the old cider poundhouse was alive with accumulated yeast cells.

However, in highly hygienic commercial and amateur cideries, where press, grinder, utensils, floors, and walls are scalded, mopped, and disinfected with chemicals to defeat the bacteria that cause cider sickness, the mortality rate among natural yeasts is high and the chance of natural fermentation low. Then, too, many cidermakers prefer to kill off most of the wild yeast along with any molds or unwelcome bacteria, then start confidently down the fermentation road with strong, laboratory-grown "wine-yeast" of known, dependable characteristics.

If you are a first-time cidermaker using new equipment and are only pressing a small amount of apples, there may not be enough natural yeast in your must to start off a good fermentation, and you may want to use a commercial white wine yeast.

If you add the yeast directly to untreated juice, it will probably overpower the weaker, natural yeasts and give you a good fermentation. However, many sickness-causing bacteria will continue to thrive in the cider and may give serious trouble before you are done, especially if you have a low-acid juice. To avoid these complications, many cidermakers, both commercial and amateur, add sulfur dioxide (SO_2) to the juice before fermentation starts. This will kill most of the bacteria and undesirable yeasts. For more on how to use sulfur dioxide, see pages 39–41.

Which yeasts to use? Commercial wine yeasts come in packets of dried yeast or in tubes of agar culture. They are laboratory-produced cultures grown from isolated strains of yeasts found on various famous wine grapes. Most familiar is an all-purpose winemaker's yeast, but you may prefer to try champagne yeast, Johannisberger, sauterne, Tokay, or Rhine wine yeasts. Baker's yeast — the kind used to make bread — will ferment cider, but the finished product is often cloudy and hard to clear and may have a strong "yeasty" flavor. Moreover, bread yeasts do not produce enough alcohol to preserve the cider. Use them only as a last resort, for they completely lack the heady vinous overtones a good yeast gives cider.

Perhaps the most widely used yeast in North American commercial and home wineries and cideries is the Burgundy-descended "Montrachet" yeast, fermenter of one of the greatest Burgundies known. This is the "all-purpose" yeast offered by all wine supply stores. Fast-acting, resistant to sulfiting, inexpensive, and with good storage life, dry Montrachet yeast has a major fault — it is responsible for the development in cider of the most objectionable of aromas and flavors — hydrogen sulfide (H_2S). Jerome Van Buren, retired professor of biochemistry at the Geneva Station, has noted that the production of H_2S, which richly confers the overpowering taste and smell of rotten eggs on anything that contains it, is closely related to the strain of yeast used, and that Montrachet 522 is a notorious producer of that overpowering product.

Of the German wine yeasts, the "Dry Vierka" (a brand name) yeasts are particularly noteworthy for giving strong grape or wine characteristics to juices made from other fruits. Some of them are suited to the dark fruits (prunes, cherries, grapes, figs), but four or five are most effective yeasts for cider, lending flavors and aromas that strongly hint at a particular type of wine even though the vehicle is apple. Rhine, liebfraumilch, sauterne, champagne, and sherry yeasts ferment apple juice into cider with some overtones of those wines. The least successful is the sherry yeast, which reputedly makes a fairly thin sherry cider that lacks the intense Flowers-of-Wine, or *Flor,* fermentation restricted to the sherry-producing regions of Spain. For the champagne-type cider-maker, champagne yeast is excellent. Although it's a long, slow fermenter, the results are well worthwhile.

Homemade yeasts. The home cidermaker can try several other yeast sources. Raisins contain an abundance of wine yeast on their skins.

Boil a quart of water, allow it to cool to 98°F (36.6°C), and then add a half pound of natural sultana raisins. Sultanas are the sun-dried, pale yellow, seedless grapes of the Mediterranean, which you can buy in many supermarkets. Keep the raisins and water warm for several days, then pour the mixture into your cider. This amount will start off ten gallons.

Cider can sometimes get a boost of yeast by pouring in the lees of table wine. This is something of a desperate measure. Care should be taken that the wine is wholesome, and that the dregs have not been allowed to go acetic. The yeasts of California wines may have been pasteurized to death.

Yeast starter. Cultured dry wine yeasts are packaged in foil or paper packets that must be kept in a cool, dry place for maximum storage life. Liquid yeasts, which come in vials that hold enough for a small batch of cider, must be guarded against temperature extremes. Depending on the yeast you choose, a packet or a vial is enough to start from five to eight gallons of cider.

Starting instructions come with most yeasts. The simplest involve emptying the packet of yeast into a cup of 98°F (36.6°C) water, waiting ten or fifteen minutes, then adding it to the cider. Other directions call for bringing a quart of cider to a boil to kill any harmful and competitive bacteria, allowing it to cool to a set starting temperature, then adding the yeast and waiting a few days for the yeast colony to multiply before adding it to the rest of the cider. The cider may have to be sweetened to provide adequate nourishment for the yeast to grow into dynamic, sugar-gulping swarms.

Yeast nutrients. In the first few days of fermentation the yeasts multiply by assimilating nutrients in the juice — largely thiamine (vitamin B_1, which essentially functions as a coenzyme in carbohydrate metabolism) and amino acids. Amino acids make up 80 to 90 percent of the total nitrogen content of apple juice.

When sugar is added to cider to increase its potential alcohol, the balance of nutrients available, which is minimal in apple juices anyway, is tipped out of proportion relative to the large amounts of sugar the yeast must convert into alcohol. The yeast growth will stop when its nutrients run low. The yeast growth brings the soluble nitrogen in the

juice to extremely low levels (10 to 20 mg of nitrogen per liter of juice). The growth can be restarted and encouraged by adding 10 to 50 mg of nitrogen in the form of ammonium sulfate per liter of cider, and 0.2 mg of thiamine (vitamin B_1) per liter. Some cidermakers, especially if they add sugar, simply put yeast nutrient in every batch of cider they start as a matter of course. Wine supply stores sell both ammonium sulfate and thiamine, usually under the simple name "Yeast Nutrient." It comes in handy, premeasured tablets or in powder form with directions.

Sulfur Dioxide

Sulfur dioxide (SO_2) is used in making both wine and cider to kill the yeasts and bacteria that can harm the fermenting as well as the finished juices.

There are both advantages and disadvantages to using this. The advantages are that you start cidermaking with bacteria-free must, avoiding the loss of the batch because of several diseases of cider, and that the sulfited juices ferment better.

The disadvantages to using it are that large amounts of SO_2, found in many processed and packaged foods as well as in wines and cider, may be injurious to your health. The amount that can be added to foods and drinks is regulated by food and drug laws in most countries. Large amounts of SO_2 may also add unwelcome flavors to your cider. The French are trying to develop a cider technology that excludes the use of SO_2 in the process.

For sterilizing barrels, an SO_2 "candle" is burned inside and it releases the gas. For sterilizing cider and equipment in commercial operations, compressed liquid SO_2 is used. The home cidermaker usually uses tablets of either sodium or potassium metabisulfite ($K_2S_2O_5$); when these are dissolved in the cider, they give off sulfur dioxide, water, and minute quantities of cream of tartar. These tablets are sold as Campden tablets of twelve grains each — enough to give fifty ppm (parts per million) of sulfur dioxide to a gallon of must, or quite enough to inhibit the harmful yeasts and bacteria but not be noticed in the finished cider.

In order for the SO_2 to nip the microflora in the bud, so to speak, it must be added to the must *before fermentation.* Juice treated with SO_2 will ferment more rapidly than unsulfited juice.

To make a bulk solution of sodium metabisulfite to a strength of 5 percent sulfur dioxide, mix together:

14 ounces sodium metabisulfite

5¼ quarts water

or

391 grams sodium metabisulfite

5 liters water

One milliliter (roughly ⅟₃₂ ounce) added to the must gives a concentration of fifty parts per million.

Long Ashton's SO₂ Chart

This chart shows how much SO$_2$ to add according to the acidity of the juice. If you have juice with a pH number higher than 3.8, you must add enough acid to bring the pH down to 3.8.

pH OF JUICES	SO$_2$ NEEDED
3.0–3.3	Add 75 ppm SO$_2$ (or 1½ 12-grain Campden tablets/gal.)
3.3–3.5	Add 100 ppm SO$_2$ (2 Campden tablets/gal.)
3.5–3.8	Add 150 ppm SO$_2$ (3 Campden tablets/gal.)
3.8–4.0	Add 200 ppm SO$_2$ (4 Campden tablets/gal.) or lower the pH to 3.8 with malic acid

---

The same basic mixture can be used to make a sterilizing solution for cleaning the grinder, press, cloths, jugs, and counters:

2 liters 5 percent SO$_2$, as mixed above

100 grams tartaric acid

Enough water to make 5 liters

Mix well.

or

2 quarts 4 ounces 5 percent SO$_2$, as mixed above

3½ ounces tartaric acid

Enough water to make 5 quarts 9 ounces

Mix well.

Studies at Long Ashton have shown that if SO$_2$ is added by dribbling it into the pulp while grinding, it inhibits the first stage of oxidation and prevents the tannins from binding with the cell tissue of the

apples. The result is a colorless juice that retains most of its flavor-giving tannins, which are so important to the final taste of the cider.

Use a 2 percent solution of SO_2 (one and one-quarter pounds of potassium metabisulfite dissolved in five gallons of water). One gallon is used for each ton of apples milled.

Do not treat all of your apple varieties with SO_2 during milling. Important as it is to have good tannin levels in the juice, and as impressive as the pale, unoxidized juice is, other vital flavors are created in the oxidation process, and cider *should* have a good rich color. If you want to grind a batch of high-tannin apples (if you're lucky enough to find some) with SO_2 added during milling to keep the tannins free, be sure to grind some other varieties, including aromatics, without SO_2 at milling and let normal oxidation proceed.

Tannins in Your Cider

Tannins, which are complex phenolics, add a slight bitter tang and astringency to cider and give the finest ciders their flavor and personality. They do not add acidity to the juice as does malic, tartaric, or citric acid. North American cidermakers who like a tannin snap to their cider will have to augment the low levels of the native dessert fruits, which have about one-fifth the tannins of European cider apples. One excellent way of getting tannin into your cider is by using crab apples or wild apple-crabs. These small apples are often extremely acidic in addition to having high levels of tannin, so measure the acid content of the must carefully to be sure it's not extreme.

U.S.P. tannic acid in powder form, grape tannin powder, and liquid tannin can be purchased from wine supply stores. About one gram to five gallons of cider will pick up the liquid considerably. Red Quebracho tannin, extracted from a South American tree bark, is chemically similar to apple tannin. It is not listed in wine supply catalogs, but may be ordered through a pharmacist.

Elderberries, whether wild or domestic, contain high amounts of tannin, but the juice will tint your cider to various shades of purple-red, from rosé to a rich garnet, depending on how much you use, and it will give the cider a delicious but not entirely subtle elderberry wine flavor.

Another excellent source of wild plant tannin for cidermakers who have an experimental streak is the staghorn sumac (*Rhys typhina*), also called the lemonade tree or vinegar tree in some areas. The bark is very

Do not confuse benign staghorn sumac, left, with poison sumac, right.

rich in tannins, and the berries, used by the Native Americans, early settlers, and today by wild food enthusiasts, also have good amounts. Pick the hairy red berries, which grow in an upward-thrusting cluster, steep them in boiling water, and strain them through cheesecloth before adding to your cider. The poison sumac tree looks similar from a distance but has smooth branches, untoothed leaves, and smooth white berries. It is an uncommon plant, growing mostly in swamps. The staghorn sumac, with its velvety branches, toothed leaves, and large tight clusters of hairy red berries, is much more common. Make sure you know the difference before you go foraging, and do not touch any part of the poison sumac. It's more virulent than poison ivy.

Acidic Levels and pH Readings

Dessert apples are fairly acidic, so the North American cidermaker rarely has to resort to store-bought acids unless he or she has really insipid fruits. The pH readings of apple juice *may* range from 2.9 to 5.4, but the best range for cidermaking is from 3.0 to 3.8. Low pH levels give the finished cider a zesty tingle and help protect the cider from various sicknesses. The malic acid is also very corrosive, so all equipment touching the cider should be stainless steel, glass, nonresinous wood, polyethylene plastic, or fiberglass.

pH Readings for Some Apple Varieties*

Variety	pH	Variety	pH
Baldwin	3.27	Melba	3.03
Cortland	3.35	Northern Spy	3.18
R.I. Greening	3.23	Red Delicious	3.81
Jonathan	3.25	Spartan	3.59
McIntosh	3.13	Wealthy	2.93

In this list the Red Delicious is quite low in acid (higher pH), and the Wealthy a bit too acidic. The variations in acid may appear to be minute but are really quite noticeable. Seven is neutral on the pH scale, and the lower the number, the more acidic the substance. The pH scale is not as simple as it looks, for the scale of values is expressed in logarithms. Each consecutive number represents *ten times* the value of the preceding number as the numbers decrease. Apple juice with a pH of 3.0 is *ten times as acidic* as a juice with a pH of 4.0. A Wealthy is nine times more acidic than a Red Delicious, and a Melba twice as acidic as a Rhode Island Greening.

The principal acid in apple juice is malic acid — 0.1 to 1.0 percent. Quinic acid and citramalic acids are also present, with trace elements of many other acids. All ciders contain *some* acetic acid, but where aceto-bacter have been able to multiply through exposure to air or through un-sulfited juice, the acetic acid level may shrivel the cider drinker's tongue.

Some people like a vinegary twist to their cider. Some of the farm ciders of the West of England are quite noticeably acetic but have their aficionados. The acetic acid level should be below 0.1 percent in the fin-ished cider for those of us who like it without the vinegar tang.

The acid level in cider decreases during the fermentation process, and many of the acids are converted in the act to other acids of lesser potency. Malic acid may undergo a *lactic fermentation* in which the malic acid is converted to lactic acid and carbon dioxide. This process usually, but not always, occurs after the primary fermentation.

If you start with a sharp, high-acid juice, a lactic fermentation is a blessing, for it reduces the acid by half and smooths and mellows the

---

* These figures, taken from E. Zubekis, "Apple Varieties as Juice," *Report Ontario Horticultural Experiment Station,* Vineland, Ontario, 1966, should be regarded as approximate, since acid levels even in the same variety vary from place to place and even from year to year of the same tree, though less markedly than sugars. Much sunshine makes for high sugar and high acid levels in apples at harvest time.

taste of the cider, which still maintains a high enough level of acid to prevent unwanted bacteria from getting a foothold in the beverage. On the other hand, a lactic fermentation in a low-acid cider can mean real trouble with a ropy, oily cider.

If you have a very acid must, remember that acidity drops in the natural course of fermentation and aging. Rather than decrease the acidity before fermentation by adding calcium carbonate or sterile water, let the cider ferment to dryness, test the acid level again, and if it is still too high, blend it with a lower-acid cider. If you have a very acid cider you should not add SO_2 before fermentation.

If you *must* decrease acidity you may use either calcium carbonate or water, or both. The flavor of the cider will be adversely affected if you use more than one or two teaspoonsful per gallon.

To Reduce Acidity	Add, per Gallon
0.1%	1 tsp. calcium carbonate or 1 pt. water
0.2%	2 tsp. calcium carbonate or 2 pts. water
0.3%	2 tsp. calcium carbonate *and* 1 pt. water

If you want to increase the acidity of your juice you can add commercial malic acid, available from wine supply stores; 3.3 grams (about one teaspoonful) will raise the acid content of one gallon of juice by 0.1 percent.

Wine supply catalogs sometimes suggest that small quantities of ascorbic acid (vitamin C) will reduce the amount of oxidation, but SO_2 is a better additive for this purpose.

Corking Your Cider

Corks are available in many sizes, and can be drilled through to take a commercial or homemade water trap. Old stone jugs, carboys, and demijohns retrieved from antiques shops and auctions with various hard-to-match openings can be used, with the right cork, for your cider-making. When you order corks, measure the diameter of the neck opening and then order corks one or two sizes smaller in diameter (measured at the narrow end) so that they can be inserted firmly. Use a manual or steel electric drill to tap a cork held in a vise. A high-speed electric wood bit tends to wobble and makes an elliptical hole or crumbles the inside of the cork.

Top Diameters, Lengths, and Point Diameters of Tapered Corks

Standard Degree of Taper 3/16" Diameter to 1" Length

Cork No.	Top Dia. (Inches)	Top Dia. (mm)	Length (Inches)	Point (Inches)
000	1/4	6.3	1/2	5/32
00	5/16	7.9	1/2	7/32
0	3/8	9.5	1/2	9/32
1	7/16	11.1	5/8	21/64
2	1/2	12.7	11/16	3/8
3	9/16	14.2	3/4	27/64
4	5/8	15.8	13/16	15/32
5	11/16	17.4	7/8	17/32
6	3/4	19.0	15/16	37/64
7	13/16	20.6	1	5/8
8	7/8	22.2	1 1/16	43/64
9	15/16	23.8	1 1/8	47/64
10	1	25.4	1 1/4	49/64
11	1 1/16	26.9	1 1/4	53/64
12	1 1/8	28.5	1 1/4	57/64
13	1 3/16	30.1	1 1/4	61/64
14	1 1/4	31.7	1 1/4	1 1/64
15	1 5/16	33.3	1 1/4	1 5/64
16	1 3/8	34.9	1 1/2	1 3/32
17	1 7/16	36.5	1 1/2	1 5/32
18	1 1/2	38.1	1 1/2	1 7/32
19	1 9/16	39.6	1 1/2	1 9/32
20	1 5/8	41.2	1 1/2	1 11/32
22	1 3/4	44.4	1 1/2	1 15/32
24	1 7/8	47.6	1 1/2	1 19/32
26	2	50.8	1 1/2	1 23/32

Adding Sugars

The amount of natural sugars in apples varies tremendously from variety to variety and from year to year in fruit from the same tree. Weather, cultivation, shade, fertilizer, and other factors affect this amount. The specific gravity of the juice will indicate how much sugar is in it from nature's hand.

If you want to increase the specific gravity of your juice by adding sugar, how much should you put in?

Specific Gravity Increase	Additional Sugar per Gallon	Additional Honey per Gallon
5°	2¼ oz.	3 oz.
10°	4½ oz.	6 oz.
15°	6¾ oz.	9 oz.
20°	9 oz.	12 oz.

In other words, add two and one-quarter ounces of sugar for every gallon of cider you wish to raise 5°, and three ounces of honey for every gallon you wish to raise 5°. Juice with a specific gravity below 1.045 will yield less than 5.7 percent alcohol and will have risky keeping qualities. It is best to add sugar and bring up the specific gravity to at least 1.045 or 1.047.

Bottles and Bottling

Wine bottle collecting is one of the scrounging arts. You may become known as an eccentric, a bottle nut, or a pack rat by your friends, neighborhood restaurants, catering services, and other bottle sources, but the important thing is to get bottles, and as cheaply as possible. Look at the alternatives.

Burgundy- and Bordeaux-style wine bottles are available through a major East Coast mail-order house for $3.94 per dozen, and champagne bottles are $16.95 a dozen. Plastic champagne stoppers are about 10¢ apiece. Ten cases make 120 bottles, enough to put up twenty-four gallons. For these you pay $139.40 or $18.50, plus the shipping. Depending on where you live and what kind of bottles you're shipping, UPS costs can be as low as $15.00 or as high as $75.00. Postal Service rates are much higher. So, with a possible bill of well over $100.00 for 120 bottles, and up to two hundred gallons to bottle off, begging for bottles is most acceptable.

What kind of bottles? The champagne bottle is the best container for cider. Molded of extra-thick glass, it will withstand years of washing and sterilizing at high temperatures and can be used for both still and effervescent ciders. A long-established symbol of elegance, the American

Specific Gravity

Specific Gravity	Total Sugars*	Percent Potential Alcohol	Specific Gravity	Total Sugars*	Percent Potential Alcohol
1.000	1.3	"	1.034	70.0	4.10
1.001	1.8	"	1.035	72.5	4.20
1.002	3.0	0.05	1.036	74.5	4.35
1.003	5.0	0.20	1.037	76.5	4.45
1.004	7.0	0.30	1.038	79.0	4.60
1.005	9.0	0.40	1.039	81.0	4.75
1.006	11.0	0.55	1.040	83.5	4.90
1.007	13.5	0.70	1.041	86.0	5.05
1.008	15.5	0.80	1.042	88.0	5.15
1.009	18.0	0.95	1.043	90.5	5.30
1.010	20.0	1.10	1.044	93.0	5.45
1.011	22.0	1.20	1.045	95.5	5.60
1.012	24.0	1.30	1.046	98.0	5.75
1.013	26.0	1.45	1.047	100.0	5.90
1.014	28.0	1.55	1.048	102.5	6.05
1.015	30.0	1.70	1.049	105.0	6.20
1.016	32.0	1.80	1.050	107.5	6.35
1.017	34.0	1.90	1.051	110.0	6.50
1.018	36.5	2.10	1.052	112.0	6.60
1.019	38.5	2.20	1.053	114.5	6.75
1.020	40.5	2.30	1.054	117.0	6.90
1.021	42.5	2.40	1.055	119.5	7.05
1.022	44.5	2.55	1.056	122.0	7.20
1.023	46.5	2.65	1.057	124.0	7.30
1.024	48.5	2.80	1.058	126.5	7.45
1.025	51.0	2.95	1.059	129.0	7.60
1.026	53.0	3.05	1.060	131.0	7.75
1.027	55.0	3.20	1.061	133.0	7.85
1.028	57.5	3.30	1.062	135.0	8.00
1.029	59.5	3.45	1.063	137.0	8.10
1.030	61.5	3.55	1.064	139.5	8.25
1.031	64.0	3.70	1.065	141.5	8.35
1.032	66.0	3.85	1.066	143.5	8.50
1.033	68.0	3.95	1.067	145.5	8.60

* Grams per liter   " Less than 0.05 percent

champagne bottle holds 25.4 fluid ounces (750 ml), or a fifth of a U.S. gallon. It is usually tinted green, which helps protect the cider from light. In addition to its strength, the champagne bottle is versatile and can be closed with straight or tapered corks, plastic "mushroom" champagne stoppers, or the all-cork counterparts known as "T" corks. It will also take crown caps affixed by hammer-driven, hand-gripper, or bench model capping machines. The American bottles are a bit narrower at the lip than European champagne bottles, with a neck finish of twenty-six millimeters, which takes plastic stoppers, and a lip for crown caps. The lips of many European bottles refuse crown caps and some are not lipped at all, but instead have pronounced glass neck bands for anchoring the wire hoods needed to hold the closures in place under CO_2 pressure.

Sturdy wine and beer bottles are good cider containers. Avoid all bottles of light "throwaway" construction that take "twist" or "snap" caps. The necks of light wine and beer bottles tend to break or chip under corking and capping-machine pressure, and they are not built to withstand the pressures from fermentation. Most good wine bottles can be closed with straight or tapered, waxed, or plain No. 9 corks. Beer bottles take standard crown caps lined with cork, plastic, or waxed cardboard. Plastic bottle stoppers and plastic "corks" are also available but are suited only to stopper bottles stored in a refrigerator. They have been known to work out with CO_2 buildup or temperature fluctuations.

Many North American wineries and Canadian cidermakers use screw-top bottles. Since the threading is there, it's easiest to close these bottles with twenty-eight-millimeter metal or plastic screw caps, but you can stop them with No. 9 corks. Some cidermakers, leery of richocheting corks from effervescent bottles, use both corks and screw caps, a practice that can result in bursting bottles.

In emergency situations soft drink bottles (twenty-eight-millimeter screw caps), whiskey bottles (twenty-eight-millimeter screw caps or No. 9 corks), and half-gallon and gallon jugs (thirty-eight-millimeter screw caps) can be used.

Corks or caps? Caps, including all kinds of metal and plastic closures, keep air away from cider. They are good where strength is required, such as with highly effervescent champagned ciders, or where all traces of air must be excluded from the bottle, as with sweet, low-acid, low-alcohol ciders.

Corks, on the other hand, are most desirable with ciders of good alcoholic preservative strengths, for corks are not impervious to air, and a cork-capped cider is able to breathe and mature. The action of air on the entrapped aldehydes and esters of high-alcohol cider enhances the bouquet and brings out rich overtones, but ciders sometimes pick up a slight corky flavor from that type of stopper.

Washing and sterilizing. Used wine and cider bottles are havens for undesirable bacteria, especially acetobacter, which find the alcoholic lees in the bottoms of bottles most tasty. Bottles for cider must be scrupulously clean. Use a bottle brush and scrub them inside with hot, slightly soapy water, rinse several times, and sterilize them, neck down, in a canning kettle by boiling them for at least ten minutes. When they are cool, drain them and cover the openings with plastic wrap and rubber bands or with screw caps until they are needed. If you have hard water, let the bottles cool to 75°F (23.8°C); then spray them with cold water. This will remove any calcium haze.

The dishwasher does a superior job of cleaning bottles. Rinse the bottles first, and be sure all the labels are removed. If they peel off in the machine they can clog the drain. The bottles must be put in upside down. If the bottles have a slight odor of detergent after their washing, rinse them with boiling water. Don't sterilize bottles in an oven.

An SO_2 solution, given on page 40 of this section, will inhibit most bacteria if the bottles are washed out with it just before bottling. If you have only a few bottles to do, dissolve one twelve-grain Campden tablet in sixteen ounces of water and pour the solution from one bottle to another, shaking each vigorously. If the bottles have a sulfite odor, rinse them with sterile water.

Bottling off. Getting the cider out of the barrel and into the bottles is a happy time, for after this operation is finished, you can enjoy the rewards of labor, care, and patience. Unlike the cider factory with its Speitz Werke high-speed bottling equipment snapping out winding miles of gleaming cider soldiers, the home bottler's equipment is only a step or two up from the primitive hollow reed, but the job gets done, and at practically no cost.

Use clear, flexible, plastic tubing of food-processing quality for your siphon. Tubing with an inside diameter of five-sixteenths of an inch will

give a steady flow that can be handled in a one-person bottling operation if the tubing has an attached flow-clamp that can halt the fluid between bottles. Since the siphon is gravity operated, it should be long enough to reach from the bottom of the cider container up through the top opening and down to the bottles, which must be on a lower level than the bottom of the cider container. It's fastest to have three people work at bottling — one person sugars the bottles (one-half to one teaspoon in each bottle for effervescence if you are making sparkling cider) and hands the empties to the siphon operator, who fills the bottles and passes them to the capper, who sends home the corks or caps.

Get the liquid moving with mouth suction. Leave at least a half-inch headspace in each bottle.

Closing machines. There are a variety of hand and bench model devices for installing corks and caps. If you are doing fewer than fifty bottles at a session, a simple, inexpensive hand-corking machine will be adequate, but if you face a long corking run, the bench model is both faster and easier on the back.

Hand cappers are not generally worth the trouble, and an inexpensive bench capper pays for itself in short order. There are two major problems with the handheld cappers: The gripper model, using your physical strength to crimp the caps, has handles that always seem to break or bend over time; the hammer-type capper has aluminum grips that compress the cap, but the hammer blow that sends the closure from the device onto the neck of the bottle frequently breaks or chips the glass of the neck. Screw-top wine bottles are the most common victims of these bad cappers.

Hand corkers that are hammer driven have the same problem. A little better are the piston-driven corkers. Best of all are the bench corkers. A French model made of bronze can be adjusted to cork fifths and magnum champagne bottles and has an attachment that converts the machine to a crown capper. American bench cappers are not as versatile; magnums can't be capped, and short beer bottles need to be brought up to position with some type of homemade platform.

Several new all-plastic cappers have also been developed. The Italian "Super Colonna" is particularly good, as it can cap a standard champagne bottle down to the squattest beer bottle thanks to a self-contained adjustable base platform.

Champagne stoppers. These mushroom closures, with as much as five atmospheres of carbonation pressing against them, must be held in place with metal collars, or with the traditional wire hoods, which may have coinlike shiny foil "helmets" at the crown. These wire hoods are designed to anchor the stopper at four evenly spaced points around the bottle's neck. You can buy them ready-to-go from wine supply stores

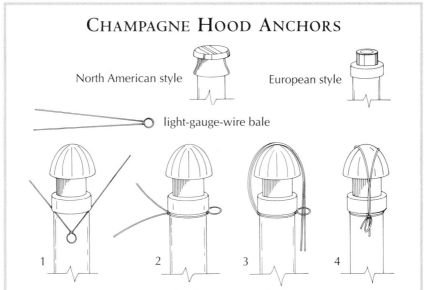

CHAMPAGNE HOOD ANCHORS

North American style

European style

light-gauge-wire bale

1 2 3 4

Homemade champagne wire hood

Cut a piece of light-gauge wire twelve inches long and fold it loosely in two. Twist the bead two or three times to form a small loop.

1. *Place the wires on both sides of the bottle's neck below the raised glass hood anchor. In this illustration a European-type champagne bottle is being used; its band is literally that, and the neck is without lip. North American bottles are lipped and have tapered hood anchors.*
2. *With a pair of pliers pull the wires tight opposite the loop and twist them around twice.*
3. *Bring the wires over the top of the stopper or cork, spreading them a bit so they pass on both sides of the crown, and position them so one is on each side of the loop.*
4. *Twist the wires and loop together with pliers to remove wire slack and anchor the closure.*

and attach them with a pair of light pliers. They cost about fifteen to twenty cents apiece. You can make your own two-point wire anchors at home for the price of some light-gauge wire and a pair of pliers. Since seepage at the end of the cork may acetify, galvanized wire will be most long-lasting.

Screw caps. Plastic and metal screw caps available at wine supply outlets will fit most twenty-eight-millimeter and thirty-eight-millimeter necks. If you are of a saving disposition, save the caps that were origi-nally threaded into your bottles. When bottling time comes, and one of your new caps just won't fit an old bottle, set the bottle aside until the end of the run. When your hands are free again, turn to the topless bot-tle and try out the caps you've saved. Screw them on tightly and see if they grasp the threading firmly. Because the original cap was machine molded to the neck, opening it distorted the aluminum and ruined a perfect seal. To make an airtight closure, heat a tiny bit of paraffin and pour a thin coat inside the cap. Give it a few seconds to cool to a firm consistency, and then screw it onto the filled bottle. The paraffin will level any highs or lows in the cap and conform to the lip of the bottle, giving a good seal.

Labels. Cider bottle contents should be marked by some sort of label. Preprinted bottle labels are available from wine supply stores, and cost ten to twenty cents apiece, though they're cheaper in lots of one hundred. The least expensive ones are simply art borders or pseudo–coats of arms, and the more expensive ones feature grape har-vest scenes, exhibition medals, fruit-laden vines, and such — nothing really suited to apples. Cidermakers will have to have their own labels printed at a local print shop (make sure the printer knows his or her gummed stock and uses one suitable for bottles), or use the plain white ones you can buy at any office supply store. If you have the talent and the time, you can make fine hand-drawn labels. Some programs for home computers will let you make your own labels, as well.

The Cider Cave or Cellar

The *cave*, or cellar, is the important locale where the cider usually fer-ments, and where the bottled nectar is stored and matured. The cave can make or break a cider; it can ruin a year's orchard work and production, can make the labor of harvesting, crushing, and pressing valueless, or it can substantially aid the cider's development into a rich, heady drink.

Most caves for the amateur cidermaker must be adapted from the cellar existing under his or her house. Homesteaders and serious amateur cidermakers who are building can make a cave separate from the main cellar, with a cidery or "poundhouse" above the cool, dark cave. If your cellar is heated, partition off the corner farthest from the furnace for your cider.

The ideal cave is underground (hence the name), neither too dry nor too damp, with fresh air circulation control and a steady, low temperature. The balance of temperature, air, and humidity has a great influence on the quality of the cave. Good proportions of these three elements can mature and conserve the cider, but imbalances may alter or even destroy it.

Temperature. A range of 10°C to 18°C, or 50°F to 65°F, is suitable for most fermenting conditions, but even cooler temperatures are best for storage. If the cellar is too warm, as most North American cellars are (thanks to the furnace), fermentation can start up again too easily, building great pressure in the stored bottles. Too-low temperatures or sudden drops in temperature are dangerous, too. Low temperatures can slow or even stop a ferment, and a sudden, sharp drop can cause a partial vacuum in the fermenting vessel that will suck the contaminated water in the water lock into the cider.

Air supply. The ventilation of the cellar should be controlled, for in a stagnant cellar where cider is fermenting, the carbon dioxide that is released tends to accumulate and will eventually make the air unbreathable for humans as well as for cider. Ventilating will also help a too-humid cellar. Too dry a cellar should also be avoided, as dryness shrinks the barrels and makes for great waste by evaporation. If you have a very dry cellar, sprinkle the floor with water.

Vibration. The cave should have areas for both fermenting ciders and cider storage. Since cider behaves in many ways like its noble cousins, the wines, the cave should be free from vibration and disturbance. Try not to place your cave near railroad tracks, where the homeward-bound dairy herd will tread close overhead, or where the school bus stops out front every morning and afternoon.

Barrel rests. Barrels should never rest directly on the floor of the cave, where they will absorb dampness and mold, to the speedy ruination of both contents and barrel. In French caves the barrels rest on foundations called *"chantiers."* These are long, planklike supports placed in parallel position far enough apart to support the two ends of the barrels. These *chantiers* should be at least one foot off the ground, and rest on stones or cinder blocks spaced along their length so that air can circulate around them. If you have only one or two barrels, they should be in barrel rests or cradles. Occasionally you see an old cellar with a high stone or heavy timber platform for a barrel. This was to make racking off easier.

Bottle storage. The bottles of cider can be stacked in piles in bins made by the home craftsman, or in those specially designed open ironwork bins available from wine supply merchants, or in stacks of old barrels whose ends have been knocked out — in almost anything that suits your purse and taste. Open ironwork bins or compartmented open storage bins in which each bottle has its own niche separate from its neighbors leave your cider unprotected from sudden temperature change. Large culvert tiles are good. They protect the bottles from rapid temperature changes.

Cider only: Neither vinegar nor beer should be made in the cave where cider is fermenting or stored. Airborne yeasts and the volatile acetobacter can contaminate the air, the containers, and eventually the cider itself. Nor should finished cider be allowed to remain in stagnation on its lees in the cave. There is one exception: If you are trying to encourage a malo-lactic fermentation in a high-acid cider, it may be allowed to stand on its lees a month or so after fermentation ends. Otherwise, rack and bottle your cider when it's ready.

Pungent substances: Because of the tendency of apples and cider to absorb aromas, no strongly scented substances should be allowed in the area where apples are stored or cider is made or stored. A musty cellar, a smelly old furnace, earthy potatoes and turnips stored nearby, scented cleaning liquids, paint, turpentine, and other pungent odors are common in cellars. Any or all of these can make a fine cider into something miserable. More good cider is ruined by bad storage conditions than by anything else.

Dirt: The cellar should be kept clean, swept, and dusted — preferably vacuumed. The dirt-encrusted bottles of nineteenth-century romantic literature are best avoided.

Acetobacter: Vinegar or pomace flies, a species of *Drosophylla* attracted to fermenting fruit juice, can carry acetobacter on their bodies and scatter these unwelcome organisms wide. The appearance of these tiny flies in your cellar demands immediate action, for acetic acid is volatile and grows rapidly in light alcoholic beverages, converting the alcohol to vinegar. Make up a sterilizing solution of SO_2 (page 40) and water and sprinkle it on the ground, on the apparatus, and on the exterior of the barrels in the area twice a day.

The Cider Log

A cellar book or cider log can not only give you an ongoing record of the ciders you have made but is also indispensable in reproducing ciders of exceptional quality, avoiding repetition of hideous mistakes, and re-creating your cider triumphs in your memory long after the prize bottle is gone. Many wine supply houses sell wine logs, and while these can do service for cider records, most of us would rather make up and photocopy or mimeo our own log pages with space for information really pertinent to the home orchardist and cidermaker.

CIDER DISORDERS

Cider may be a victim of a number of ills, because of its relatively low alcoholic content, its low levels of acid or tannin, poor storage conditions, or a dozen other reasons. The home cidermaker can remain happily ignorant of most of these problems by keeping utensils, equipment, fruit, cider room, and storage room scrupulously clean; by avoiding the use of metal containers, except stainless steel; and by using SO_2 in low-acid ciders in the early stages of cidermaking.

But sometimes, despite a watchful eye and good cidermaking techniques, the cider goes awry. Some of these disorders can be partially corrected, though the cider will never be as good as before, but others are fatal to the cider and may infect the whole cellar if neglected. The disorders that befall cider are of three kinds: biological, chemical, and accidental.

Cider Log

Date: _____

Orchard and Harvest Comments

Varieties Used in Blend:

_____

_____

_____

Apple Amount: _____

Juice Yielded: _____

% of Blend: _____

Acid: _____

Sugar: _____

Tannin Est.: _____

Aromatic: _____

Blend Acidity: _____

Blend Sugar: _____

Sugar Added: _____

Yeast Type: _____

Other Additives: _____

_____

Comments: _____

_____

Fermentation Notes

Dates Racked Off: _____ Weather: _____

Comments: _____

Date Bottled: _____ Weather: _____

Comments: _____

Storage Notes: _____

_____

Taste Test

Type of Cider: _____   Bouquet: _____

Percent Alcohol: _____   Body: _____

Color: _____   Flavor: _____

Comments: _____

_____

Acetification. This is one of the most common cider disorders, caused by one of several *aerobic* (living in oxygen) bacteria, usually referred to as acetobacter. These convert alcohol into acetic acid, the basic vinegarmaking process. Although the bacteria need oxygen to multiply, they are present in the juice — *all* juice — before fermentation starts, and can survive the *anaerobic* (without oxygen) conditions of fermentation, can survive sulfiting, and, after all this, can revive and launch an assault on the cider during storage — *if they have air.* First, a translucent gray film forms on the surface of a cider exposed to air, which gradually turns to a jellylike vinegar "mother."

If you notice a rise in acidity during or after fermentation, acetification is probably under way. Immediate pasteurization will save the cider as "apple juice" if fermentation hasn't gone far, or as rough farmhouse cider if it's nearly complete. Alternatively, with a cider just beginning to turn acetic, you may save it by adding to the cider one to one and one-half pounds of potassium carbonate per fifty gallons, and then one hundred parts per million of SO_2. If the acetification has happened in storage near the apple harvest time in the next year, freshly pressed pomace may be soaked in the acetic cider and then repressed. The new must will have a much-reduced acetic level and plenty of sugar. If this is fermented and then stored carefully out of all contact with air, the cider is drinkable.

Flower. This is a greasy, ashlike surface film that forms on the cider and is caused by mycoderma film yeasts, which need air for their growth. They break up easily and make the cider cloudy, or insipid, or give it an unpleasant moldy flavor. Prevention is the best cure. Keep air out.

Cider sickness, *la tourne,* or *framboisé.* An infamous cider problem. It occurs in low-acid ciders containing unfermented sugar, especially in warm weather. It is caused by an organism called *Zymomonas mobilis,* which produces acetaldehyde in the cider. A heavy, milky turbidity or haziness, a horrible aroma of rotten lemons or banana skins, and sometimes a white foaming head are the symptoms, caused by the tannins uniting with the acetaldehyde. After four to twelve months, the dreadful odor and taste *may* disappear, but the tannins will be gone, and the cider will be thin and insipid, without character, a weak and feeble thing that has made only a partial recovery from a serious and debilitating illness.

The causative bacteria, which probably live in the soil and get into the juice from the fruit skins, are not affected by even huge doses of SO_2. However, these bacteria cannot survive at a pH below 3.7, nor without simple sugars such as the glucose and fructose found in unfermented cider. In England, where acidity is kept at 3.8 or lower, and the sugars are completely fermented to dry ciders, the sickness is rarely seen now. In France, where low-acid, sweet ciders are stored, there are many problems with this bacteria.

If your cider develops this sickness (unlikely due to the high acidity of North American dessert apples), increase the cider acidity with citric or malic acid. If you catch the disease in its early stages, you may now add a strong pure yeast culture and yeast nutrients to compete with and vanquish the *Z. mobilis* by converting the sugars. At the end of the renewed fermentation, store the cider *below* 50°F or 10°C.

But if the process is well under way, there's not much you can do to stop it. Let the cider proceed to completion, rack it off, and store it for at least six months. After this decent interval, interspersed by prayers, add fresh sugar, a good strain of yeast and yeast nutrients, and start a new fermentation. The cider, if saved, will be drinkable but thin and lackluster. Use it in blends with more flavorful ciders and try to forget.

All vessels and equipment that have been in contact with this cider must be thoroughly sterilized.

Thickness, oiliness, ropiness. This is a disease caused by anaerobic lactic acid bacteria rods and cocci, which attack the sugars in the cider, building slimy polysaccharides — usually after fermentation, during storage. It is most apt to attack low-acid ciders left standing on their lees. The flavor is not much affected, but the cider pours first like light oil, then in thick slimy ropes of raw egg-white consistency. This sickness does not occur when SO_2 is added to the freshly pressed must.

The condition can be slightly remedied. Let the acid level decrease naturally as it does in lactic fermentation, then pour all the affected cider into an open mixing vat. Stir and whip up the cider until the slimy, oily element disappears. Add SO_2 at one hundred parts per million.

If you have a large amount of cider that has gone oily, and the thought of hand-stirring fifty gallons back to health is overwhelming, you can fine the cider with tannin and gelatin (see directions on page 33), then rack off the cider and add SO_2 as above.

Sterilize all equipment and containers that have been in contact with the cider.

Mousiness. Unobtrusive at first, a "mousy" flavor and aroma in the cider soon intensifies to the highly unpleasant odor and taste of an over-populated mouse cage. Some lactic acid bacteria, among others, are held responsible for the affliction.

Putrid fermentation or putrefaction. Both putrefaction and fermentation are the decomposition of organic matter that occurs in the presence of organisms and in the absence of air. The major difference is not one of process, but of basic materials. Sugary substances generally produce end products with a pleasant odor and taste (fermentation), while protein-laden substances produce evil-smelling substances (putrefaction).

Cider can putrify rather than ferment if the utensils used in its manufacture are not clean, if dirty procedures occur during its manufacture, or if protein-rich additives are put into it. If you make cider with apples that haven't been washed, that have dirt, manure, grass, and other vegetative matter clinging to them, if your crusher and press are filthy with dust and old pomace, if your bottles and barrels are dirty and crusted with ancient deposits, if a mouse or rat falls into your fermentation vat, if you add rotten apples or worse to the juice, if you forget to mill the fruit for six weeks after the harvest is in, if you simply do not care enough about the process to keep your equipment clean, you are destined to produce a disgusting and vile liquid that is the result of putrefaction, not fermentation. The problem is 100 percent avoidable.

Blackening cider. When the juice has come in contact with iron, either in the mill or collection vessel, the tannins combining with the dissolved iron in the juice may give the cider a blackish or greenish black color when it comes in contact with air. Such cider will also have a harsh metallic flavor. Other factors can discolor cider, such as enzymic darkening through oxidation of the tannins when exposed to air.

To test for the cause of darkening: Fill two small glasses with the suspect cider. Put a pinch of citric acid in one and let them both stand overnight. In the morning, if the glass with the citric acid is still pale, and the untreated cider has darkened, the problem is iron-darkened cider. To correct the disorder, add fifty grams of citric acid for every hectoliter (twenty-six U.S. gallons) of cider. Dissolve the citric acid in a little cider, then mix it in well.

If both glasses of test cider turn dark overnight, the problem is not iron contamination, but most likely enzymic oxidation, which causes the tannins to combine with the air in an open bottle and "tan" the cider a disturbingly dark brown color. This doesn't often happen unless you have used quantities of overripe apples in your cider. You can correct the problem by crushing and dissolving two Campden tablets per gallon. If you have to treat a large batch, use one and one-half ounces of potassium metabisulfite for every fifty gallons of cider. Once the cider has actually darkened it cannot be restored to the golden pallor of its youth. You must treat it before it goes black.

Green cider. This is caused by allowing cider to come in contact with copper. Copper not only gives cider a greenish color, but markedly taints the flavor. There is also a biological cause for green-colored cider. Some ciders, low in acid, tannin, and nitrogen, but with high mineral levels from the soil in which the apple trees grow, can occasionally develop an olive green color, stop fermenting, and form starch. The problem is just about impossible to cure.

— 2 —
MAKING DIFFERENT CIDER VARIETIES

*I*n *this section* we list six ways to make various ciders. Some of them are descriptions of a state of mind, some of them specific recipes. Still, sparkling, champagne, barrel, French, and an ancient recipe for flavored cider are all given here.

For the beginner, we recommend the Basic Still Blended Cider. The cidermaker who has success with this is ready to try any of the other methods in this book.

BASIC STILL BLENDED CIDER FROM NORTH AMERICAN VARIETIES

The basic directions that follow are for a fifty-gallon batch, but the recipe can be reduced or doubled.

Apple Characteristics

Select varieties that fall into the four categories below for the best blending results.

Neutral base. Thirty to 60 percent of the total juice. Use seven to twelve bushels of sweet, low-acid apples, which will merge and blend with the juice flavors of more zesty and aromatic varieties. Baldwin, Ben Davis, Red Delicious, Cortland, Rambo, Rome Beauty, Stayman Winesap, Westfield Seek-No-Further, or York Imperial.

EQUIPMENT FOR CIDERMAKING

Grinder	Vinometer
Press	Siphon
20–25 bushels apples, several varieties	SO_2
Two 50-gallon barrels or polyethylene tanks	Yeast culture
Fermentation lock	Sugar, sweet cider, or boiled cider concentrate
Fining agent or filter (optional)	About 250 wine bottles or 50 one-gallon jugs, caps, and capper
Titration equipment	
Hydrometer	

Tart. Ten to 20 percent of the total juice. Two to five bushels of medium-acid apples. Jonathan, Cox's Orange Pippin, Eospus Spitzenberg, Newtown, Northern Spy, Rhode Island Greening, Wayne, Wealthy, or Winesap.

Aromatic. Ten to 20 percent of the total juice. Two to five bushels of aromatic apples to give the cider bouquet and "nose." Cox's Orange Pippin, Red Delicious, Fameuse, Golden Russet, Gravenstein, McIntosh, Ribston Pippin, Roxbury Russet, Wealthy, or Winter Banana.

Astringent. Five to 20 percent of the total juice. One to four bushels for tannin content. Three cultivars with higher tannin levels than most are Newtown, Lindel, and Red Astrakhan. The crab apples Martha, Dolgo, Red Siberian, and Transcendent are excellent, but remember that they are also high in acid, too high for most people's tastes, so blend in their juice carefully, or eliminate the tart acid category of apples from the blend. Wild apples also usually have higher tannin and acid levels.

Juice Composition

Dessert apples will give you a juice with a good sugar-acid ratio, low amounts of tannin, and a high nitrogen content, unless you are using apples from grassed-over, long-unfertilized, abandoned orchards, where the nitrogen content will be lower. Nutrient-rich, high-nitrogen juices ferment violently, keeping the yeasts in constant suspension. It is usually

Cidermaking, William Sidney Mount, 1841.

difficult to stop such a fermentation short of dryness (the total conversion of the sugar in the juice into alcohol), which you must do if you want a naturally sweet cider. This is unfortunate, for the naturally sweet ciders are usually of superior quality and better hold the aromatic and fruity character of the original juice than cider fermented to dryness. It is easier to ferment these dessert juices to dryness and then to add sweetener later in the form of unfermented, pasteurized sweet cider, boiled cider, or sugar. If you use low-nitrogen apples from old unmanured orchards, you will have better luck at making a naturally sweet cider by stopping the fermentation process short of completion.

You may want to keep the different categories of juice separate during fermentation, blending them before either storage or bottling until you work out a cellar formula balance to your taste, or you may prefer to blend the apples at milling and pressing time — an easier way to go, but with unknown ends for the first-time cidermaker. It is more practical, with large amounts of cider, to blend before fermentation.

Here are the steps to follow in making Basic Still Blended Cider.

Step 1: Apple harvesting and "sweating." Harvest or buy only mature, ripe, sound apples. Avoid windfalls. Store the apples in a clean, odor-free area for a few days to several weeks, "sweating" them until they yield slightly to the pressure of squeezed fingers but retain their soundness.

Step 2: Washing. Wash the apples in a large tub by directing a water stream from a garden hose with the nozzle set on high pressure directly on them. Discard all rotten or moldy fruit.

Step 3: Milling and pressing. Grind the apples into pomace, and press, one category at a time; keep the different groups separate in carboys or vessels unaffected by the acid juice until prefermentation blending. You may want to sulfite the astringent apples during grinding to retain as much of the tannins as possible. See directions on page 39.

Step 4: Testing and blending. Take quart samples of each category of juice for blending trials. Keep notes of the comparative amounts needed to get a good balance of juices. Test for tannin content first. Add small amounts of the astringent juice to the base until the astringency is right for you. Look for a sensation of drying and puckering in the mouth when isolating tannin taste reactions from acid sensations. Next, work in the aromatic juice and finish with the acid juice, being careful not to get too acid a blend. Keep an eye on the acid level with titration equipment or test strips. When you have a satisfactory balance, blend the bulk of the juice to the same ratios as your blending samples and pour it into the fermenting tank.

Step 5: Testing specific gravity. Immediately measure the specific gravity of the must with your hydrometer, and, if necessary, add the sugar needed to bring up the potential alcohol reading to a good level — at least 9 percent for a stable unpasteurized cider, less if you are going to pasteurize. Anything below 5.7 percent alcohol is risky. Stir in the sugar until it is dissolved.

Step 6: Adding pectic enzymes. You may add pectic enzymes at this point to help in later clarification.

Step 7: Adding sulfur dioxide. Unless you have a very acid juice with a pH of 3.0 or lower, add SO_2 according to the chart on page 40.

Sulfited juice may take up to two weeks to begin fermenting the natural yeasts that have survived but only several days if pure yeast cultures are added. Let the sulfited juice stand for twenty-four hours. The temperature should be constant, between 55°F and 65°F (12.7°C and 18.3°C). Put aside a gallon or two of the sulfited cider for topping off during the boiling-over stage of fermentation, or prepare a topping-off solution of one and one-half pounds of sugar dissolved in a gallon of sterile water.

Step 8: Adding yeast culture. Read about yeasts, starting on page 36, decide which kind you are going to use, and add it now.

Step 9: "Boiling over" or primary fermentation. Leave the barrel or tank open until the foaming, frothing stage of primary fermentation slows down to a regular slower fermentation. This stage may take several weeks. Keep the fermenting vessel topped off with the set-aside cider or sugar-water solution. The cider is protected from aerobic contamination by the SO_2 and the vigorous ferment.

Step 10: Fermentation. When the boiling-over stage has subsided into a regular bubbling ferment, top off the cider level and fit a water seal to the tank or barrel. Let the fermentation proceed until dryness at a constant temperature of 55°F to 65°F (12.7°C to 18.3°C), until the cider reaches a specific gravity of 1.005 or less. The specific gravity usually drops about 1 degree a day in the fermentation process.

Step 11: Dry cider. Take specific gravity readings from time to time as fermentation slows. At dryness, test for acid and note the level. It should be lower than the reading you took before the fermentation began. (If it is higher, the cider has probably been infected by acetobacter, which are busily converting your alcohol to acetic acid. See *Cider Disorders*, pages 55–60.) If you have had a vigorous, high-nitrogen ferment, and the acid reading (and taste) of your cider is still higher than you like at the end of fermentation, let the cider stand for a month on its lees before racking, to encourage a malo-lactic fermentation. The temperature should not be lower than 50°F (10°C). This fermentation may not occur until storage. Titrate and taste samples from time to time until the cider has lost enough malic acidity to be mellow and pleasant to taste. Rack off, filter if you feel you have to, and you may add one hundred parts per million SO_2 to protect the cider from storage contamination. You may bottle the cider now or store it in other containers.

If your cider has a low acid reading at the point of dryness or a specific gravity of 1.005, you may rack off, filter, sulfite, and bottle it immediately or put it into airtight storage. Do not let a low-acid cider stand on its lees.

Sweetened still cider. If the cider you have just made is too dry for your taste, you can make a sweet still cider. Store the racked, dry cider for four to six months before bottling to allow all the yeasts to die out, thus avoiding a bottle fermentation. Then you may add sugar to taste. Six ounces per gallon will give a medium-sweet cider. You may also mix the dry cider with pasteurized, unfermented sweet cider that you processed immediately after pressing in the fall harvest. Leave a headspace of a half-inch as you siphon-fill the bottles. Cap and store the bottles in a cool cellar or cave. If you used dessert-variety apples, a bottle fermentation may occur in such sweetened cider that can produce a foaming "pot-gun" cider, a naturally effervescent cider, or an exploded bottle. Pasteurizing the bottled cider will prevent uncontrolled bottle fermentation but may damage the delicate flavor of the cider. Cold storage is a good alternative.

Naturally sweet still cider. If your apples were gathered from the wilds or from long-unfertilized grassy orchards, and the fermentation has been rather slow, you may be able to stop the process short of dryness for a naturally sweet cider.

As fermentation slows, take occasional samples of the cider with a wine thief or length of tubing. Test the specific gravity. At around 1.030 rack off the cider into an empty, sterile barrel or tank and attach a water seal. A slow, second ferment will eventually start. Keep a close eye on this, and after one or two weeks, or when the specific gravity drops to the range of 1.020 to 1.025, taste a sample for sweetness. If it's too sweet, let the ferment continue until the specific gravity drops a few more points. When it pleases your taste, rack the cider (and filter if you have decided to risk it). With the juice from true cider varieties you would probably have a stable, naturally sweet cider at this point, but with dessert apple juice, it is a good idea to store this cider in a container with a water seal against the very real possibility of a third ferment. If it does start up again, rack off, bottle, and either pasteurize the cider or, if you don't like pasteurization, store it in a very cool place — 30°F to 40°F (1.1°C to 4.4°C).

THE CIDER'S GITTIN' LOW

Cider has inspired a good deal of doggerel dialect poetry, but this one has a certain anxious poignancy that moves all cider lovers.

When the Farmer's stock of
  fodder
He has placed within the barn,
When he's gathered all the
  apples
And has placed them safe from
  harm,
When the butchering is over,
Then the farmer feels so-so;
But he's always sort of worried,
Fears the cider's gittin' low.

He sees the signs of Winter
In the breast-bone of the fowl;
And he fears a spell of weather,
For he's heard a tooting owl.
As he fills the yawning wood-
  box,
He remarks, "It's going to snow."
Then he says, "We must be
  keerful,
For the cider's gittin' low."

When the cold and snapping
  breezes
Bend the sere and leafless trees,
When a pile of feathery
  snowflakes
Is the most a farmer sees,
Then he comes in from the
  tavern,
And he whispers rather slow,
"Goin' to be a freezin' winter,
And the cider's gittin' low."

So throughout the Winter season
And a part-way through the
  Spring
The farmer feeds the cattle,
And doesn't say a thing;
But when he sees us drinking,
With his face expressing woe,
He remarks, while helping
  mother,
That "the cider's gittin' low."

— Unknown

Naturally Sparkling and Champagne Ciders

The home cidermaker who tries his or her hand at making naturally sparkling and champagne-type ciders is an avocational descendant of Dom Pérignon, the seventeenth-century cellarer-monk credited with the discovery of champagne. These lightly sweetened bubbly ciders are the most popular of all ciders. When they are made commercially, assembly-line fashion, bottles of full-flavored, low-acid, slightly sweetened cider are injected with CO_2 in amounts ranging from a "crackling" two or three atmospheres to five or six atmospheres in the champagne types. Another way they are made commercially is by the Charmat Closed Cuvée and related methods, in which the apple juices are processed into bottled cider by passing through hermetically sealed pasteurization, fermentation, and refrigerated aging tanks without being exposed to air. CO_2 in tank form is not practical for the home cidery without special bottling equipment and pressure gauges. (A sample, of sorts, can be made by charging a seltzer bottle with cider and then squirting the apple bubbly directly into glasses.) The natural carbonation of cidermakes a much finer drink and is a simple process for the home cidermaker.

Start with a supply of well-flavored, clear dry cider, as made by the preceding directions, that was fermented with champagne yeast. Champagne yeast is important, for the yeast must convert all the sugars into alcohol during the first fermentation and still retain enough vigor to convert a small quantity of added sweetener into CO_2 and a bit more alcohol during the bottle fermentation. Since alcohol in greater strengths has an inhibiting or deadly effect on yeast, a dry cider of not more than 7 to 10 percent alcohol by volume will give the best results. The added CO_2 helps counter acetification in later storage.

Naturally Sparkling Cider

Dry cider
Hydrometer
Heavy glass bottles, champagne, cold duck, or beer
Thermometer
Sugar

Crown caps and capper (for naturally sparkling cider)
Champagne stopper and wire hoods (if cider is to become champagne type)

1. Temperature. See that the dry cider is the correct temperature for an accurate hydrometer reading. The specific gravity of absolutely dry cider is 1.000 — no sugar present.

2. Testing the yeast. Determine the strength of the residual champagne yeast by making a test bottle run. Fill a champagne bottle three-quarters full of the cider, add two teaspoons of sugar, then stopper and anchor the stopper with a wire hood. Wrap the bottle in a towel and place it on its side for three weeks, maintaining a steady temperature of 68°F (20°C).

Unwrap the bottle carefully and see if any lees or silty haze has formed in the bottle, the welcome sign of fermentation. Open it. Since the bottle was only filled three-quarters full, carbonation should have built up in the headspace, enough to make the stopper pop or pull out freely. Pour some into a glass — if it fizzes lightly, you're in business.

3. Bottling. Bottle up the batch, sugaring each bottle with two teaspoons of sugar, or, more efficiently, adding enough sugar to the dry bulk cider to bring the specific gravity up to 1.010, and then bottling. This amount of sugar will add 1 percent of alcohol to the finished batch of cider.

4. Storage. Store naturally sparkling cider bottles on their sides in a cool place if you have closed them with corks. If you have used plastic stoppers you do not have to keep liquid in the neck, and you may stand the bottles up.

But suppose the stopper does not come easily out of the bottle in Step 2? If there is no haze and the cider seems to be as still as the day it went in after three weeks of the test run, a nutrient may be needed to rouse the yeasts from their torpor. Add to the bottle one-quarter of the amount of yeast nutrient prescribed for a gallon of cider (or for the specific sugar weight of the liquid). Reseal the bottle and wait another twenty-one days. If your trick has worked, sugar the cider to 1.010, add the appropriate amount of nutrient tablets or powder for the whole batch, let it all mix for a day, and then bottle it off.

Any cider that won't respond to the yeast nutrient is best drunk just as it is — still.

Naturally sparkling cider is like natural beer, a drink that tends to be cloudy because of the dead yeast cells and other precipitates of fermentation as well as pectin. Depending on the clarity of the still cider when you added the heading sugar, the cloud in each bottle of your cider bubbly can range from an intangible haze to Mississippi murkiness. Therefore, these ciders should be placed in an upright position a day or so before serving so that the lees will settle around the punts in the bottoms of the bottles. Often it's possible to pour sparkling cider with the lees remaining in the bottle, and other times the sudden release of pressure will send CO_2 bubbles hurtling up and disturbing the sediment. The taste isn't affected by the haziness, but, for reasons of pride, training, and aesthetics, cidermakers may demand absolutely clear beverages. When naturally sparkling cider is cleared, it becomes cider of the champagne type.

Champagne-Type Cider

Closures to duplicate those in
   the bottles to be cleared,
   and wire hoods
Shallow tub and *dégorgement*
   rack

Rock salt
Crushed ice
Bucket of ice water
Double-ended cotton swabs
   (sterile)

1. **Settling lees.** Let your bottled, naturally sparkling cider sleep for six months to a year. Now, place the bottles neck down in crates so that the lees, which have settled along the side or in the bottom, will slide down to rest on the cork, or in the hollow plastic stopper stem. If some bottles have impacted sediments that won't drop of their own accord, give the bottles a brisk twist with glove-protected hands to dislodge the lees. In the French champagne business, the twisting of bottles is an art and the man who does it is known as a *remueur*. A good one can handle more than thirty thousand bottles daily.

Production in the home cidery is somewhat smaller, but the twisting is just as important and takes caution. The lees *must* be on the corks in order to be removed, and if you jolt a bottle with high-pressure contents, there is the danger of bursting and a handful of broken glass. While it's doubtful that the carbonation resulting from two teaspoons of sugar, which will generate perhaps two or three atmospheres of pressure, will burst a stout champagne bottle that is designed for twice that pressure, still, glass does crack and accidents do happen. The cider *remueur* who wears leather gloves is wise.

Lees settled in the bottom of the bottle.

2. Removing lees. Settled lees are removed by a process known as *dégorgement* that involves getting the sediment into such a position that gas and foam will propel it from the bottle when the stopper is popped. To curtail excessive foaming and loss of beverage the modified technique commonly used calls for freezing the cork and that portion of the bottle-neck liquid containing the lees, then removing both as a solid core.

Fill a shallow tub with a freezing bath made by mixing two parts of crushed ice and one part of rock salt. Rest a *dégorgement* rack across the tub. The *dégorgement* rack can be made from a wide plank or a sheet of plywood drilled with rows of two-and-one-half-inch holes through which the necks of the bottles protrude. Load the bottles carefully into the racks as they were taken from the crate, upside down. The level of the brine should rise half an inch above the lees.

The brine quickly freezes the tops of the necks. Each bottle is then promptly dipped into a bucket of ice water to remove any salt, the wire hood is removed, and the stopper is popped. The frozen core of lees usually flies out with the stopper, either stuck to the back of the cork or frozen in the hollow plastic stem, but if the cork has to be pulled free, the sediment plug usually comes with it. Aim the corks into an elevated box or barrel.

3. Replacing the liquid. Wipe the interior necks of the bottles with cotton swabs to remove any traces of residue. Liquid lost through the foaming should be replaced with cider of the same batch, poured from an open bottle, or with a *dosage* of sugar, or cider or apple brandy. If a

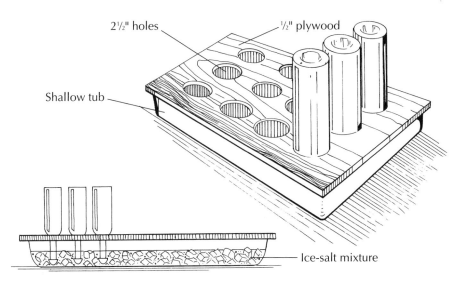

Dégorgement *rack. Note that the bottles are submerged so that the liquid is half an inch above the lees on the cork or stopper.*

dosage is used, the cider should be consumed within several months because the sugar content will ferment and make new deposits.

4. Restopping. Insert fresh stoppers, wire them down, and put the cleared cider back to sleep for several weeks before consuming it.

Cidermakers with deep freezers can try degorging this way after a test run: Put an inverted bottle of cider into the freezer and allow it to freeze. Pull the stopper. A hollow-stemmed plastic stopper is the best for this as the lees come out with the stopper and won't have to be gouged out with a knife. Replace the stopper with another sterile one. Unlike soft drinks and beer, cider of fair alcoholic strength does not freeze into a solid mass that expands and bursts the bottle; it turns into a mushy "slip-ice." If the *dégorgement* by freezer works well with the test bottle, then the process can be carried out in case lots.

OLD-FASHIONED NEW ENGLAND CIDER

The ciders of rural New England a century and more ago were made in wood and had a rugged and well justified reputation for alcoholic strength. The most powerful ciders were the most prized, and "receipts"

THOMAS'S DIRECTIONS

Isaiah Thomas, Jr.'s Town and Country Almanack *for 1819 gives directions for making cider. The advice is a mixture of common sense and tradition.*

All apples fit to be eaten will make good cyder. The grand secret is in cleaning it from the filth and dregs as early as possible. Each sort of apples are to be beaten and pressed by themselves. Two kinds of juice, both good, would, if mixed, often make bad cyder. Throw out all imperfect, sorry, sunburnt apples, as well as dust and trash: beat your apples before much mellowed, as they lose their strength, soundness and spirit, if too mellow; let them stand half a day after being beaten, before putting into press; then press them slowly; discontinue it as soon as the liquor discharged appears to grow thin and watery. The advantage of low pressure is in making the liquor run pure. Let your casks, previously well cleansed, be filled quite full to let the froth and pomace to discharge itself at the bung. When the fermentation abates, cover the bung closely with something that may be lifted by the fixed air that escapes during the future fermentation. In a week rack off the cyder carefully — ceasing the moment you observe it to run muddy. Now stop the cask more firmly: in ten days rack it off a second time, and in fifteen days the third time.

for locally famous ciders usually directed the cidermaker to add boiled cider, raisins, sugar, molasses, honey, and other sweeteners to his mix. These were designed to raise the spirituous element of cider to a level more tolerable to the palates of New Englanders who regularly downed prodigious amounts of rum. That same kind of cider can be made today. You don't have to use potassium metabisulfite, hydrometers, titration tests, or cultured yeast strains. You might even be able to make decent cider without a water trap, an acid tester, or a bottle capper. It was done for centuries, but in those days people had more time to spend in the cider room; plenty of child labor to pick apples, cart them home, and grind them; and quantities of apples, so any barrels lost to the vinegar fly were recouped via the vinegar barrel without great regrets.

Equipment and Materials for Barrel Cider

The primary fermentation vessel is a clear, fumigated barrel. (See the section on barrels beginning on page 18.) It should lie in the cradle or be elevated in some other way to allow for siphon racking and bottling. If the cider is to be racked into another barrel of comparable size, its bunghole must be lower than the bottom of the fermentation barrel. In the old days barrels used for fermenting were sometimes rolled up into place on stone or heavy timber rests three or four feet above the cellar floor.

Since colonial days sweeteners have been added to New England cider to give it a higher alcoholic content. Potency was one goal, and another was to make a product that would keep.

Of the sweeteners, sugar, boiled cider concentrate, and honey are the most suitable for modern tastes. The sugars can be cane or corn — white, brown, or golden. The darker sugars slightly flavor the finished cider. The best honeys are apple blossom, orchard, and clover honey, all delicate and harmonious with apple aromatics. Buckwheat and golden-rod honey overpower the cider.

Fresh cider, reduced from one-half to one-quarter of its original volume by boiling, was called "boiled cider" and was often used as a prefermentation sweetener to boost the alcohol. Molasses and maple syrup were other traditional sweeteners, but neither is favored today. If molasses is used, the entire barrel of cider, potent though it may be, will taste powerfully of sorghum. Maple syrup is an old farm sweetening standby and there's still nothing like it on pancakes and snow, but it can do strange things to cider. Today's high cost prevents its use as a bulk sweetener by all but the very wealthy, but some sugar producers who also make cider have tried it and reported the finished cider has an off-flavor faintly resembling mold.

Raisins — natural, sun dried, and untreated with preservatives — have served as both yeast and nutrients to cider for centuries. Depending on the microflora of the cider mill, the apple juice will be rich or marginal in fermenting yeasts, and raisins can encourage a vigorous fermentation. In addition to carrying wine-type yeasts, raisins provide the cider with sugars in the form of dextrose and levulose. The grapes contain between 12 and 27 percent sugar and 70 to 80 percent water. If the water is evaporated you have raisins — little dots of fruity sugar. The raisins also supply the yeasts in the cider with nutrients — amino acids and proteins — and make a small contribution to body with malic and tartaric acids and tannin. Raisins were also used in the old days in low-alcohol stored cider. A handful of raisins dropped into the cider kept a slight fermentation going, and the CO_2 bubbles rising through the cider kept acetification at bay.

Other items were added besides raisins. Unground wheat was a favorite. Some people sprinkled it into a fermenting barrel, where the wheat supposedly made a thick dust coat on top of the cider, protecting it from air and making a water lock unnecessary. Others claimed that half a peck of wheat (unground) put into cider that was "harsh and eager" would make it "more mild and gentle." Less savory items were added too, the most infamous being the aged beefsteak beloved of "scrumpy" freaks. There is some validity to the belief that a slow fermentation would "pick up" after a piece of meat had been worked through the bunghole, for the steak added nutrients to the juice, probably enough to encourage the yeasts to proceed.

New England Barrel Cider

Fermenting barrel on planks or in a barrel cradle
Honey or sugar or boiled cider concentrate
Raisins

Water lock, siphon hose, and racking stick
Small draft barrels or bottles and closures

1. **Primary fermentation.** Fill the barrel with cider. Siphon out and reserve two or more gallons to allow space for the sugar for topping off. Add the sugar — about eight ounces per gallon, or about ten ounces of honey per gallon. Top off the barrel, leaving the bung open, and put the remaining cider in the refrigerator to use for topping off during the next few weeks. The natural yeasts present in the juice should be enough to start the primary fermentation, a "boiling-over" process that is marked by foam and bits of fruit cascading out of the bunghole and down the side of the barrel. Keep the barrel filled to the bunghole so the cider can purge itself, and wipe the barrel off daily with a damp rag.

When the foaming ceases, add the raisins — one pound to every ten gallons of cider — and insert a water lock. In earlier days when water locks were unknown, the cider was protected from airborne bacteria by loosely fitting bungs or layers of muslin held in place by the bungs or by sandbags. Both are risky procedures. Top the barrel up before you leave it. Allow the cider to ferment for the next two or three months without removing the water trap.

2. **Dryness.** When the bubbling of the water trap stops altogether and is quiet for two weeks, pull the trap, sterilize the water-lock tubing in boiling water, and use it as a wine thief to sample a little of the cider. If it's dry, bung the barrel tight, and let the cider stand on its lees

until bottling time, traditionally in March. If the cider is still a bit sweet — too sweet for your taste — add more raisins, replace the water lock, and wait a few weeks to see if fermentation will start again. If it doesn't, consider bottling and pasteurizing it as lightly alcoholic sweet cider, or, if you're unscrupulous, consider cheating by slipping in a couple of decks of yeast and a handful of nutrient tablets when no one is looking.

3. Bottling. When the cider is ready to bottle, pick a good clear day in the middle of March for "bottlin' off." Cloudy days make cloudy cider. If you want sparkling cider, put a little sugar in the bottom of each bottle — one-half to one teaspoon — and cap them. Sometimes the residual yeasts in barrel cider won't be strong enough to convert the small amount of sugar added into sparkle and alcohol. In that case you'll end up with lightly sweetened still cider. Usually there are enough yeasts, so the bottles should be strong enough to withstand pressure — champagne and beer bottles.

4. Draft cider. Draft cider is what you'll have if you store your cider in wood instead of bottles. If your barrel of cider has made it from October to March, you can rack it into another big barrel for aging, which could be a year or two, or into smaller barrels and kegs. Once a big barrel is tapped, however, it must be emptied swiftly, because as the *ullage* (the air space between liquid and wood) increases, so does the danger of acetification. It's better to rack off into smaller barrels. As long as they're capped full and bunged tight the cider is safe. Once you open one you must drink it up within a few weeks or risk vinegar. Barrels in three-gallon, five-gallon, and ten-gallon sizes are most useful.

5. Avoiding acetification. Storage in a barrel means constant attention to the peril of evaporation, and topping off every few months. Acetification has always been a nagging problem in barrel-stored ciders. Efforts to keep the air away from the good liquid were ingenious in old New England. One method was to pour into the barrel a bland oil — usually olive oil — which spread over the surface and effectively sealed the cider away from air. In the days of wooden bungs, very long bungs — six to eight inches long — would be wrapped in waxed canvas and driven in so that one end of the peg was submerged in the cider. The moisture-swollen wood kept the bunghole tightly sealed.

FRENCH CIDER

French ciders made by the following method are superb, and many cider connoisseurs consider them the finest in the world. No SO_2 is used in the juice, no yeast cultures, and no added sugar to bring up the alcohol level. The cider is completely natural, and very difficult to make. At its best it is exquisite.

The French cidermaker must have experience, skill, and a passion for cleanliness; even then cider sicknesses often attack. North American cidermakers who want to try this method should not use dessert apples, but either grow their own cider stock (a long-term proposition) or experiment cautiously with small batches squeezed from wild apples or crab apples. The following directions are taken from the pamphlet *"Comment Faire du Bon Cidre"* ("How to Make a Good Cider"), published by the *Comité des fruits à cidre et des productions cidricoles* for home and farm cidermakers.

Choice of Apples

Use only cider apples with a high specific gravity of *at least* 1.055, or more than 115 grams of sugar per liter of juice, and *low amounts* of nitrogenous material.

MOONSHINE

There are persons who think, that the influence of the moon affects the making of cider, and they assert, in support of their opinion, that, such as is pressed out, when it is decreasing, by being less disposed to ferment than the other, retains a more pleasant taste.

— A Treatise on the Cultivation of Apple Trees, and the Preparation of Cider, Being a Theoretical and Practical Work for the Use of the Inhabitants of the Island of Jersey, *the Reverend Francis Le Couteur, 1806*

Blends. Sweet and bittersweet varieties make up the base of the blend, and these sugar-rich apples produce the high alcohol levels necessary for preservation. Acidic apples improve the cider's taste and give a certain amount of protection against oxidation and *framboisé.* The bitter or astringent tannin apples give body to the cider and facilitate the formation of the *"chapeau brun"* (literally the "brown cap" or crust).

Harvesting. Use only clean, sound, mature apples for quality cider that will keep well. Of the early, midseason, and late-ripening cider varieties, the early September apples are the softest and must be pressed immediately, for they won't keep; the semihard midseason apples, which are ready from early October to mid-November, must be stored awhile before they are ready to press; the late hard apples are not ripe, though mature, at harvest time, and must be stored for a long while before they are ready to press in December or even January. The early apples tend to ferment too quickly and make a poor cider. The later apples are the most aromatic. Harvest the fruit in dry weather and handle the apples carefully.

A turn-of-the-century advertisement urging French cidermakers to make champagne cider for greater profits.

Preparation for Cidermaking

French cidermakers must keep their cidreries and caves fanatically clean to avoid contamination problems. The following is routine:

Before beginning, thoroughly clean the press room and cave. Whitewash the walls with a solution made up of ten kilograms of quicklime and one kilogram of copper sulfate.

At the end of every work period, wash down the area where the cider is being made, clean every metal part, wash and scrub down the press at the end of every day it is used, and wash the pumps, pipes, tubes, and press cloths to avoid the development of unwanted bacteria.

When the pressing is over, rinse and disinfect the press cloths with 0.5 liter of liquid bleach per 100 liters of water. Use nylon press cloths to facilitate cleaning.

Cleaning wood casks and barrels. The extremely thorough cleaning of the storage containers includes these steps:
1. Prepare a solution of three to four kilograms of washing soda in one hundred liters of water. Pour this into the barrel, bung it, and keep it there for forty-eight hours, vigorously rolling the barrel many times a day.
2. Empty, then rinse the barrel twice with clear water.
3. Rinse the barrel with a mixture of 150 grams of citric acid in twenty-five liters of water to neutralize any residual soda.
4. Drain and rinse with clear water again.
5. Drain, dry, and bung up the barrel for one week.
6. Fumigate the barrel with sulfur. Bung until needed.

To ensure good storage and to reduce the evaporation of cider during barrel storage, treat the exterior of the barrels every two to three years with a mixture of three parts linseed oil and one part turpentine.

Procedure for French Cider

The eight steps to French cider may look a bit complicated, but if you take them one step at a time, being careful to perform each step completely, you will be amply rewarded when it's time to drink the cider.

Milling. Do not grind green, unripe apples. They give a juice that is low in sugar, ferments rapidly, and makes defecation very difficult, leading to a poor cider low in alcohol and subject to various cider troubles. Throw out rotten apples. Wash the apples before milling. Use a grinder mill that slivers the fruit by means of sawtoothed knife blades that give a very fine, consistent pulp and a pure juice.

Cuvage or maceration consists of lightly packing the freshly milled pulp into vats where it is stored for six to eight hours. This gives a greater yield of juice, better success in the defecation stage, as well as better coloration and more pronounced aromatics in the finished cider.

Pressing. Use a press with a central screw. Avoid all contact of the pulp with cement or iron. Use racks and nylon press cloths. The pressure should be applied slowly and regularly to assure the quality and maximum quantity of juice.

Defecation and racking off. The expressed must, except the juice from very acidic apples, now has to undergo a natural purging, or defecation, before fermentation. (In England this process is called "keeving.") Defecation is the very slow beginnings of fermentation and is successful only at low temperatures. As soon as the juice has been pressed out and poured into a defecation vat, add to each hectoliter of juice thirty grams of calcium carbonate and forty grams of fine table salt. In a few days the pectic material in the juice coagulates through enzymatic action, and when the process is well established, it covers the surface of the must with the brown scum called *chapeau brun* that is kept buoyed up by the rising bubbles of CO_2. The lees sink and are deposited at the bottom of the vessel. Most of the yeasts, bacteria, and molds are captured in the lees and the *chapeau brun*. This process also brings about an important decrease in the nitrogen content of the juice: Deprived of nitrogen, the must ferments very slowly and gradually purifies itself, becoming increasingly likely to give a naturally sweet cider.

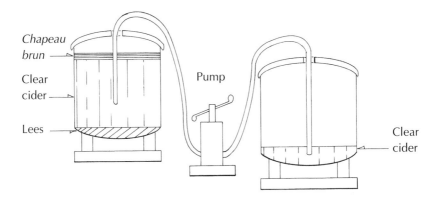

Racking off the clear cider at the critical moment after defecation. Note the position of the pump between the containers.

The defecation process should be finished no more than eight days after pressing. When the *chapeau brun* is well formed, the must is very clear, sandwiched between the *chapeau* and the lees. It should be racked off immediately into another tank by siphon or pump. Both defecation and racking off should be done in cool weather.

Fermentation. The must is now set to ferment very slowly in airtight containers fitted with air locks in a cave kept at 10°C to 12°C (50°F to 56°F). This slow fermentation may take months to complete.

Ullage. If the fermentation takes place in a barrel, some cider will evaporate. Therefore, the barrel must be topped off every month with quality cider.

Second racking off. A second racking off will slow down the fermentation even more and help clear the cider. The racking off should be done on a clear, calm day with a high barometric pressure reading. Low pressure puts the lees back into suspension to some degree. Avoid racking the cider when the density of the must is between 1.025 and 1.035, for there is a risk then of *framboisement.*

Storage. For cider to keep well, it must be cut off from contact with the air. If you store the cider in barrels, they must be topped off every three to five weeks. Bottles are the best way to protect a quality cider. The cider may be bottled without danger when the specific gravity does not vary more than 2 points (degrees) in three weeks.

Specific Gravity	Cider Characteristics
1.000–1.005	Dry cider
1.010–1.015	Semisweet cider with 20–30 g sugar per liter
1.018–1.020	Sweet cider with 30–40 g sugar per liter
1.020–1.025	Very sweet cider

Bottling. Bottle in clear weather when the barometric pressure is high, using champagne bottles. Fill the bottles gently, using a siphon long enough to reach to the bottom of each bottle. Do not let the cider cascade down into the bottles. These precautions will prevent the cider from losing its carbonic gas. Fill the bottles so that the corks will touch the liquid when in place. Use good quality corks, made flexible by soaking in hot water. Fasten down the corks with wire and store the bottles on their sides in a cool cave.

CIDER IN A HURRY!

Sparkling sweet cider, a light alcoholic refreshment that is speedily made in small quantities, is popular. Little space is required, basic experiment expense is one-time and minimal, and, since the project calls for only five gallons of apple juice, the supply can be obtained at a mill or farm stand and transported home without too much trouble.

A blend of apple varieties of your own choosing is best, but since most cider mills blend two or more cultivars, it's possible to come home with a prefermentation blend that will be as pleasing as finished cider. A basic blend could be 25 percent aromatic and 75 percent base juice.

The bottle on the left has too much headspace above the cider. The bottle on the right is filled correctly, with the cork just touching the cider in the bottle.

Sparkling Sweet Cider

5-gallon carboy with water trap	Siphon tube
Yeast	Heavy beer bottles
Potassium bisulfite or sodium metabisulfite	Crown caps and capper
	Canner or deep kettle with rack

Fill carboy with juice and add fifty parts per million of potassium bisulfite or sodium metabisulfite, mix, and let stand for twenty-four hours. Inoculate with yeast — some dry yeasts can be added directly to the juice — and protect with a water lock. Place the carboy near a radiator, furnace, or stove so a temperature of 75°F to 85°F (23.8°C to 29.4°C) can be maintained for three or four days after CO_2 first escapes from the trap. When no more bubbles rise to the surface, remove the trap and taste the cider for sweetness. If a sweeter drink is desired, add sugar to the bottles at the rate of one-half teaspoon per twelve-ounce bottle, one teaspoon per sixteen-ounce bottle, or one tablespoon per quart. Slightly larger amounts of honey can be used as a substitute. Fill and cap the bottles, leaving one to one and a quarter inches of headspace, and move them to the warm radiator or stove position for three or four more days. During this period residual yeasts will ferment the added sweetener to produce a small quantity of alcohol and CO_2 sparkle, or "head."

Chill a bottle, pop the cap, and check it for effervescence. If you want more sparkle, let the bottle work several days longer, then pasteurize (see below). This is necessary because if the yeast is left unchecked, it could convert all the desired sweetener into alcohol and generate enough gas to burst the bottles. Also, since this cider is sweet and low in alcohol, it can be prone to bacterial contamination unless pasteurized.

To pasteurize, place the bottles in a canner or, for the tall quart bottles, in a deeper kettle. The bottles should be in racks and covered with water to a level an inch above the caps. Bring the water to a boil, boil for sixty seconds, then turn off the heat and raise the rack to let the bottles cool. When the bottles are cool enough to handle, lift them out carefully, avoiding drafts or stray splashes of cold water. Place them on their sides on towels or layers of newspaper. Don't let the bottles touch; the air should circulate around them. When the bottles are cool, store them in an upright position so the slight sediment will settle. Storage in a cool dark place for a month is all the aging needed. This cider is best drunk thoroughly chilled.

Flavored Cider

Anyone who has ever enjoyed thyme- or marjoram-flavored apple jelly with a roast bird, or noticed the ability of apples to carry and blend other flavors with their own, knows that aromatic herbs combine with apple to the mutual enhancement of both, a rare and happy marriage of the medium and the flavoring.

Experiment-minded cidermakers with herb gardens may enjoy testing this seventeenth-century recipe:

Though Cider needs not any, 'tis yet a very proper *Vehicle* to transfer the vertue of any *Aromatic,* or *Medicinal* thing: . . .

Ginger renders it brisk: dried *Rosemary,* Wormwood, juice of *Corints,* &c. whereof a few drops tinges, and adds a pleasant quickness. Juice of *Mulberries, Blackberries,* and (preferable to all) *Elderberries* press'd among the *Apples,* or the *Juice* added: Clove-July-flowers dry'd, and macerated both for the *tincture* and *flavor* is an excellent *Cordial:* Thus may the *Vertues* of any other be extracted: Some stamp *Malago Raisins,* putting *Milk* to them, and letting it percolate through any *Hippocras* sleeve: A small quantity of *this,* with a *spoonful* or two of Syrup of *Clove-July-flowers* to each Bottle, makes an incomparable drink.

Clove-July-flowers, or "gilliflowers," are clove pinks *(Dianthus caryophyllus)*. A "Hippocras sleeve" was a filter used to strain a highly spiced wine, Hippocras, much favored in the period.

BENEFICIAL VOYAGE

English cidermakers sometimes sent their cider on a sea voyage, as did winemakers with Madeira, to improve it. One ciderist wrote in 1801:

> *I had three hogsheads of cider which I left to work on the lees, after which I had it racked three times; and, in March, 1789, I put half a gallon of Coignac brandy into each hogshead, and soon after I had it bottled off. I had exactly sixty dozens, which I put on board the Peggy, (Captain Thomas Bandinal), and sent them to the Bay of Honduras.*
>
> *The heat of the climate made a great many of the bottles fly during the passage. The remainder, (the bottles included), was sold as mountain wine, at the rate of forty-three shillings a dozen.*

This sharp practice of doctoring up cider and then selling it as Málaga, the Spanish dessert wine known in England as "mountain wine" or "mountain," was quite common.

APPLES FOR CIDER

It is almost impossible to decide precisely which is the apple that affords the best cider. The qualities of this fruit . . . depend . . . on the climate, the soil, the exposure, and the age, of the tree. Some persons have extolled l'amerel *or* gentilhomme *and the red streak has enjoyed a high reputation; but the one and the other are now worn out. Every thing that is the work of man impairs itself, and passes away like him.*

— The Reverend Francis Le Couteur, 1806

The bouquet, color, flavor, and body of cider depend almost as much on the varieties of apples used in making this ancient drink as on the method of fermentation. The single most important step in cidermaking is acquiring fine-flavored, well-ripened apples with good levels of acid and tannin. The fame of your cellar is linked to the trees from which the fruit came, and, accordingly, a cidermaker should know how to appraise an apple just as a viticulturist knows how to judge a bunch of grapes.

THE APPLE — BODY AND SOUL

Begin this appraisal by looking at an apple, feeling and hefting it, smelling, and, finally and most important for the cidermaker, biting into it and tasting it judiciously. It is worthwhile taking a little time to examine and categorize apple varieties that are new to you, not only for

the pleasure of it, but also to sharpen your senses and observations as to which apples will make the best cider for your palate.

Size

The sizes of apples vary from the huge, hand-filling Wolf River to tiny crab apples. A crab apple is any apple less than two inches in diameter. A large apple can be fairly light, and a small, juice-packed one quite heavy. Apple sizes can vary on the same tree from year to year, depending on soil nutrients, disease, rainfall, sunshine, the intensity of orchard care, and thinning of the fruit. Very small, hard apples such as crabs often give trouble at crushing time. True European cider apples tend to be small and dense, while North American table varieties are usually of good size. Europeans prefer the small apples because they do not bruise easily when they fall, and because the proportion of the skin and pulp is small — important parts of the fruit in cidermaking.

Form

The form of an apple is its geometric shape. If it is tall and tapered, it is conical; if tall and untapered, cylindrical. Apples that are broader than they are tall are described as "flat." Additionally, apples may be regular, lopsided, ribbed, or a combination of these.

Skin

The skin of an apple contains essential oils and odorants that give the apple its aroma, plus acids, tannins, certain bitter substances, yeasts, and pigments that color it. The color variations in apples are uncountable. Young apples are all green. As they ripen, the green turns yellow, the "ground" color. The red that overlies the ground color in many apples is called the "surface" color. Some varieties, such as the Golden Delicious, do not develop a surface color, while the pronounced surface color of others totally obscures the ground. Red, brick red, carmine, crimson, russet, or black-red surfaces are often marbled, washed, streaked, or stippled with other colors. Even apples that appear at first glance to be a solid color are usually sprinkled with tiny dots of another color.

The pigments that give apples their color are trapped inside the cells of the apple skin and will not dissolve in the juice during crushing or pressing. The skin pigments contribute very little to the color of the cider since it is extremely difficult to rupture the stout, strong cell walls

in apple skins. Even in a hammer mill, which smashes the apples into a near-liquid in preparation for pressing, these skin cells remain intact.

As you hold an apple in your hand, notice whether it is smooth, semismooth, or rough to the touch. Some table apples have oily skins. Many of the old-time cidermakers used skin texture as a loose general rule for identifying cider apples, believing that fruits with rough or russeted skins usually made superior cider. These russeted apples were often referred to as "leather-coats." John Newburgh wrote in the seventeenth century, "Tis with us an observation, That no *sweet-Apple* that hath a tough rind, is bad for cider." Many of the European cider varieties are russeted apples, and two North American varieties that make an excellent cider — the Roxbury Russet and the Golden Russet — are "leather-coats."

The odorants that give an apple its distinctive perfume or aroma are most concentrated in the skin and develop fully as the fruit matures. There are also odorants in the pulp of the apples, though to a much lesser degree, and they are most pronounced in ripe apples. One reason why it is important to use only ripe apples for cider is to get the most of these interior odorants, for the perfumes trapped in the skin cells, like the pigments, are not easily released. Some of the aroma will be lost during fermentation, blown off with the carbon dioxide, but enough will remain for the cider lover to detect the characteristic bouquets of many aromatic varieties.

Apples have many kinds of yeasts both on their skins and internally. In the past it was believed that different varieties of apples had characteristic yeasts, but studies at Long Ashton Research Station show that no individual yeasts can be associated with particular varieties. However, there are yeasts on the apples from various orchards characteristic of certain geographical areas. Naturally fermenting yeasts (particularly those of the genus *Saccharomyces*) found on apples are widely scattered and quite sparse. It is these yeasts that have accumulated in the cider room and massed on the crushing and pressing machinery and cheesecloths that start cider fermenting, not the yeasts on the skins. Today most cidermakers, both home and commercial, kill the wild yeasts, not all of which are desirable, and add a strong, laboratory-grown "wine yeast" of dependable behavior. If you are making cider for the first time with new equipment, it's best to add yeast to the juice to ensure a controlled and thorough fermentation.

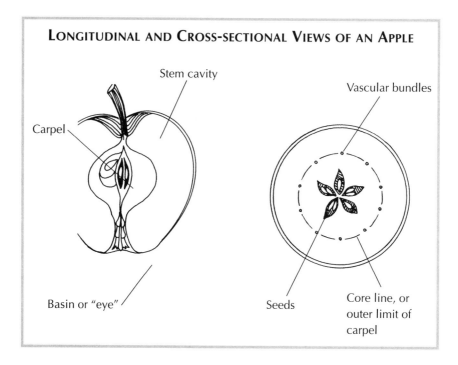

LONGITUDINAL AND CROSS-SECTIONAL VIEWS OF AN APPLE

Stem cavity

Vascular bundles

Carpel

Basin or "eye"

Seeds

Core line, or outer limit of carpel

At the bottom of the apple is its basin, or "eye," which can be large, small, entirely open, or closed. The eye is sunk in a depression variously broad, shallow, narrow, or deep, according to the "cultivar," or variety.

Stems also take different forms. They may be long, semilong, or short. Additionally they are thick, slender, or twisted, and when a twisted stem fills up its cavity, it is called "caruncular." The stem cavity itself takes various forms. One old variety of cider apple, the woodcock, took its name from the long, tapered stem that protruded from the oval fruit, and resembled, to its imaginative namer, a woodcock's head.

Inside the Apple

The interiors of fruits have always fascinated humans. This is reflected in the designs of our textiles, ceramics, and paintings. The firm globe of an apple cut open either longitudinally or horizontally reveals a secret world inside its chambered heart. The cores of apples — which are the real fruit — may be symmetrical, asymmetrical, or irregular. The life passage of the apple from blossom to brown-seeded fruit is displayed. If an apple is cut in half horizontally, you'll notice that the center contains five chambers in the shape of a star. Each chamber, or carpel, contains

two seeds if the fruit has been fully pollinated. Apples with fewer than ten seeds are only partially pollinated and may be lopsided. Farther out from the star in the body of the apple are tiny points like miniature tubes, forms left by the petals and sepals of the blossom, the so-called vascular bundles. Sometimes these points are connected by curved lines — anastomoses — that mark the outer margin of the true fruit, the core.

Apple seeds contain a volatile essential oil. This can give cider a penetrating, bitterish taste, pleasurable to some people and distinctly noxious to others. Anyone who has ever eaten an apple seed has noticed the taste of bitter almonds. Hammer mills, which crush apples, break some of the seeds in the process, with a chance of some of the bitter flavor in the finished cider. Grinding-type home apple crushers generally do not break the seeds. Small-scale amounts of cider made in an apartment kitchen with the aid of an electric blender may also have a "seedy" taste unless the seeds are scooped out before the apples go into the machine.

The Pulp

The pulp of an apple is the cidermaker's prime raw material. The consistency of the pulps of different cultivars is extremely variable — dry, juicy, hard, soft, or "cottony." English cider apples tend to be rather dry. The pulp makes up roughly 95 percent of the total weight of an

---

CIDER STATISTICS

→ A standard apple tree will produce about ten bushels of apples.

→ A semidwarf tree will produce about five bushels of apples

→ A dwarf tree will produce about one and a half bushels of apples.

→ A bushel of apples weighs about forty-five pounds (twenty kilos).

→ One bushel of apples will yield two to three gallons of fresh cider.

→ In an area eighty feet square you can grow four standard-sized apple trees, or forty-two dwarf trees.

→ A standard apple tree has a life span of around a hundred years.

---

apple, solubles and insolubles. The soluble part is, of course, the apple juice, which in cidermaking becomes the must. The insolubles are largely starch, pectin, cellulose, nitrogenous material, and ash, some of which stubbornly remain in suspension in much homemade cider after all efforts to clear it. The fibrous tissues — about 3 percent of the pulp — along with the skins, seeds, and other insoluble substances are known as the pomace or the *marc.*

The must, or syruplike liquid expressed from the crushed apples, has a higher density than water. It is made up of 75 percent to 90 percent water, several sugars (glucose, levulose, and saccharose), malic and other acids, tannins, pectin, starch, albuminoids, oils, ash, nitrogenous substances, and trace elements. In ripe apples the proportions of sugar vary, not only from one variety to another but also in apples on the same tree from year to year, by as much as 30 percent. The must contains roughly 8 percent to 14 percent sugar, most of which will be converted into alcohol in the fermentation process.

Apple juice contains many different acids, but the principal one is malic acid, ranging from 0.1 to 1.0 percent. The acid, which decreases in volume as the apples ripen, gives tartness both to the raw apple and to the cider. Malic acid contributes toward the stability of the must. A juice low in acid darkens rapidly when it comes in contact with the air, while a must that is rich in acid keeps a pale, light color and makes a pale cider. The acid level also protects the must to some degree from the invasion of harmful bacteria and promotes the normal development of yeast. The level of malic acid will drop during the fermentation process, but remains one of the most brisk fruit acids going. A juice with a pH reading higher than 3.8 is not acidic enough to make good cider.

The range of tannins in apples extends from less than 0.1 percent, typical of North American dessert apples, to 0.5 percent, a level approached by the "bitter" class of European cider apples. High tannin levels are important in making a good cider. Tannin exercises an antiseptic action against the diverse bacteria that attack cider, and is especially effective in keeping at bay *Zymomonas mobilis,* bacteria that cause a disorder known as cider sickness, as well as acetobacter, which turn cider into vinegar. Apples highly prized by cidermakers for making a good "keeping" cider contain large amounts of tannin. Tannin is important in cider apples for another reason: It gives the cider character and "body," a rich sensation on the palate of roundness or substance.

Educating Your Taste Buds

It is fairly simple to test the freshly expressed juice for acid levels, either with litmus paper or an acid-testing kit. Sugar volume can be measured with a hydrometer. Testing for tannin is more difficult. There is no simple way of determining the tannin amounts in apples or juice outside a laboratory except through careful tasting. Experience and the concentrated desire to isolate various taste sensations will make you a good judge of whether an apple has appreciable levels of tannin.

While crab apples are high in tannin, they are also high in acids, and the two taste sensations are apt to be confused by the beginning taster. A better test apple is one with some tannin and *low* acid levels, such as a Red Delicious, which will allow you to isolate the tannin taste. Look for a drying, puckering feeling in your mouth, and a sensation of astringency and bitterness on the palate. Apples with high acid levels will taste sharply sour. So-called "sweet" apples do not necessarily contain more sugar than "sour" apples. Sweet apples contain less malic acid, not more sugar, which our taste organs and brains interpret as "sweet."

GOOD CIDER APPLES

There is a yawning gulf between the two questions, "What makes a good cider apple?" and "What apples make good cider?" There is a rough consensus on what the desirable properties of cider apples are, from the rules of ancient cidermakers to the measured levels of acid and tannin of modern cider scientists. But just ask cidermakers which varieties of apples are the best for making cider, and you will get either evasive comments on the weather or wildly contradictory recipes touting all sorts of apples, from the ubiquitous McIntosh and Delicious to the wild apple-crabs, as the "only" proper fruits for cider.

Specific apple varieties prized for cidermaking have come and gone. Many of the old-timers believed that cider cultivars reached a peak of quality for a few decades and then faded away, the stock worn out and exhausted, to be replaced by a new variety.

In England, the most esteemed cider apple in the seventeenth century was the Red Streak, which gave "the richest and most vinous liquor." Other favorites were the Bromesbury Crab, "smart and winey," the Red and White Must apples, one sweet and the other acidic, the

Harvey, the Pearmain, the Foxwhelp, and the Gennet-Moyle, this last considered to have an "effeminate" flavor especially suited to "tender palates." But 135 years later, in the 1813 *Worcester County Report to the Board of Agriculture*, W. Pitt remarked dolefully that "the old fruits which raised the fame of the liquors of this country, are now lost, and the Red Streak is given up . . . little genuine red-streak cyder is now made."

In the United States, Baldwins, considered good cider apples in the nineteenth century, are rarely seen today, and the most famous American cider apples — the Harrison, the Campfield, the American Hagloe Crab, the Grindstone, Hewe's Virginia Crab, and others — seem to have vanished.

In this century the Long Ashton Research Station, where the world's primary cider research is carried on, has classified cider apples as follows:

Apple Group	Acidity (g Malic Acid/100 ml)	Tannin (g/100 ml)
Sweets	*<0.45	<0.2
Bittersweets	<0.45	>0.2
Sharps	>0.45	<0.2
Bittersharps	>0.45	>0.2

Very few varieties of cider apples contain within their globed fruits the correct balance of acid and tannin to yield an excellent single-variety (not a blend) of "vintage" cider. Only three English cider apples make a single-variety cider — the famous Kingston Black, a bittersharp; the New Foxwhelp, a sharp; and the Stoke Red, a bittersharp. Almost all other ciders, in Europe and North America, are blends that balance out the sugar content, tannin, and acid. North American apples reputed to make a good single-variety cider are the Golden Russet, the Roxbury Russet, and the Ribston Pippin. The St. Jean Experimental Farm in Québec has made "satisfactory" single-variety ciders from a number of developing or experimental varieties with fairly high tannin levels. However, what is a "good" cider in Québec or Ontario or the United States may not be judged good at all in other cider-drinking countries.

In North America, where the supply of Kingston Blacks and Stoke Reds is either severely limited or nonexistent, and where sweeter taste sensations are more popular, the question of which apples make the best

---

* The sign < means "less than"; > "greater than."

cider is something of a headache. Nor is there agreement on what a good or poor quality cider is; tastes vary markedly from person to person. This disagreement was well illustrated in a report under the direction of Dr. Willard P. Mohr at the Smithfield Experimental Farm in Ontario:

> The matter of assigning quality standards for apple cider, on the basis of fruit properties and levels of specific components, remains unclear. Replies from correspondence with leading cider research centers around the world suggest that there is ambiguity and lack of general agreement over what constitutes high quality cider and what constitutes poorer quality cider. As yet it does not seem feasible to assign overall scores to cultivars.

Many a home cider maker has had the humbling experience of proudly presenting a bottle of "Special Reserve" to a friend and then months later, in a subsequent visit, discovering the bottle with only one drink taken from it, hidden away in a dark corner of the cupboard.

Ciders and cider tastes vary from country to country, even from one region or township to another, and in the final judgment, from person to person. For amateur cidermakers, it is not so much a question of which apples make the "best" cider as of becoming familiar with the very broad spectrum of flavor and aroma combinations of different apples and experimenting until the most pleasing blends are found.

In North America cider will be made for a long time from whatever apples people can get their hands on. Nevertheless, Oscar Mendlesohn's comment in *The Earnest Drinker* should flash before the eyes of every cidermaker who presses low-tannin, insipid dessert apples, culls, or otherwise inferior fruit, the varieties all mixed willy-nilly, and who yet somehow expects the mélange will give him or her a prime cider:

> Cider of a sort can be made from any variety of apple juice, but for a fine beverage it is essential to use "vintage" apples, which are distinguished by a chemical composition which makes them inferior or even unusable for general purposes. Cider varieties of apples are broadly distinguished by comparatively high acidity and tannin. They are therefore somewhat sour and bitterish.

Of the three major alcoholic drinks — wine, beer, and cider — cider is the least known, the least appreciated, and the least developed in North America. Here cidermaking is in its rebirth, and only years of experimentation, careful selection, and quality control by the amateur cidermakers can create a variety of "vintage" ciders in different areas of the two countries. You may not have a single apple tree in your life at this moment, but this fall you can make your own cider and within a few years be experimenting with your own blends from apples you've grown yourself — and be well on your way to creating superb and unique ciders.

"Wild" Apples versus "Tame" Apples

For centuries spokesmen have promoted the wild apple as superior cider material. In the seventeenth century, surrounded by orchards of Harvey, Foxwhelp, Red Streak, and Parmain, all famous cider apples of the time, John Evelyn wrote in his *Pomona*, "We do seriously prefer a very wild orchard." The late Herbert Ogden, former proprietor of Ogden's Cider and Grist Mill near Hartland Four Corners in Vermont, advocated wild apples as making very good natural cider. In his pamphlet, "How to Make and Age Apple Wine," he remarked:

> Wild apples are best — strictly WILD, not just from some run-out orchard. The soft, early wild ones are no good, though. They must be hard and sound. Don't worry about the worms; they sort of add "body." The better an apple tastes to EAT the poorer the cider it makes.

But what are "wild" apples? Orchard and dooryard apple trees planted by long-gone farmers still stand beside the cellar holes of the houses they once shaded. Decades after their planters have been forgotten the old trees, whose lifetimes often extend into their second century, are still blooming and bearing fruit despite water sprouts, broken limbs, scars from mouse and deer damage, and insect infestations. They are neglected and uncared for, but they are not "wild" apple trees.

The true wild apples of North America are the native crab apples, which, with one or two exceptions, were here long before the white settlers brought over European apple stock.

Generally, crabs are hardy, highly resistant to fire blight, but quite susceptible to cedar rust. They blossom late, as do English cider varieties, thereby escaping spring frost damage to the blooms, and produce fairly heavy crops of tiny fruit. Only a little of their juice, which has high acid and tannin readings, can pick up a bland cider remarkably. Wild food enthusiasts as well as other cidermakers may like to experiment with wild crab juice additions to their cider blends.

A third group of apple trees has been termed "wild" apples, and it is these that both John Evelyn and Herbert Ogden have in mind as good cider apples. These are the offspring of different varieties of *Malus sylvestris*, the common apple, which have escaped from cultivation through sexual reproduction by seeds. These *apple-crabs*, as they are properly called, are the seedlings of old cultivars whose seeds were spread abroad by humans and other animals. John Chapman, better known as Johnny Appleseed, was the famed broadcaster of these seedling-grown trees in the eighteenth and early nineteenth centuries.

Since domestic apples do not reproduce true to type by seeds, their offspring revert to characteristics in their ancient ancestry, which includes dominant crab apple forebears in the Asian-European family tree, ancestors that had small, sour, and astringent crabby fruit. The wildings that sprout from the seeds of the most placid, tame apples ever grafted will most often take after these crotchety high-acid, tannin-rich ancestors and lack the more genteel table characteristics of their immediate parents. They make good cider, generally, although you take what you find with unknown results.

The fruit of wild apple-crabs will make a decent — often a good — cider because of the high tannin levels in some of them, but specific aromas and desirable flavors associated with various cultivars will not be there. The wild apple way of making cider is literally a mixed bag, and it's impossible to know what you're going to end up with until you drink it. You can exercise greater control over the contents of your cider barrel by using cultivars with known desirable qualities and judiciously blending in the juice of wild apple-crabs, cultivated crabs, or even, in experimental doses, the fruit of the truly wild native crab apples.

EUROPEAN CIDER APPLES

England, France, and Spain are the major countries with true cider apple orchards. These apples are characterized by high acid and tannin levels, which make them unfit for table fruit but give ciders distinctive flavors and body. French varieties mostly fall into the classification of bittersweets, as do the Spanish cider apples. Swiss and German cider apples tend to be high in acid and sugar, with fairly low tannin levels, and are often used for table apples as well as cidermaking, as are North American varieties.

JOHNNY APPLESEED

Part of American folklore is the legend of Johnny Appleseed, a wanderer who shunned the company of people and planted apple seeds wherever he went. In real life Johnny Appleseed was John Chapman, a nineteenth-century Swedenborgian eccentric who left his apple seedling nursery and orchard in Pennsylvania to move westward with the pioneer settlers, planting small orchards wherever he went. His ragged clothes, strange ways, and religious enthusiasms made him something of a character in his own time, and both popular legend and the press made a folk hero of the man who went into the wilderness with nothing but a Bible and large bags of apple seeds.

Born in Leominster, Massachusetts, in 1774, Chapman believed that the Divine Spirit was visible in all living things — plants, animals, humans. He was famous for his extreme kindness to animals and his refusal to eat fish, flesh, or fowl. He would gather his apple seeds from cider mills east of the Ohio and take them westward. His pioneer orchards were set in small woodland clearings, protected by brush barriers, and received minimum cultivation. They were intended as rootstock for grafting cultivars by the new settlers of a region, and he always planted in areas where he thought the future expansion of civilization would make them appreciated.

For more than forty years he wandered through the west planting orchards until apple trees dotted a huge region. Many people still believe that a wild apple tree in an out-of-the-way place can be attributed to Johnny's presence in the last century. By the time he died in 1845, he had become the patron saint of orcharding and conservation.

Some of the superior English cider varieties are being phased out in England, since they are either poor producers or subject to many apple ailments. In their place more productive cultivars are being planted to catch up with the increasing demand for cider apples. No longer is cidermaking the leisurely affair of the farmer with the small orchard. It is an expanding big business.

Cider apples, since they are grown for the crusher and the press, instead of the table, need not be perfect fruits and are less demanding of intensive care than the gold and ruby beauties of bon voyage baskets. English cider orchard management traditionally involved little pruning or thinning of the fruit, though this is changing now with the greater use of new rootstocks and the desire for heavier crops and larger apples.

EXAMPLES OF ENGLISH CIDER CULTIVARS

English apples are divided into four major cider classifications, as we mentioned earlier.

SWEET	BITTERSWEET	SHARP
Sweet Alford	Harry Master's	Bramley's Seedling
Woodbine	Jersey	Frederick
Eggleston Styre	Dabinett	New Foxwhelp
Sweet Coppin	Knotted Kernel	Dymock Red
Court Royal	Royal Wilding	Crimson King
	Bulmer's Norman	Brown's Apple
	Sherrington Norman	Tom Putt
	Yarlington Mill	Cap of Liberty
	Ashton Brown	
	Jersey	**BITTERSHARP**
	Chisel Jersey	Kingston Black
	Médaille d'Or	Stoke Red
	Michelin	
	Nehou	
	Brown Snout	
	Reine des Hâtives	
	Stembridge Jersey	
	Vilbrie	
	Taylor's	
	Trembletts Bitter	
	Somerset Red	
	Streak	

Cider varieties are usually late bloomers, so they are safe from spring frosts that nip early blossoms.

Organic gardeners should note that the cider orchard needs only minimum spraying, usually for scab and canker, unless you want perfect fruits. Grafted onto the new rootstocks, true cider varieties now come into bearing in six to eight years — almost half the time of the old standards. To learn more about the growing habits of individual European cider apples, consult *Long Ashton Annual Reports,* published by the University of Bristol, and available in the libraries of many agricultural stations and colleges, particularly in apple-growing regions.

EXAMPLES OF EUROPEAN CIDER CULTIVARS

In the Northeast today the New York State Experiment Station at Geneva includes thirty-six European cider cultivars in its one thousand-variety collection.

VARIETY	HARVEST DATE	VARIETY	HARVEST DATE
Alamanka	October 15	Lyman Prolific	August 25
Amère de		Major	September 15
Berthecourt	October 25	Maréchal	October 5
Amer Forestier	November 1	Marin Oufroy	October 1
Argrile Gris	October 10	Médaille d'Or	September 25
Bedan		Muscadet	
(de Jaune)	October 10	de Bernay	November 1
Bramtot	October 1	Muscadet	
Cap of Liberty	September 20	de Lense	October 25
Cimitière	October 10	Nehou	September 10
Crofton (Black		Peau de Vache	October 10
Crofton)	October 25	Pomme Gris	October 20
Crow Egg	October 10	Reine des	
Dabinett	September 25	Pommes	September 25
Dufflin	September 10	Souvenir	
Feuillard	September 25	de Cognet	September 25
Foxwhelp	October 1	Sumatovka	November 1
Geevenston		Tremblett's Bitter	September 25
Fanny	October 10	Twistbody Jersey	September 25
Goolsbey	August 15	Vagnon Scarlet	September 5
Gros Bois	September 25	Winston	November 1
Kingston Black	September 15	Yarlington Mill	October 10

CANADIAN APPLES

Apples for cider can be grown in many parts of Canada, although the climate is more beneficial on the Atlantic and Pacific Coasts, the Great Lakes, and the St. Lawrence River plains than in the heartland. Longer growing seasons and a greater number of growing-degree days offer a chance of a broader varietal cider blending base in Nova Scotia, Québec South, Ontario, and British Columbia, but this doesn't mean that cider-makers in other regions, except the Far North, should despair of ever having a good barrel. Given the hardiness of many high-tannin crabs, it's possible to pep up innocuous early-season juices by making sure the bitter little fellows are growing in your orchard.

Prince Edward Island and Newfoundland

Apple trees flourish throughout Nova Scotia, and in Newfoundland, New Brunswick, and Prince Edward Island they grow best in those areas with the most favorable conditions.

Any cider production in Newfoundland will have to be on the home level, as apples aren't grown commercially.

Exposure to cold, moist wind is a problem in many areas of Newfoundland, and to combat this it is recommended that dwarf or semidwarf trees on rootstocks adapted to relatively damp soil conditions, such as EM 7, be planted. Trees should be planted in a sheltered location with a southern exposure, with an artificial windbreak such as a high fence.

RECOMMENDED FOR PRINCE EDWARD ISLAND

McIntosh	Cleveland

RECOMMENDED FOR NEWFOUNDLAND

Quinte	Yellow Transparent
Melba	Ranger
Close	Caravel
Vista Belle	Lodi

*Turn-of-the-century apple picking at Kinsman's farm,
Lakeville, King's County, Nova Scotia.*

Nova Scotia

Nova Scotia's early orchards developed along the Annapolis Valley. One of the varieties planted by Charles R. Prescott in Wolfville in 1812 is still recommended today, the early Gravenstein. Two other varieties that he planted are the Rhode Island Greening from the United States, and the Blenheim, imported from England.

Cider is produced commercially in the Annapolis Valley, and the research station at Kentville has used McIntosh and Golden Russet juices in its studies related to improving the flavor and color of cider.

Among the newer varieties, the midseason Nova Easygro, an apple developed by the Kentville Station and introduced in 1971, is valued as scab resistant and is a long keeper. The Nova is a cross between a Spartan and the experimental PRI 565. Organic orchardists will be pleased that it needs no spraying for scab, though it is susceptible to mildew. The striped and blushed, medium-sized fruits are crisp and good-flavored. The Idared, an Idaho cross between Jonathan and Wagener, introduced in 1942, has also been used in cider blends.

Close	Cortland
Quinte	Spartan
Gravenstein	Red Delicious
McIntosh	Idared
Nova Easygro	Northern Spy

New Brunswick

New Brunswick apples are grown primarily along the St. John River, from Woodstock to St. John, or along the coast. Most of the interior and northern regions of the province have severe temperatures, making many of the popular but less hardy varieties unsuitable for growing. E. N. Estabrooks, retired fruit crops specialist in Fredericton, has noted that minimal lows in the apple-producing areas are around -30°C (-22°F), while in the interior and the north, minimum temperatures can be even colder.

There are no commercial nurseries in the province, and most trees come from Ontario or Michigan nurseries.

Crimson Beauty	Lobo
Vista Belle	Dudley Winter
Melba	McIntosh
Jerseymac	Cortland
Paulared	

Québec

None of the apples listed in the present recommendation group will grow *everywhere* in Québec, the largest Canadian province. Even in 1916, Dr. W.T. Macoun, first Dominion horticulturist, accounted for the diversity in climate by simply dividing the province in two: Québec No. 1, the south, and Québec No. 2, which encompassed all territory north of 46° latitude, including Rimouski and the Gaspé. In the Rimouski-Gaspé area he suggested Duchess and Yellow Transparent and, in sheltered areas, Antonovka, Wealthy, and the crabs.

While excessive use of McIntosh and Mac family apples in Québec's commercial cideries has somewhat stereotyped the product, there's hope for the home cidermaker who would like to try other varieties. Included in the collection of the Agriculture Canada Research Station in St. Jean are ten European cider cultivars: Dabinett, Bulmer's Norman, Tremblett's Bitter, Bohnapfel Schmidt, Brown Snout, Harry Master Jersey, Somerset Redstreak, Taylor's, Yarlington Mill, and 3223 A Güttinger 203.

RECOMMENDED FOR QUÉBEC

Cortland	Cox's Orange Pippin
Red Delicious	Golden Russet
Fameuse	
R.I. Greening	*Crabs*
Wealthy	Dolgo
McIntosh	Geneva
Lobo	Hyslop
Melba	Redflesh

Ontario

Divided into six districts for apple census purposes, Ontario's farm and commercial orchards are located in the southern part of the province. According to the 1995 census, McIntosh, Red Delicious, and Empire were the big three, but also of note were the gains of Mutsu (Crispin) and especially Golden Russet, which is grown for bittersweet blending in apple juices and ciders. But the dramatic news was the increased planting of trees on controlling rootstock. The number of standard-sized trees dropped from 605,490 in 1976 to 200,000, while size-controlling rootstock numbers soared from 1,859,706 in 1976 to 5,600,000 in 1995. This should be encouraging for the home cider orchardist, because commercial demands for dwarf and semidwarf stock will be reflected in larger nursery inventories.

RECOMMENDED FOR ONTARIO

Quinte	Delicious
Lodi	Golden Russet
Melba	Golden Delicious
Early McIntosh	Northern Spy
McIntosh	Red Spy
Wealthy	Spartan
Fameuse	Empire
Cortland	Idared
R.I. Greening	

Manitoba

Manitoba is still studying its apple varieties as cider cultivars, as well as for juice, slices, and cold pack. "We're still struggling to succeed in growing them," retired provincial fruit specialist P. J. Peters said, adding, "Most of our varieties are cross-bred with crab apples in order to breed in hardiness." The apples that succeed should make good cider.

The hardiest rootstocks and stem builders, cultivated and grafted in the province, are recommended for all apple varieties, and home orchard growers are advised to choose well-drained sites, not too alkaline or salty. Crucial to survival in areas exposed to prevailing northwest winds are shelterbelts that will give some measure of protection against wind and snow.

The minimal-temperature map of North America defines the province as falling into two cold zones, 2 and 3, but the Manitoba Horticultural Association uses a more detailed map divided into six zones. The warmer zones, 1 to 3, are generally southern, while the colder 4 is west central, and 5 and 6 cover the north. All the crabs will grow in the north, but only several of the apple-crabs and apples will. In planning an orchard, cidermakers who live in Manitoba should obtain a copy of this helpful map.

RECOMMENDED FOR MANITOBA

Heyer 12	**Apple-Crabs**
Battleford	Rescue
Breaky	Reknown
Carroll	Trail
Moscow Pear	Shater
Collet	Kerr
Goodland	
Miami	**Crabs**
Manitoba Spy	Dolgo
Luke	Robin
	Colombia

Saskatchewan and Alberta

Orchards planted on the Plains must have shelter. This is of primary importance, before the other requirements of hardiness, drought tolerance, and early bearing are considered. The greatly increased number of varieties available today as compared to 1916, and the success of fruit growing, can be attributed to the development of shelterbelts as well as hairy rootstocks. Saskatchewan spearheaded the drive to plant protective wind-, snow-, and erosion-controlling breaks around fruit trees starting at the turn of the twentieth century. In 1914, the Forest Nursery Station at Indian Head and its Sutherland substation began a program of distributing shelterbelt trees to farmers free of charge. The project, more than eighty years old and still going strong, has been both a fruit-production and a farm-landscaping blessing.

Depending on the terrain, soil, and region in the prairie provinces, the shelterbelts are comprised of several varieties of deciduous or coniferous trees in spaced varietal phalanxes to create snow traps and wind-slowing breaks. Areas in which the different varieties are most suitable, supply sources, and planting instructions are detailed thoroughly in the *Guide to Farm Practice in Saskatchewan*, available from the University of Saskatchewan, Extension Division, Saskatoon, Saskatchewan S7N OWO. This guide is updated every three years and is free to Saskatchewan residents.

RECOMMENDED FOR SASKATCHEWAN AND ALBERTA

Goodland	*Apple-Crabs*
Harcount	Kerr
Heyer 12 and 20	Rescue
Patterson	
Reid	*Crabs*
	Osman
	Dolgo
	Dawn
	Red Siberian

Apple workers in Salmon Arm, British Columbia.

NATIONAL PHOTOGRAPH COLLECTION, PUBLIC ARCHIVES OF CANADA, C 63307.

British Columbia

The list of recommendations is unrealistic from the cidermaker's viewpoint as the province contains within its boundaries zones 2 through 8, with all the benefits of the warmer regions, and many, many varieties of apples will grow here happily. British Columbians have long been interested in cidermaking, and tests on the desirability of table fruits as cider apples date back to 1931 at the Long Ashton Research Station.

Apple cider is now produced commercially in British Columbia. Until 1977 all cider and wine were made and marketed on an industry scale, but now these products can be made and sold by individuals on their own orchard or vineyard premises.

The future for British Columbian cidermakers and home orchardists is bright. Many traditional North American varieties suited for cider as well as true European cider apples can be comfortable in some part of the province. Blends of North American and European apples there could produce unique regional ciders.

Older varieties grafted onto newer climate-fighting rootstocks, new cultivars developing and expanding each year, trees naturally resistant to scab, effective pest controls, and the experiments of the research stations give Canadians a head start in apple growing. Trees that once would never have survived in rigorous climates can now mature fruit, all to the good of the cider barrel.

<table>
<tr><td colspan="2" align="center">RECOMMENDED FOR BRITISH COLUMBIA</td></tr>
<tr><td>McIntosh</td><td>Newtown</td></tr>
<tr><td>Jonathan</td><td>Winesap</td></tr>
<tr><td>Delicious</td><td>Stayman Winesap</td></tr>
<tr><td>Rome Beauty</td><td></td></tr>
</table>

North American Astringents

The tannin needed to give a full, round body to cider is missing in most North American apple varieties. Someday, perhaps, the high-tannin European cider apples will be easily available to the home orchard grower, or North American pomologists and breeders will come up with cultivars with the same attributes. Both are likely if there's a demand, but the amateur cidermaker needn't wait until that day, if he or she takes a page from history and turns to the crabs and apple-crabs.

By adding these tannin-high apples to the blander table varieties, you can build and intensify the body of your cider. Some cidermakers add them proportionately while grinding, but since the fermented acid and tannin levels are unknown, it's best to grind and ferment the varieties separately, and blend them at bottling time.

Cidermakers with a supply of "wild" apples available may want to experiment with them, while others plant apple-crabs or crab apples in their orchards. The crabs are popular, because they're also good pollinators. Two apples with appreciable tannin levels are the Red Astrakhan and the Lindel. The Red Astrakhan has been in North America for a long time, and is one of the most productive summer apples. It is also very acidic, considered almost too tart for eating, but can be a good apple for the cidermaker. The Lindel variety, according to Dr. W. P. Mohr of the Smithfield Experimental Farm in Ontario, has a 0.14 percent tannin content, one of the highest of normal apple cultivars.

Remember that acidity and astringency usually go hand in hand in these small apples, so if your basic blending juice is made from rather acidic dessert apples, be cautious while mixing in the acidic astringent.

A rough general rule holds that no more than 20 percent of an astringent cider should be added to a blend, and in the case of an already acidic cider, 10 percent or less is a safer proportion. Apples, apple-crabs, and crab apples providing tannin include:

Red Astrakhan	Red Siberian	Okanagan
Martha	Geneva	Whitney
Lindel	Soulard	Hyslop
Dawn	Redflesh	Osman
Yellow Siberian	Transcendent	

Pollination

The apple blossom contains both the male and female sexual components needed for reproduction into a fruit. Minute grains of pollen form on the male stamen in the mature blossom and are transferred to the female pistil primarily by bees in their normal nectar-gathering operations. The pollen is transported by the pistil to the blossom's ovule, where a growing cell forms to develop seeds and, ultimately, a thick, protective wall of juicy, edible flesh.

Very few varieties are capable of self-pollination, and in most cases at least two cross-pollinators are required for maximum fruit-setting. Strong pollinators include McIntosh, Red Delicious, Cortland, and Dolgo crab; poor pollen is produced by Gravenstein, Baldwin, and Northern Spy. Jonagold, a cross between Golden Delicious and Jonathan, is sterile, with triploid chromosomes, and cannot be depended on to pollinate other varieties, and, since it's in the same family, the parent Golden Delicious is cross-incompatible with Jonagold.

In your orchard, plant varieties from different families to ensure cross-pollination. Since the duration of blooming and fertility varies according to cultivars, it's safest to select trees that will reach full bloom within two days of each other, and to make sure no tree is placed more than fifty feet from its pollinator.

Hivebees, solitarybees, and bumblebees aren't the only agents of pollen transfer, but they're the best because they work in large numbers, are thorough, and the hairs on their bodies and legs make good pollen traps. As the bee crawls in and buzzes about in the blossom, the grains of pollen collected in earlier forays on its legs shower on the pistil. If your trees are too far apart, the bees can be blown away by the wind or lose the pollen in transit.

In large orchards or in remote homestead plantings, hives of bees are imported about two days before the blossoms are fully open. One good hive can pollinate an acre of trees, but the hive should not be brought in before bloom, or the bees will disperse throughout the countryside. Most small orchards will be efficiently pollinated by wild bees, and this is easily checked. Simply walk through your trees in bloom and look for any bee activity. If there is little or none, you had better plan on importing hives.

If you have only a few trees you can do it yourself. Take a cup and a soft artist's paintbrush. Gently tap the pollen from pollinating trees into the cup. Then go to the trees to be pollinated, and carefully dab at least ten particles of pollen on the head of each pistil. Continue this process until all the trees are cross-pollinated. It doesn't take long in a dwarf orchard, since just those blooms six inches apart need to be tickled — a nonselective thinning process.

NORTH AMERICAN CULTIVARS USED IN MAKING CIDER

The following lists of apple varieties that have been, and are, used in making cider have been compiled from many sources, both old and modern. Most of these apples are available through a number of North American stock suppliers, though not all of them can be grown in every area. The reader is urged to experiment with blends in his or her cidermaking room and to make the final decision as to what "good" cider apples are.

BALDWIN

OTHER NAMES: Woodpecker, Pecket, Steele's Red Winter
ZONES: 5–7
PARENTS: Unknown
RIPENS: 140–150 days after full bloom
CIDER CLASS: Medium acid, medium sugar

Once a leading variety in the Northeast, the Baldwin's numbers were decimated by several severe freezes in the 1930s, and most were never replaced. Vigorous, upright, spreading, and long-lived when grown in normal conditions of their range, Baldwins lose sprightliness, fruit firmness, and acidity when grown in the South. They have strong biennial tendencies and are not resistant to apple scab, sun scald, fire blight, or spray injury, but, on the positive side, they are not affected by cedar rust. The most common rootstocks today for Baldwin are the semidwarfs. The Baldwin is a poor pollinator but is very productive, with trees commonly bearing twenty bushels of fruit. Harvest of the large, bright red, round apples is short, as they all ripen at once.

While Baldwins have been used for cider for more than two hundred years, and have received good marks in the past, several experiments have shown the juice to be flat and insipid. Baldwins are best when blended with other, more flavorful varieties.

BEN DAVIS

OTHER NAMES: Baltimore Pippin, Kentucky Pippin, New York Pippin, Red Pippin, Victoria Pippin
ZONES: 5–8
PARENTS: Unknown
RIPENS: 150–155 days after full bloom
CIDER CLASS: Low to medium acid, neutral

Ben Davis is an upright, spreading tree with medium vigor, but very productive, and an annual bearer. The trees are resistant to fire blight and cedar rust but not to apple scab. Some sprays will injure this tree.

The fruit is hard, dry, and tough, poor for table use but good for cooking and as a basic cider blend. Ripening over a long season, the apples are large, with a round-conic to oblong-conic shape, and are striped with red. They are faintly fragrant, with dull, white flesh. The cider by itself is flat and characterless. Other varieties should be added.

CORTLAND

ZONES: 3–4
PARENTS: Ben Davis x McIntosh

RIPENS: 125–130 days after
full bloom
CIDER CLASS: Medium acid, sweet

Frequently considered to be an "old" apple, Cortland is one of the early "new" varieties, created at the New York State Experiment Station in 1898. Medium in size and vigor, the Cortland is an annual bearer and continues to be a popular commercial orchard variety. It is a good pollinator for other varieties.

Cortland apples are dark red with a dusky, blue cast; they are oblate in shape and of medium size. The fine-grained flesh is very juicy, tender, and white. One of its good features for cidermaking is the long time it takes to discolor at grinding time. A Cortland cider tends to be light colored, and its mildness makes it an excellent blending base. The juice is slightly pink.

COX'S ORANGE PIPPIN

OTHER NAMES: Cox's Orange
ZONES: 5–8
PARENTS: Ribston Pippin Seedling

RIPENS: Mid-September to early
October
CIDER CLASS: High acid, aromatic

Cox's Orange Pippin is the favorite English dessert apple, possessing a delightful perfume, incomparable flavor, and a pleasant, lingering aftertaste. The trees are hard to grow in North America, where they are considered unthrifty and not very fruitful on standard stock. They are prone to apple scab. Through the use of size-controlling rootstock and better orchard care, the Cox's Orange is becoming more popular here. Of medium size, with a small core, the apples are red and yellow, blending into orange.

DELICIOUS

OTHER NAMES: Red Delicious, Stark
  Delicious
ZONES: 5–8
PARENTS: Unknown

RIPENS: 140–150 days after
  full bloom
CIDER CLASS: Very low acid, sweet,
  aromatic

One of the three favorites in North America, the Delicious is first and foremost a table apple, but many of them are pressed for cider because of large production and strict grading standards. The Delicious is an upright, vigorous, and spreading tree, resistant to fire blight and cedar rust, but it must be protected against apple scab. It's a good pollinator for other varieties. It has an intermediate tendency to biennial production. The familiar dark red conical fruits have five distinctive bumps on the end, and are juicy and sweet with a distinctive aroma. The amber juice makes a fragrant blending base, much improved by the addition of juice with more character, such as crab apples, apple-crabs, Jonathan, or Newtown. Delicious is also good to add to a cider blend that has little aromatic quality.

EOSPUS SPITZENBERG

OTHER NAMES: Spitzenberg
ZONES: 4–8
PARENTS: Unknown

RIPENS: 145–150 days after
  full bloom
CIDER CLASS: Medium to high acid

Upright, vigorous, and full, the Esopus Spitzenberg must be pruned regularly and allowed plenty of room in the orchard. The tree is fairly hardy, an intermediate bearer, and will not do well on all soils, favoring silt or sandy loam. It is resistant to apple scab, fire blight, cedar rust, and spray injury. The fruit is medium to large, bright red with gray dots, and has a conic-oblong shape. The yellow-white flesh is juicy and rich with a delicious, brisk flavor. The Spitzenberg makes a good acidic addition to more innocuous ciders.

FAMEUSE

OTHER NAMES: Snow, *Pomme de Neige, Sanguinesse,* Snow Chimney
ZONES: 3–6
PARENTS: Unknown
RIPENS: Late September to early October
CIDER CLASS: Medium acid, aromatic

At home in Canada and the higher altitudes of the United States, the Fameuse will grow in warmer zones, but its fruit tends to soften. Moderately vigorous, medium-sized, and very hardy, it is susceptible to scab and tends to be biennial.

The apples are of medium size and round, crimson, with a blue blush. Its popular secondary name, "Snow apple," is derived from the color of its flesh — stark white. The apples are very finely grained, tender, and juicy with a hint of tartness. It makes a flat, mild-flavored cider and needs picking up by more spirited juices.

GOLDEN RUSSET

OTHER NAMES: English Golden Russet
ZONES: 5–8
PARENTS: Unknown
RIPENS: Mid-October to early November
CIDER CLASS: Medium acid, aromatic

The Golden Russet is one of the best North American apples for cider. Passed by for the more colorful red apples, these small yellow, bronze-russeted "leather-coats" are good table fruit. For cider they are nearly unmatched in North America. The juice is rich, syrupy, aromatic, and tart, and these qualities translate well into the fermented product.

As with another North American apple that makes good cider by itself, the Nonpareil, which came from England, Golden Russet is of European origin. The difference is that while Nonpareil has just about vanished from North America, the Russet continues to hold on.

GRAVENSTEIN

ZONES: 5–8
PARENTS: Unknown

RIPENS: 110–115 days after
full bloom
CIDER CLASS: Medium to high acid,
aromatic

Vigorous, upright, and spreading, the Gravenstein can be an annual bearer in some areas and biennial in others, depending on soil richness and the previous year's yield. The trees are quite productive when they yield, but are susceptible to cedar rust and spray injury. They are resistant to apple scab and fire blight. Gravenstein is an unsatisfactory pollinator.

The fruit ripens over several weeks, requiring two to three pickings. The apples are bright red, striped, and splashed with another shade of red, and are oblate, angular, and rather lopsided. The medium to large fruits are firm, juicy, and have an aromatic, crisp, white flesh. The juice is rich and vinous, and is good to pick up more subdued blends.

JONATHAN

ZONES: 5–7
PARENTS: Seedling of Esopus
Spitzenberg

RIPENS: 140–145 days after
full bloom
CIDER CLASS: Medium to high acid

Jonathan is a very accommodating tree that will adapt to different soils and climates but does best in cooler regions. Bearing early and annually, this variety is self-sterile, as are most cultivars, and so must be planted with other varieties. Jonathan is resistant to apple scab, but not to fire blight or cedar rust.

The fruits are small to medium, uniform bright red splashed with lighter red, and sprinkled with small white dots. The apples are round, truncated cones, and the yellowish, red-tinged flesh is juicy with a spicy, mildly aromatic flavor. Good for eating and cooking, but a poor keeper, Jonathans make good cider, with a clean, tart, refreshing flavor, especially when pressed immediately after picking the ripe fruits. Jonathan can be used to blend with cider of less character, such as Delicious, and many claim it makes an acceptable single-variety drink.

McIntosh

Zones: 3–7
Parents: Probably a Fameuse
seedling

Ripens: 125–130 days after
full bloom
Cider Class: Medium acid, very
aromatic

Few need an introduction to McIntosh, one of the three most popular apples in North America, and the parent of many other table varieties. Very productive, with today's high yields protected by hormone sprays that combat a tendency to drop fruit just before harvest, the McIntosh is also one of the kings of pollination. When planting Macs as cross-pollinators with newer varieties, be sure that McIntosh ancestors aren't somewhere in the background. Especially prone to apple scab and susceptible to fire blight, Macs resist cedar rust and spray injury.

Round-oblate in shape, the apple is of medium size, and light to dark red with a bluish bloom in some climates. The smooth, thin skin is stippled with tiny yellow dots. The tender, juicy white flesh is savored by many as a superior table apple. For cider, its use is best determined by personal taste.

Newtown

Other Names: Yellow Newtown,
Albermarle, Green Newtown
Pippin, Mountain Pippin,
Newtown Pippin, Yellow Pippin
Zones: 5–8
Parents: Unknown

Ripens: 160–165 days after
full bloom
Cider Class: Medium to high acid,
more tannin than most dessert
apples

Without thinning and good nutrition, Newtown tends to be a biennial bearer. The upright and full trees are not resistant to scab, fire blight, or spray injury, and produce medium-sized, round-oblate apples. The trees are grown to commercial perfection in Hood River, Oregon; Albermarle, Virginia; the Hudson Valley of New York; and British Columbia. With controlling rootstocks and more intense orchard care, their range should expand.

Popular table fruit, the Newtowns are superior eating apples — hard, crisp, and juicy, with a faint aroma and a tart nip on the palate. For cider they're usually used in blends. Stored, or tree mellowed for two weeks past maturity, the apples make cider with a bitter, oxidized flavor.

Northern Spy

Other Names: Spy
Zones: 4–8
Parents: Unknown

Ripens: 145–155 days after
full bloom
Cider Class: Medium to high acid

Like McIntosh and Delicious, the Northern Spy is the parent of numerous later varieties and also has the distinction of contributing genetically to the success of the Malling-Merton rootstocks. A good cross-pollinator, the Northern Spy resists scab, fire blight, and spray injury, but can be attacked by cedar rust. An intermediate bearer, tending toward the biennial habit, the Spy takes longer than most varieties to reach bearing age. The fruit is large, conical-round in shape, striped with bright red, and sometimes has a delicate bloom. The flesh is of fine-grained texture, slightly aromatic, and juicy. The Spy is particularly noted for its high vitamin C content, which is four times higher than that of McIntosh.

Rhode Island Greening

Other Names: Greening, Burlington
Greening, Jersey Greening
Zones: 4–6
Parents: Unknown

Ripens: 135–145 days after
full bloom
Cider Class: Medium to high acid

Spreading, and a bit sensitive to cold, the Rhode Island Greening is not an early bearer but is long-lived. It can be broken of a biennial tendency by thinning especially heavy crops, and it becomes more productive with age. It is not resistant to scab and fire blight, but will fight cedar rust and spray injury.

The fruit is colored grass green to yellow-green and is roundish-oblate. Sometimes slight ribs are visible through the smooth, oily skins of the medium to large apples. The flesh is yellowish, crisp, very juicy, and with a lively, rich acid taste. The flavor is distinctive and the apples store well. The Rhode Island Greening makes an interesting, somewhat tart cider and is very good to add to duller juice.

Ribston Pippin

OTHER NAMES: Ribston, Essex Pippin
ZONES: Sheltered areas of 3–6
PARENTS: Unknown

RIPENS: Early October
CIDER CLASS: Medium to high acid, aromatic

Hardier than Baldwin or Rhode Island Greening, the Ribston Pippin does well in New York, New England, and Canada in zones 4 through 6, and there are reports that it will grow in zone 3 if protected from wind and snow damage. Although it is only a moderate producer of small to medium-sized fruits and is an unsatisfactory pollinator, the Ribston is another of those special North American varieties that can make a good cider all by itself.

The fruit is a slightly small to medium apple with rough-textured russeting over a skin of orange-red. It is very aromatic, with yellow, granular flesh and sharp, rich juice. Only the Ribston, the Nonpareil, the Roxbury Russet, and the Golden Russet make acceptable cider in North America without blending.

Rome Beauty

OTHER NAMES: Rome
ZONES: 5–8
PARENTS: Unknown

RIPENS: 160–165 days after full bloom
CIDER CLASS: Low to medium acid

Annual bearing and good production make the Rome Beauty a fine choice for home cidermakers. The trees do well in most soils, but a rich soil enhances color. The apples tend to be hard, dry, tough textured, and mealy when overripe, but the tree is resistant to scab, fire blight, and cedar rust. Rome Beauty is a late bloomer, making it a good variety for cross-pollinating other late-blossoming varieties. The apples are medium red, with color blushed onto the round-oblate fruits. The juice has a mild, sweet flavor and is excellent for a blending base. Rome Beauty is a good blending base that can be used in large amounts because of its ability to pick up the flavors of other varieties with greater character.

Roxbury Russet

OTHER NAMES: Boston Russet, Roxbury
ZONES: 4–8
PARENTS: Unknown

RIPENS: Mid-October
CIDER CLASS: Medium acid, aromatic

Perhaps the oldest named variety still grown in the United States, the Roxbury Russet originated in Roxbury, Massachusetts, around 1649. It has a long and deserved reputation as a fine table apple and as a superior cider apple. More productive than the Golden Russet, the Roxbury has similar characteristics — "leather-coats" of full russet over greenish yellow-brown skins with brownish red cheeks. The fruit are round-oblate and of medium size with unequal, asymmetrical sides. The flesh is coarse and juicy with a mild subacid taste described as "russet flavor" — a mixture of aromatic oils and nuttiness. The trees are vigorous and spreading, and grow best in the rich intervale soils found in areas from New England to Michigan.

Stayman Winesap

OTHER NAMES: Red Stayman Winesap, Stayman
ZONES: 5–8
PARENTS: Winesap

RIPENS: 160–165 days after full bloom
CIDER CLASS: Medium acid

Not very hardy, and needing a long growing season, the Stayman Winesap comes into production early, bears annually, and produces highly flavored apples that keep exceptionally well. Medium-large, full-blushed red apples are round-conic in shape. The cider from this variety can be rounded out by blending with several other varieties.

Wealthy

ZONES: 3–6
PARENTS: Common apple x Siberian Crab

RIPENS: 120–125 days after full bloom
CIDER CLASS: Medium to high acid, aromatic

The Wealthy is an upright, spreading, medium to small tree of only medium vigor. The trees bear early at four to six years and are biennial in habit. They are resistant to scab, fire blight, and cedar rust, though subject to spray injury. They yield heavy crops. Wealthy is a good tree choice for the organic gardener because of its resistance to disease. The trees tend to become much less vigorous as they reach maturity. Wealthy adapts well to different soils, especially sandy and gravelly soils, and is very hardy in cold areas.

The medium-sized fruits are blushed red. The aromatic, tender but crisp and juicy apples are of high quality for dessert and cooking and make a mild and slightly tart cider.

WINESAP

OTHER NAMES: Wine Sop
ZONES: 6–8
PARENTS: Unknown

RIPENS: Late October to early November
CIDER CLASS: Medium acid

The Winesap originated in England, and was well known in that country and in early America as a cider-blending apple. The tree thrives on light, sandy soil. The apples, of medium size and rather oblong, have the quality of hanging late on the tree without injury. They are smooth skinned and of a fine dark red color with a few streaks and a little yellow ground showing on the shady side. It is best used in blends based on bland, sweet varieties.

YORK IMPERIAL

OTHER NAMES: York
ZONE: 5
PARENTS: Unknown

RIPENS: Mid- to late October
CIDER CLASS: Medium acid

Growing well in the southern Pennsylvania, Virginia, and West Virginia apple belt, the York will also grow in colder climates. It prefers heavy, fertile soils, with substantial clay foundations. Yields of the bright red, carmine-striped, lopsided fruit are good, and when fully ripe the yellow flesh yields a mildly flavored sweet juice. The York is a good blending base for more lively ciders.

— 4 —
THE HOME
CIDER ORCHARD

The fragrant stores, the wide-projected heaps
Of apples, which the lusty-handed year,
Innumerous, o'er the blushing orchard shakes,
A various spirit, fresh, delicious, keen,
Dwells in their gelid pores, and active points,
The piercing cider for the thirsty tongue.

— Thomson in *William Pitt,* 1813

This section is a guide for the home cidermaker who wants a small stand of apple trees for the purpose of making "the piercing cider for the thirsty tongue." If you have an established orchard, you will probably want to add certain varieties to improve your cider. Old apple trees of low vigor produce apples with sweeter juices, higher specific gravities, and lower fermentation rates than young trees of the same variety.

If you are planning to grow true cider varieties, a complete guide is *An Introduction to Modern Cider Apple Production* by R. R. Williams, written in conjunction with his work as chief cider pomologist at the Long Ashton Research Station, Bristol, England.

And while the orchard is still in the planning stage, it's good to talk with state or provincial Agricultural Extension Service pomologists. Not only are these men and women extraordinarily knowledgeable and unfailingly helpful, but they are usually aware of what cider research is being done at the experimental stations in each country. The stations at

Geneva, New York, and those in British Columbia, Nova Scotia, Ontario, and Québec have made many tests on North American apples seeking good cider characteristics, and several have European varieties in their collections.

THE ORCHARD — FROM DREAM TO REALITY

Your decision to plant a cider orchard means an ethical commitment to the care of the trees for many years. The satisfaction gained from growing your own fruit and making your own unique ciders are rewards worth the effort, but you must plan to give your orchard thoughtful, loving care and close personal attention. Experience in the cider room will give you an intimate knowledge of the qualities of the varieties you grow and their blending characteristics. The same teacher will show you the right moment in the stage of ripeness to harvest fruit, and how long the apples may be stored before milling and pressing. Experience and a keen sense of observation, coupled with sound orchard care, are the best guides to making cider of outstanding quality.

THE BROOKLYN MUSEUM: DICK S. RAMSEY FUND.

Apple Gathering, Jerome B. Thompson, 1856.

The size of your orchard will depend upon the amount of growing space you have, the number of trees you can care for, and the number of varieties you want for cider blending.

If you live in an area where commercial orchard-run apples are abundant and reasonably priced, you may prefer to buy these in bulk or under a "U-Pick" arrangement. Generally these will be table apples, juicy, rich in sugar, and with medium to high acid and very low tannin levels — good eating apples but most without enough tannin to make a tangy, full-bodied cider. If you plan to use such apples for your cider, you will want to plant complementary varieties with higher tannin levels for use in blending and will, therefore, need fewer trees than a person without a good local apple supply.

If, on the other hand, the area in which you live is devoid of commercial orchards, or apples are prohibitively expensive, varieties covering the whole cider spectrum may be planted — rich sugars, heavy juicers, individualistic bouquets, good levels of acid and tannin.

Knowing Your Way around Rootstocks

Apple seeds carry within their brown coats a myriad of possible genetic combinations. Apples do not reproduce themselves true to type. Whenever you plant an apple seed, you are planting a horticultural surprise package, and, unfortunately for growers of table fruit, a surprise package that's usually a disappointment. Seedlings, though hardy, tend to make trees with low yields of small, bitter fruit. Many of these crabby chance apples will make good cider — hence the popularity of "wild apple" cider — but for the home cider orchard it's also nice to grow specific varieties with known aromas and flavors that also give good yields. Distinct cultivars, or different kinds of apples, are reproduced vegetatively, most commonly by grafting a scion or bud of the desired variety onto sturdy rootstock.

There are many different kinds of rootstock in existence, suited to a diversity of soils and climates, and producing apple trees of variable sizes, vigor, and disease resistance. Basically, there are two different sources of rootstock — clonal and seedling.

Clonal rootstocks, such as the Malling and Malling-Merton, are produced in *stool beds.* A stool bed is made by cutting off a tree a few years old of the desired variety at ground level early in the spring.

Suckers shoot up from the severed stump, and, as earth is heaped around them, put out roots. The following spring these rooted shoots are dug up and moved to a nursery.

Seedling rootstocks are grown from the seeds of apples. Until around 1935 seeds for the stock were imported to North America from France, and the resulting seedlings were known as "French Crab" seedlings. In the decades since then, seedling stock has most often come from the pips collected at North American cider mills. In general, seedling rootstock is hardier than clone stock, unless the seeds come from varieties with nonhardy parents.

Major experiments carried out in England sixty-five years ago at the East Malling Research Station brought order into the then-confused world of rootstocks by the selection of sixteen rootstocks with various characteristics, which were numbered M 1 to M 16. The original identifications were in Roman numerals, and you may still find them listed this way in some nursery catalogs, though the current trend is to use Arabic numbers. Later work at East Malling resulted in rootstocks numbered M 17 to M 27. Still another series was developed by East Malling in conjunction with the John Innes Horticultural Institute, known as the Malling Merton (MM) collection, and numbered MM 101 to MM 115. One of the parents of the MM rootstock is the good old Northern Spy, whose vigor has made it a favorite in rootstock-building experiments. The Central Experimental Farm in Ottawa, Ontario, has developed a very hardy crab apple rootstock, *Malus robusta 5*, as well as a whole series specifically suited for northern apple growing, Ottawa 1 to 22.

Although there are intermediate sizes, rootstocks are generally classified as to the size of the tree they support: standard (trees fifteen or more feet in height), semidwarf (up to fourteen feet), and dwarf (less than nine feet tall). In catalogs these sizes are abbreviated S, SD, and D.

You should check with your county agent before ordering trees to find out what kinds are best for your area. Thousands of healthy young apple trees die each year because their rootstock was unsuited for the soil and climate in which their hopeful but unknowing purchasers planted them. Try to buy your trees from a good local nurseryman or -woman who uses rootstock that is at home in your locality.

Which Size Tree for You?

The standard apple tree, tall, robust, and stately, symbol of a hundred memories in yellowed photographs of the old home place, is fading away. The big trees, like many things, have surrendered to the forces of progress. Gone is that first early-spring swing on the lowest branch, the fireworks of blossoms and the sky-high robin's nest. While we'll all miss the standards, big is not necessarily best. And gone, too, is the thirty-foot pole pruner with a blade so high up you could scarcely see it, much less put it around a secondary leader; gone, too, the aerial dueling with yellow jackets, the daring ladder-act routines; and gone is the up-the-ladder, down-the-ladder, boxing, sorting, boxing, and resorting, for sale, for storage, for cooking, for cider.

Standard apple trees take a lot of hard work and considerable growing space and time. In rows they need a minimum of thirty-two feet between trees and forty feet between rows. If you plant standards, figure on a forty-foot square for each tree. While they're great bearers, with fifteen to twenty bushels per tree not uncommon, they'll take from seven to ten years to bear fruit, and decades to mature.

Today, orchardists are turning increasingly to dwarf and semidwarf trees. Termed "high-intensity" orchards, these trees can be planted six or twelve feet between trees on the line, and fourteen to twenty feet between the rows.

Orchard care and harvesting, particularly by mechanical means, is an important concern of growers faced with a shrinking orchard labor force and a crop that won't wait. The same advantages of dwarf and semidwarf trees that appeal to commercial growers make sense for the cidermaker's small orchard.

More Trees and More Varieties in Less Space

In the space required for one standard apple tree, you can plant eight or nine dwarfs or four or five semidwarf trees. By planting the smaller trees, the cidermaker can count on several varieties of juice for the all-important cider blending.

Quality fruit. Because the smaller trees are simply a definite variety grafted onto a dwarfing rootstock, the fruit is of the same quality and size as a standard tree of the same variety would bear.

Earlier production. While it takes a standard tree many years to bear, dwarf trees often come into production the second year after planting, and the semidwarfs in their third season. And they produce! Dwarfs, when mature, can yield a bushel of apples, and the semidwarfs, four or five.

Easier care and harvest. Dwarfs reach a height of eight feet at maturity, and semidwarfs around fourteen feet. Pruning is easily done with hand shears and short poles, where standard trees require longer poles and ladder work. Dwarf fruits are picked by hand from the ground, while the slightly higher semidwarf branches are emptied with a short pole picker or by hand from a short ladder.

Better pollination. Most apple varieties are self-sterile or produce poor pollen. One or, better, two other varieties are needed in fairly close proximity for good cross-pollination. Since a number of small trees can fit in the space required by one standard, the chances for effective pollination are increased.

CLIMATE AND WEATHER

In most areas of the United States, and in many parts of southern and coastal Canada, dwarf trees can be grown successfully. Yet, because apple trees grow in temperate regions all over the world and have a reputation for being hardy and adaptable, many people believe any apple will grow anywhere. Ordering a York Imperial grafted onto dwarf rootstock propagated in a Virginia nursery and expecting the delicate little tree to "adapt" and flourish in northern Minnesota is a hope lost. The odds against its survival are overwhelming, because a severely dwarfing stock, such as M 9, is shallow and brittle and cannot tolerate a deep freeze location in the North.

Check the Map

The climate you live in will determine the final flavor and quality of your cider. Cultivars vary in hardiness and the length of growing season they need to mature fruit. To get a general idea of which trees can grow in your area, it's important to know in which average minimum-temperature zone you live. You can determine this by looking at the

USDA map, below. Orchard hardiness and fruitfulness vary on a lot more, however, for even within such relatively small areas as townships, there are microclimates that can vary considerably from the zone map's norm.

Various rootstocks have been developed to meet many soil and climate situations, to combat cold, drought, and extreme moisture, and some have deep-grabbing roots to stabilize the tree against winds. Take these factors into account as you leaf through the stock catalogs.

The weather itself can have a marked effect on your cider. A dry, sunny summer will produce apples that yield juice of a high specific gravity

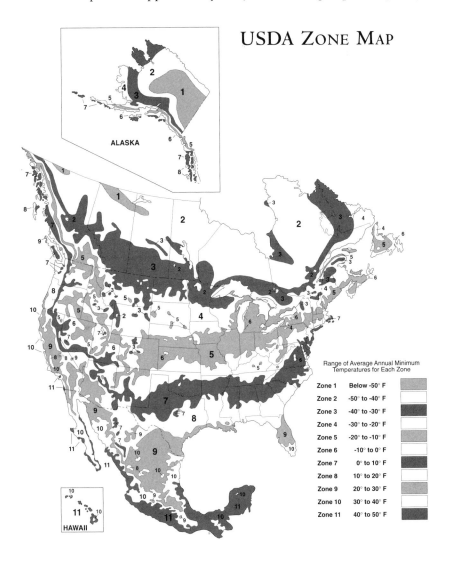

USDA ZONE MAP

Range of Average Annual Minimum Temperatures for Each Zone	
Zone 1	Below -50° F
Zone 2	-50° to -40° F
Zone 3	-40° to -30° F
Zone 4	-30° to -20° F
Zone 5	-20° to -10° F
Zone 6	-10° to 0° F
Zone 7	0° to 10° F
Zone 8	10° to 20° F
Zone 9	20° to 30° F
Zone 10	30° to 40° F
Zone 11	40° to 50° F

with a low rate of fermentation, very desirable qualities in cidermaking. Conversely, a cold, wet summer makes juice with a low specific gravity and fast fermentation, a combination that can give poor-quality cider.

Following are North American apple varieties used for cider and the zones in which they will bear usable fruit, based on the U.S. Department of Agriculture's average minimum temperature zonation map.

Zone 3
Cortland (in most favored regions), Fameuse, McIntosh, Ribston Pippin (with care), Wealthy, and Siberian and Hyslop crabs

Zone 4
Cortland, Esopus Spitzenberg, Fameuse, McIntosh, Northern Spy, Rhode Island Greening, Ribston Pippin, Roxbury Russet, Wayne, and Wealthy

Zone 5
Baldwin, Ben Davis, Cox's Orange Pippin, Delicious, Esopus Spitzenberg, Fameuse, Golden Russet, Gravenstein, Jonathan, McIntosh, Newtown, Northern Spy, Rhode Island Greening, Ribston Pippin, Rome Beauty, Roxbury Russet, Stayman Winesap, and Wealthy

Zone 6
Baldwin, Ben Davis, Cox's Orange Pippin, Delicious, Esopus Spitzenberg, Fameuse, Gilpin, Golden Russet, Gravenstein, Jonathan, McIntosh, Newtown, Northern Spy, Rhode Island Greening, Ribston Pippin, Rome Beauty, Roxbury, Russet, Stayman Winesap, Wealthy, and Winesap

Zone 7
Baldwin, Ben Davis, Cox's Orange Pippin, Delicious, Esopus Spitzenberg, Gilpin, Golden Russet, Gravenstein, Jonathan, McIntosh, Newtown, Northern Spy, Rome Beauty, Roxbury Russet, Stayman Winesap, and Winesap

Zone 8
Ben Davis, Cox's Orange Pippin, Delicious, Esopus Spitzenberg, Gilpin, Golden Russet, Gravenstein, Newtown, Northern Spy, Rome Beauty, Roxbury Russet, Stayman Winesap, and Winesap

---

European cider apples will grow in Zones 5–8.

Growing-Degree Days

Perhaps even more important than the average minimum temperature is the length of the apple-growing season and the incidence of late-spring and early-autumn frosts that can injure fruit-producing blossoms and retard tree growth and the ripening process. One meteorological measurement used by horticulturists is the concept of *growing-degree days.* These are calculations based on the minimum amount of heat a plant requires before growth will occur. Some areas, even though they have temperate winters and long, frost-free seasons, may have a low number of growing-degree days. An example is Newfoundland, classified on the zone map as a very desirable Zone 5 and 6. Would-be cider orchardists in Newfoundland should not start filling out massive multivariety tree orders, however, for cool summers and chilly ocean winds bring the province's growing-degree days down to a low average of two thousand. If you live in a region with a low number of growing-degree days, you should plant early-maturing apples, for while late bearers will grow, as Northern Spy in northern Vermont, the fruit will not mature before killing frosts. Again, before ordering trees, be sure to check with a local fruit nurseryman or -woman or your Extension agent, who will suggest which rootstocks and varieties are best suited for your place.

How Many Trees Do You Need?

The amount of juice you get from your apples will vary with the variety, the summer weather, and the efficiency of your grinder and press. You can expect to get a minimum of two and up to three or just under four gallons of juice from a bushel (forty-five pounds) of apples. If your goal is to fill a fifty-gallon barrel with estate-produced cider, you will need twenty-five dwarf trees or seven semidwarfs.

Trees = Apples

1 dwarf tree = 1 bushel of apples

1 semidwarf = 4–5 bushels of apples

1 bushel of apples = 2–3 gallons of cider

25 dwarfs = 50–75 gallons of cider

Sizing Up the Site

The best place to plant your orchard depends on the nature of your land. Before staking out the site, consider the larger area in which you live, especially if it's in the North. In addition to climate and growing-degree days, the elevation and land contours, soil, nearness to bodies of water, and exposure to winds will affect the young trees.

Rolling hillsides are good orchard sites because the slopes provide good air drainage. Colder air seeks a lower level, so cold, moist, and potentially frost-bearing air will roll down the hillsides away from the blossoming or ripening trees. It is not unusual in a cold snap for these lower flats and pockets to be as much as 20°F (6.6°C) colder than slopes only a few miles away.

Prevailing westerly and northwesterly winds driving cold air before them in the Northern Hemisphere are deflected by mountain ranges, which offer a degree of protection to orchards planted on their eastern and southern slopes. Trees are also protected if they are planted on the leeward side of large bodies of water. Water serves as a temperature modifier in two ways — holding warmth on into early winter, and pro-longing cooler temperatures in the spring, which delays blossoming until the frost danger is less.

Avoid a windy, exposed site unless there is no other place to plant. Wind and blowing snow can raise havoc with trees. Wind may uproot or permanently malform trees, break limbs, knock down immature apples, dry out the soil, and make spraying difficult if not impossible. Windblown snow can drift over small trees to break them, at the same time providing surface or tunnel footing for rodent depredation above wire or plastic tree guards.

While it's always better to cooperate with nature than to fight it, if you must plant the orchard in a wind-ravaged location you can break the force of howling gales with strategically located windbreaks. Pines, Lombary poplars, and other shelterbelt trees or tall hedges can be planted in a strip to break the prevailing winds, or can be set in a box shape to enclose the entire small orchard.

Your orchard should receive the maximum amount of sunlight. Cider cannot be made from unripe apples, and the trees need plenty of sun for good growth and well-ripened fruit. Be on guard against tall shade trees, sun-blocking terrain, and shadow-casting buildings.

If your orchard is going to become part of the permanent shelter landscaping, put it on the sunny side of the house. The site of a former vegetable garden — if it was a success — is usually a good location, indicating a fertile, well-drained soil. Be careful not to plant the orchard over a lush septic tank leach field, as the roots may be burned by liquid waste and might clog or break lateral pipes.

Getting the Picture

So you think you've got the perfect spot? If the planting will be just several varieties spotted around the house to be used for blending, or something on a larger scale, you'll probably wonder how it will look. A preview is possible. Take a black and white photograph of the location and have an enlargement (eight by ten inches or larger) made. Go through old nursery catalogs and horticultural magazines cutting out appropriate and proportionately sized pictures of apple trees. Then, using a dab of rubber cement, tack them onto the print in the desired locations. Use of rubber cement makes it possible to move the pictures from point to point. By squinting your eyes to blur the composition a bit, you can get a fairly good idea of how it's all going to look.

SOIL

Ideally, your home cider orchard should be planted in good deep silt-loam soil. The starting orchardist, however, frequently discovers that the soil of his or her chosen site consists of heavy clay, rock, and hardpan, sand, or muck. But through a bit of improvement and the judicious choice of specialized rootstock, most undesirable soil can support apple trees, as long as you have a cooperating climate and good air drainage. Extremely sandy soils are poor because they lose moisture rapidly, and although it might be possible to dig ditches for a water supply and feeder trenches, such an irrigation project may be financially unreasonable. The determined cider orchardist cursed with semidesert may be heartened to know that it can be done. In South Africa, which has some 7.3 million apple trees under cultivation, the best orchards are found in the Elgin area. These orchards are planted in pure sandstone decomposé, and are grown hydroponically with fertilizers fed to the trees through the irrigation water.

Apple trees will grow in sandy or heavy clay soils and will do their best to adapt to the unfavorable conditions. Tolerant rootstocks can help. MM 111 is more tolerant of drought than most other stocks, and M 7 can stand fairly wet sites, while M 13 will even manage to produce apples in swampy soil.

Percolation Testing, Ditches, and Drain Tiles

Once you've chosen your site, dig several holes in the area to determine soil composition and drainage. The test holes should be two feet deep. Notice the makeup of the soil as you dig — topsoil, depth of rock and hardpan, wet or dry soil. If the holes fill with water and won't drain naturally, you've probably got a drainage problem and will have to ditch or tile-drain the site. While some rootstocks can stand very wet feet, standing in water can drown the trees.

If the holes are dug in dry weather and you discover hardpan, use a hose or buckets to fill each hole with water, then see how well it drains. Some hardpans are so impervious that they act as cementlike reservoirs that will collect and hold water during wet seasons. Your trees cannot live long in these watery prisons. If the land slope shows the possibility for drainage, you can correct the problem with footing tiles. Drainage ditches pitched to run along the rows and dug to a depth deeper than the tree root systems will carry water away. To avoid erosion, be sure to ditch along natural contours and not crossing the rows down the side of a hill. Where you have hardpan reservoirs, place the drainage tiles so they drain the trees' roots and empty into the ditches, before planting. Cover tile openings with wire screening to keep them from becoming root-chewing rodents' highways.

Soil Testing for pH

The right pH (potential of Hydrogen) is important to your trees because it determines the point at which they will make maximum use of the nutrients in the soil. Using samples of topsoil uncovered during the percolation test, check the pH rating with a soil test kit, which determines the alkaline-acid balance of the soil. These are available from state agricultural services or garden supply stores. This pH measurement is a simple scale in which the number 7 represents a neutral soil; numbers above 7 indicate increasing alkalinity, and those below, increasing acidity. Some grains prefer a "sweet" soil of 7 or 8, while blueberries do best in extremely acidic soil, around 4. Apple trees grow best in slightly acidic soils, about pH 6.

Some regions, such as the Canadian prairie provinces, have alkaline soils with pHs above 7, but most areas will be acidic, with readings going way down due to longtime agricultural use and other leaching factors. Alkalinity can be reduced by adding powdered sulfur or acidic organic materials such as oak leaf or pine mulch to the soil. The more common problem of acidity is corrected by mixing limestone into the soil. The cidermaker can create his or her own chalk soils with a few bags of limestone from the nearest garden store. Dolomitic limestone may be the best, for it supplies the additional element of magnesium needed for vegetative growth, but if your soil test shows magnesium is already present, calcitic limestone will be fine.

Nitrogen

Cidermakers know that the rate of cider fermentation depends upon the soluble nitrogen content of the juice. Higher levels of nitrogen in the juice mean faster fermentation. The slower the fermentation, the better the cider, but some commercial makers add nitrogen to speed up the process and get the product onto the market faster. The true cider apple varieties are lower in nitrogen than North American dessert varieties. Trees absorb the nitrogen naturally present in the soil through the action of a soil bacterium, *azotobacter*, which converts atmospheric nitrogen into a form the tree can absorb. Grass competes with apple trees for the nitrogen, so if you want a slow-fermenting cider, let the grass win. A grassy orchard not only produces better cider apples, but provides a cushion for falling apples as well. Since both insects and animals can find good cover if the grass is long, keep it mowed, especially in the fall. Nitrogen levels may also be higher in shaded fruit, so prune to let the sun into the trees.

STAKING OUT YOUR ORCHARD'S CLAIM

Let's say you've decided that a fifty-gallon cider barrel looks good, that you've selected the site and ordered a mixed variety of twenty-five dwarf apple trees for spring delivery. You should stake out your orchard and prepare the site for planting well before the young trees arrive — the autumn before, if possible. A few days' work will contribute to a lifetime of good drinking.

Figuring the placement of the trees is easier for most people if they block space requirement in terms of rectangles rather than the natural circular shape of the tree. When the trees are planted in rows, the imaginary rectangles will include the needed room for aisles between the rows. Allowing enough aisle space is important for spring pruning, machine cultivating, mowing, and harvest.

Work out your plan on paper first. If your orchard is going to be made up of little trees grafted onto very dwarfing M 9 stock, the trees, which attain a mature height of eight feet, should be planted at least six feet apart in the row and twelve feet apart in the aisle. To plant a block orchard of five trees in five rows, you'll need a minimum space of thirty by fifty-four feet. Semidwarfs and standards will need more space.

Space Requirements

ROOT-CONTROLLED TREE SIZE	SPACING (ROW × AISLE)
Standard	40 × 40
Seedling, M 16, MM 109	24 × 32
M 13 or MM 104	20 × 28
M 1 or Alnarp 2	18 × 26
M 2, M 4, or MM 111	16 × 24
MM 106 or M 9 Interstem Standard	14 × 22
M 7 or M 9–MM 111 Interstem	12 × 20
M 26 or M 9–MM 106 Interstem	10 × 18
Ottawa 3	7 × 14
M 9	6 × 12

Contour Planting

An orchard planted to follow the contours of a small knoll is very handsome, and the staking is easily done with a swing line. Anchor the line at the crown of the knoll and place the stakes at the proper places along the swing of the arc. Be sure to allow for the aisle spacing as the concentric arcs diminish. A semidwarf standing at the crown stake will complete this beautiful orchard. Planting all trees in sweeping arcs while keeping them in line from top to bottom makes for easy machine care, with less chance of machines ricocheting off the little trees.

Getting the Site Ready

Nursery trees — potted, boxed, or balled — can be planted anytime frost is out of the ground. In warmer areas apple trees are often set out in the fall, but in the North, it's safer to plant them in the spring. It's not essential to start getting ready for the spring tree shipment the previous fall, but many orchardists facing virgin territory do, and with good reason.

By digging the holes in the fall, you can determine what must be done in the way of soil conditioning. Since inert material such as large rocks and hardpan has to be replaced with good soil, an early start makes the spring push a lot easier. The soil will get an extra turning in the spring, and though this may seem like double work, the benefits are worth it. People with that perfect orchard soil — naturally deep, rich, and well drained — will have fewer problems with spring planting.

There's an old saying that contains a lot of good advice: "Don't plant a fifty-cent tree in a two-bit hole." For dwarf trees, dig a hole at least two feet deep and two feet wide. Spread a tarpaulin or sheet of heavy-gauge plastic on one side of the hole, and place a garden cart or wheelbarrow on the other. Shovel all the turf and richest soil down to the hardpan onto the tarp. The rocks and hardpan go into the cart to be permanently removed. If you have a drainage problem, this is the time for remedial ditching and tile laying. If it's cement hardpan, set the tiles at the bottom of the hole, well below root depth. Now, depending on how much material has been removed, add the good soil, old manure or compost, sand if the basic soil is heavy clay, lime, and any other nutrients the soil test has indicated your soil lacks. Mix it all thoroughly with a hoe or rake before shoveling it into the hole.

In fall preparation, a dry chemical fertilizer such as 5–10–10 may be mixed in with the soil in *very* small amounts. The chemical will break down in winter moisture, and most often it won't be necessary, as the

Planting apple trees, a woodcut from the title page of Joseph Blagrave's *The Epitome of the Whole Art of Husbandry,* London, 1675.

well-limed and manured soil will keep the young tree happy through its first year. No chemical, raw poultry, or livestock manure should be mixed into the soil in the spring, as those will almost certainly burn tender roots. If, for some reason, your soil is still below par in nutrients come springtime, after the tree is planted you can spread fertilizer in a circle on the ground well away from the trunk.

PLANTING

On that great day when your young apple trees arrive, and the site is ready for them, it's important to get them into the ground as soon as possible.

Trees shipped from distant nurseries are usually bare-rooted and packed in plastic sleeves. When the tree is packed at the nursery, the medium protecting the roots is damp, but nursery-pruned roots usually puncture the plastic in transit, and they can become dangerously dry. Be ready with plasma — a rich mixture of topsoil and water, about the consistency of old-fashioned pea soup. Plunge the root into this mixture after removing the plastic sleeves. Old washtubs are fine for this. Water the tops of the trees, and keep the container out of sunlight and wind. It is possible to delay planting several days this way, but the root should be soaked daily with fresh water. During planting, keep the tree protected with damp burlap until it goes into the ground. Balled, potted, or boxed trees should be kept watered and out of the sun and wind until they are planted.

All trees should be planted slightly deeper than they were in the nursery if the graft or bud union is as high as a foot or more above the roots. Make *sure* that the grafting union, no matter where it is on the tree, is not covered with soil, or the grafted-on stock may put down its own roots and revert to its inbred standard habit, canceling out the dwarfing effect of the rootstock. The rootstock itself will often put up suckers. These must be removed, or before long you'll have a lusty crab crowding out your fancy young apple.

Ready to Plant!

Shovel enough soil out of the hole onto that handy tarp so the tree's root system can be placed to such a depth that the graft union will be above ground level. If you are planting bare-rooted trees, carefully spread the roots and clip clean all that are broken. Then place the root system in the hole, straighten and smooth the roots into a flat natural position, and cover with soil. If your trees are balled, snip the strings holding the burlap or plastic wrapping so the covering lies flat on the bottom of the hole. Burlap will soon rot away, but the plastic must be removed and discarded. Do not disturb the soil around the roots, but clip off any obviously broken roots. Hold the tree straight (it's handy to have a helper at this stage of the work) and sprinkle soil around the rootball. Fill the hole with the conditioned soil, tamping firmly to fill in any air pockets, until the soil level is one inch below ground level. This slight depression will act as a rain trap.

Pour two gallons of water into this depression to help settle the soil and bring it into contact with the roots, as well as to remove small pockets of air. Some orchardists add a small amount of liquid starter fertilizer such as 10–52–17 to help bare root sets take hold. This fertilizer is hot and should be used sparingly. If your soil mix is rich, you don't need it. There may be an urge during the tree's early years to give it a good fertilizer shot and thereby induce speedier and heavier bearing. Resist it. Extremely vigorous growth in young, just-bearing trees produces juice that is high in nitrogen and therefore likely to ferment very rapidly, producing a lower-quality cider.

New trees should be pruned by cutting the previous year's growth shoots back to the midbud, and removing excess or crossed branches. Make the cut clean and close to the trunk and diagonal to the bud.

Trees on dwarfing rootstock, such as M 9, have shallow roots and must be staked. A strong wind, or later growth, can topple them. Five-foot lengths of hardwood two-by-twos or metal pipe are good for stakes. Hammer them in five or six inches from the tree and deep enough to give good support. You may tie the trees to the stakes with clotheslines, but a section of wire, covered with a piece of garden hose to keep the wire from cutting into the tender tree, is more lasting.

In areas of the North where winter sunscald is a problem, painting the tree trunks white with a rubber-based paint will help reflect sunlight and reduce sunscald injury.

Protect your trees from mice and rabbits, a real winter problem, by enclosing the trunks in fine-meshed hardware-cloth sleeves that extend from two inches below the earth's surface to just below the first branch. This protects against both sunscald and rodent damage.

ORCHARD CARE

That's it. Your orchard is planted and off to a good start. Within a few years you'll be carrying boxes of fragrant, rich apples to your cider room, if you give the trees the degree of care you did in preparing their permanent homes. While cider orcharding takes less care than growing perfect table fruit, some jobs must be done if you want the best yields of high-quality fruit from the little trees.

Pruning

Complex pruning manuals with esoteric vocabularies exist in abundance, but the home cider orchardist can usually manage pruning chores by remembering that the point of nipping off growth is to concentrate the tree's energy into producing large fruits on a minimum of strong branches, and to open the tree's interior to the sunshine for good fruit ripening. Cider apples *must* be well ripened, preferably on the tree.

Beginning in your apple trees' second year, prune in the late winter or early spring while they are still dormant. Use sharp pruning clippers or shears, and cut all branches flush with the parent growth. Projecting stubs frequently won't heal and will develop rot, or the stub will waste the tree's energy by sending up vigorous water sprouts. When you cut back branchwood, make the cut just above a leaf bud on the diagonal so that it will shed water. Fruit buds are thicker and more blunt than leaf buds.

Cut out all obvious deadwood and drooping weak branches. When you notice two crossing branches, cut the weaker of the two level with the trunk, unless it has better characteristics, such as the direction or angle of its growth. For example, if one of the crossed branches has a nice horizontal line instead of reaching up straight for the sky, you will want to keep it, since it will expose the fruit to the sun.

Shoots springing up from the roots are aptly called *suckers* and should be cut level with the ground. Growth starting on the trunk below the first main branch, and fast-growing upright shoots among the branches, especially above previous pruning cuts, are *water sprouts* and should be cut flush with the main trunk or branch.

Thinning

In the second or third year after planting you will be rewarded by fragrant clusters of apple blossoms in May or June. As the tiny apples develop you may feel that the goddess Pomona has rewarded your dedicated labors with an incredible embarrassment of fruit riches — then you may be horrified when many of the immature apples fall to the ground. Both your horror and the apples' fall are natural. This is the "June drop" or the "July drop," and there's nothing you can do about it. It's the tree's way of getting rid of fruit it can't support. Sometimes, however, the tree doesn't do a thorough job, and then the thinning is up to you.

Very heavy fruiting is undesirable. The small branches of dwarf trees will break under heavy loads of fruit. The apples will be smaller, because there's just so much nourishment to go around. Finally, the unthinned tree may go into a biennial bearing habit — heavy crop one year, sparse or no crop the next. This happens because the tree has put so much into one crop that it needs to regain its strength.

To prevent these conditions, apples should be thinned to allow five or six inches between fruits. Snap the little apples off, making sure you don't tear the stem from the branch, opening a wound. Don't leave the fruit on the ground to rot and attract pests, but collect it and dump it into your compost heap.

DISEASES, INSECTS, AND WILDLIFE

You are not alone in loving apple trees. Unfortunately, your affections are shared by all manner of ravaging diseases, more than four hundred kinds of damaging insects, and hungry wildlife. There is evidence that apple trees are less resistant to diseases and pests today than they were in the past. Perhaps this is the price we pay for the destruction of many pests' natural enemies, and for large, commercial plantings that diseases and insects find highly attractive.

Some rootstocks are disease resistant, as are some varieties, and companion planting of certain strongly scented plants will deter a few insect pests, as will good orchard hygiene, insect traps, and physical deterrents, soil tillage, and the encouragement of natural enemies.

But for the most effective control of these scourges, a spraying program is important, whether it is with simple, "organic" sprays, botanical sprays based on insect-toxic plant tissues, or chemical sprays. Some of the more common diseases and insects that attack apple trees are listed in the following pages.

Apple scab. A fungus that starts in periods of wet weather and infects fruit and foliage with green-black splotches. The maturing fruit is disfigured with gray, scabby areas. Sprays can fight this disease. There are resistant varieties.

Apple scab

Fire blight. A bacterial disease and a serious problem for both cider and table apple growers. Leaves, twigs, and branches suddenly wither and die, as though the tree had been singed with a giant blowtorch. Action must be taken when it first appears or blight can kill the entire tree. Cut off each diseased sprig or branch, sterilizing your clippers in a chlorine-water solution (2:10) between cuts, and burn the cuttings. A streptomycin antibiotic spray is available to cure this sickness.

Fire blight

Apple canker. Also known as "apple blister," this canker appears as an ulceration on the tree's trunk, and can start as an infection of an untreated wound. Cankers can spread, girdle, and kill the tree if they aren't removed. Cut out the diseased area with a saw and paint the wound with a tree sealer. Sterilize your saw by dipping it into a chlorine-water solution.

Apple canker

Wilt, cedar rust, and powdery mildew. Wilt attacks vegetation by cutting off its water supply. Mildew covers both fruit and foliage with a frosty mold. The chances are good that leaves and fruit will be affected by cedar-apple rust if the orchard contains susceptible varieties and red cedar grows near the orchard. While it's painful to cut down durable evergreens, the variety is an alternate

Cedar rust

host of the disease — remove the cedar and the cycle is broken. Rust attacks leaves, speckling them with dead blotches, and causes large, circular rotten areas in the fruit. Sprays will control all these problems.

Powdery mildew

Codling moth. A common and destructive pest, the larvae of this moth tunnel through the flesh of the fruit to the core in midsummer. They can destroy a whole crop. Telltale piles of dried droppings around the surface hole indicate the codling moth is your guest, but by the time they're seen, the damage is done. Traps, baits, simple sprays using oils, fine clays, or even plain water help check the codling moth. The botanical insecticide ryania offers fair crop protection. Woodpeckers are major enemies of codling moth larvae.

Codling moth damage

Codling moth

Tent caterpillar. The familiar weblike tents are usually found in three-branch junctions. In the small dwarf or semidwarf orchard these voracious eaters can be removed by hand and crushed underfoot or burned, away from the tree.

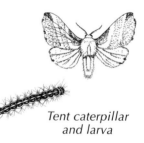

Tent caterpillar and larva

Apple maggot. This is the familiar apple worm that everyone looks for after the first bite into an apple. It is the larva of a two-winged fly and burrows through the flesh of the apple, leaving a brown wavering track. Host apples turn soft and fall prematurely from the tree. Infected apples should be picked up and destroyed to break the growth cycle.

Apple maggot

Aphids and European red mites. These minute pests, which are barely visible, can cause mammoth destruction to leaf and fruit. The aphids' work produces brittle leaves and grotesquely deformed fruits, while the mites injure vegetation. The botanical spray ryania is effective against apple aphids. Frequent spraying of the trees with plain water in a standard sprayer is effective in controlling aphids, while chemical sprays will control both. Nature helps in the aphid "red mite" control by providing more than forty natural enemies.

Aphids

Oystershell and San Jose scale. These tiny insects, which suck the nutrients from branchwood, get their name from the crusty scale that protects them and appears somewhat like tiny barnacles. Sprays will give protection.

Scale

Curculios. These insects penetrate the apple's skin to lay eggs, causing visible puncture wounds and premature fruit drop. Weak saltwater sprays, simple traps, and good orchard hygiene will help to keep their numbers down, while a spraying program offers greater control.

Curculios

Borer. A drilling worm that leaves a gelatinous excretion around the hole it makes into a tree's trunk. If left alone, borers can seriously weaken a young tree, and they should be bayoneted with a flexible wire skewer.

Borer

Organic Apple Growing

In a day when the use of chemicals in food and agriculture is under severe scrutiny and criticism, the mere mention of the word "spraying" is sure to raise hackles in some quarters. Yet sprays are made up of all kinds of substances, from pure water to botanicals composed of plant tissue to chemicals, used in varying strengths. USDA grading standards, market fruit grades, and consumer expectations make it necessary for commercial growers of table apples to use potent chemical sprays. The public expects attractive and flawless fruit, and the grower can't gamble on quantity or quality.

The cider orchardist is in a better position to work with nature and experiment with less toxic sprays, physical deterrents, insect traps, companion planting, and the encouragement of natural predators. Apples used for cider alone can be blemished, a bit wormy, smallish, and scabby. If you are not bothered by the thought of lighter crops, less-than-perfect fruit, and a few inhabitants in your apples, try an organic approach to cider apple growing. Choose varieties resistant to scab and fire blight, make use of companion planting to help check insects, and let your chickens range through the orchard to pick up other insects. Wood ashes thrown onto dewy trees have been used for centuries to discourage various apple banes, and even a well-directed jet of water from hose or sprayer can knock off many insects. Homemade sprays of oil or soap and water, or a Bio-Dynamic tree spray made up of a very fine clay and botanical toxins, generally harmless to anything but insects, are used by many organic gardeners. Be heartened by the fact that some regions are less severely affected by disease and insects than others. In northeastern Vermont, for example, the codling moth is no problem, while some one hundred miles to the west and south it will devastate a crop if not checked. If you live in a fairly isolated area with few orchards, it may take the bugs a long time to find you.

Botanical Sprays

Fair protection can be achieved through a spraying program that utilizes such insecticides as rotenone, pyrethrum, ryania, and others that are made of plant tissues. These sprays must be applied more frequently than chemicals since they are less toxic. Rotenone, which is made from the roots of different tropical plants, kills insects by slowing their metabolisms. Pyrethrum is manufactured from the flowers of a variety of perennial chrysanthemum, sometimes called the "bug-killing daisy." One of the safest insecticides, pyrethrum acts directly on the insects' nervous systems, works quickly, but it has a short life when exposed to sunlight. Insects do not develop a tolerance to pyrethrum. Ryania, which is made from a Latin American shrub, is an effective although somewhat

INTEGRATED PEST MANAGEMENT

Integrated Pest Management, or IPM, is the most commonly applied pest management approach used by growers today. Its goal is to make decisions that produce economically and environmentally optimum results.

IPM requires that a grower monitor his or her orchard regularly to determine which pests may be present in numbers large enough to require spraying. So-called thresholds are set for each pest, with the assumption that an orchard can tolerate a certain quantity. If the pests exceed the threshold and the grower decides to spray, IPM dictates using selective pesticides so that damage to helpful species is minimized.

IPM can range from reasonably priced and easy-to-do to expensive and labor intensive, depending on your level of involvement. A full-blown IPM program has four levels of treatment; many growers get by with only one or two levels, which holds down cost and time expenditures.

As an example, a modified two-level IPM program could spray for, say, plum curculio. That uses Imidan, a synthetic chemical, at petal-fall and again 10 days later.

The first line of IPM defense, however, is visual. Get out and look at the trees. Such baits as pheromone lure and sticky spheres will capture enough of the critters to give you an idea of their numbers. Only if the number of trapped bugs indicates approaching crisis would you spray.

Four-footed pests, such as deer, can be discouraged by nontoxic means as well. Try hanging out slices of soap in the lower branches to discourage browsing. Irish Spring, Dial, and Cashmere Bouquet are three proven anti-deer bars.

selective killer of codling moths. It acts by paralyzing the insects, and, although it does not kill them outright, they stop eating. Ryania is also effective against apple aphids.

If You Choose Chemical Sprays

Chemical sprays may be very effective in the short run, and seemingly safe for humans when used properly. However, growing concerns about limiting dangerous chemicals on produce and protecting the environment has led many farmers and gardeners to adopt an effective practice called Integrated Pest Management (IPM), which combines organic techniques with limited and carefully targeted chemical controls.

With any spray program, it is important to remember several important "dos" and "don'ts" that will make your spraying safer and more effective.

→ Chemical spraying should be halted two to four weeks before harvesting.
→ Don't spray when the sun is hot and there's a possibility of burning foliage, nor when the trees are in full bloom, since bees and other pollinating insects will be killed.
→ Don't spray during or just before a rain, or the spray will be washed off and you'll have to do it all over again. Don't spray on windy days.

There are all-purpose orchard sprays formulated for insects *and* fungi. However, the most effective spray programs are targeted to specific conditions — there is no reason to use a chemical designed to work on pests that are not found in your area. Always consult your local Agricultural Extension Service for advice.

The Schedule

Early spraying is timed to the blossoming of individual trees. Different varieties blossom at different times, sometimes over the period of a month. Treat each tree or variety as an individual until all the blossom petals have fallen. Then all can be sprayed at the same time. Botanical sprays will have to be applied more frequently, and a thorough covering job is important.

Green tip: Spray when the green tips first appear on the buds, and before the first rainfall, to ward off apple scab and mildew.

Prepink: Spray when the blossom buds first show pink, against scab, mildew, aphids.

Pink: Just before the blossoms open, against scab, mildew, aphids, wintermoth, and green fruitworm. Do not spray while the blossoms are open.

Calyx: Spray after all the petals have fallen, against scab, mildew, aphids.

First cover: One week after the calyx spray, against scab and insects.

Second cover: Ten days later, against scab and codling moth.

Third cover: Ten days later, against scab, codling moth, mites, and apple maggot.

Fourth cover: Ten days later, against apple maggot.

Fifth cover: Ten days later, against apple maggot.

Stop spraying two to four weeks before harvest.

Spraying Equipment

Spraying dwarf and semidwarf trees is easy and inexpensive. Compared to the mammoth compressors and lumbering fogging fumigators that are used in orchards of standard trees, your weapons seem like toys. But they're just as effective and are easy to handle, generally not more than five gallons and under fifty pounds when full.

You may want to use a simple tank, pumped up to operate by compressed air, or a backpack sprayer powered either by compressed air or a hand pump, or just a "trombone" pumping device itself, one fed from a

---

PRECAUTIONS FOR USE OF SPRAYERS

1. *Read and follow all directions carefully.*
2. *Don't spill chemicals on yourself when mixing and loading the sprayer. If you do, flush immediately with water. Wear protective clothing — a raincoat, boots, hat, and goggles.*
3. *When spraying, stand upwind, and watch out for other people and animals.*
4. *Do not smoke or eat while you spray.*
5. *Store all chemicals and equipment in a safe place, out of the reach of any children.*

pail containing the spray solution. This little pump is the cheapest of all and just fine for a small orchard used in conjunction with a five-gallon bucket and a section of broom handle to stir the solution.

Clean all equipment thoroughly after each spraying. And remember — pesticides are lethal by nature.

More Uninvited Guests

Creatures, from the meek mouse to the bold bear, will find your orchard irresistible. Like the bug and blight, they'll savor it all — buds, twigs, bark, and fruit. Small rodents such as mice and rabbits will often do greater harm than raccoons and bears by gnawing enough bark off the tree to kill it. In a dwarf tree, a raccoon can break just as many branches as a bear will while stealing fruit from a standard variety. Porcupines can chew trunks and branches clean, while squirrels will bite the apples, and birds will peck them or drill holes in the tree. The worst of all, perhaps, are the deer, for they do a lot of everything. During the fall they'll come down and eat your apples. In winter, when food gets scarce, they will browse on your trees, nibbling off tender buds and twigs, and when they're done with that appetizer, long strips of bark make up the next course.

Tree trunks can be protected from girdling by mice and rabbits by installing narrow-meshed wire sleeves, or plastic tree guards, or even thick layers of newspaper wrapped around the trunk. This is fairly effective except in deep snow, which allows the mice to run their tunnels on a higher level and come in above the guards. Traps set in the orchard from early fall until snow will help reduce the mouse population, as will poison baits spread on the orchard floor just before snowfall.

High fencing, blood meal, mothballs, human urine, and other repellents are used in combatting deer but they are ineffective when the snows come. A fence is not protection against bears or raccoons — if it's a

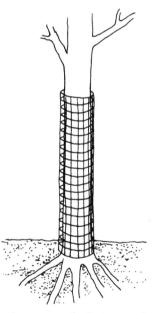

A tree guard of wire mesh or plastic will discourage mice and rabbits from dining on your apples.

strong fence they'll climb over it, and if it's weak they'll knock it down
A good hound dog that's concerned about respect for your property
lines will make them think twice, though.

The most obvious safeguard is to walk often through your winter
orchard. Look for tracks in the snow, or droppings — they'll tell you
what to expect. And if you find Porky dining on an apple branch, use a
good lead-based spray, such as .22.

THE HARVEST

Within two or three years your small trees will begin rewarding your
care with baskets of rich fruit ready to be transformed into golden cider.
In some years of fine summer weather you will have a bumper crop, each
fruit large and bursting-tight with aromatic juice. In the old days cidermakers referred to these extraordinary harvests as "a hit of fruit," and
more than two hundred years ago cider lovers wrote nostalgically about
the "great hit of 1784" when, for lack of enough barrels, cider was
stored in water cisterns in the ground. It's a great moment when the
tangy sweet juice flows from the first pressing of your own apples.

One sure sign that your apples are ripe is when they start falling
from the trees without the help of the wind. Squeezing an apple isn't a
good test of ripeness because some varieties, though perfectly ripe, are
rock hard. Color is not a true test either, for green and yellow apples
may blush a bit, but there's no real color indicator of ripeness, and red
apples may reach one tone and stay that way. A good test is to pick an
apple. Always pick apples by twisting them clockwise, being careful not
to tear the branchwood away with the stem. If the fruit separates from
the tree easily, it's ripe, but if you have to tug, you'd better wait a little
longer. Another good test is to pick an apple, cut it in half, and check
the seeds. If the seeds are a dark brown, the apple is ripe. The seeds in
unripe fruit are greenish tan.

Some cidermakers allow picked apples to "mellow" for a week or ten
days before pressing, in the belief that juice is increased and flavor
improved. Others prefer to let the apples hang on the trees after they
ripen, instead of storing them inside. This is fine unless wind and gravity harvest the fruit in the meantime. For those who would store their
apples, remember that such varieties as Newtown and Jonathan do not
store well for cider and should be pressed as soon after picking as possi-

ble. Drops have been used for cider since ancient times, but they can be the source of possibly deadly botulism. However tempting they may seem, *do not use drops* in your cidermaking. Softened apples or apples with brown spots indicating the beginning of rot are best tossed into the compost heap, as are windfalls.

Picking apples in dwarf and semidwarf orchards goes fast, because there's little or no ladder work, and the dumping station, usually a garden cart, moves right along with you. Four or five bushels of apples can be loaded directly into the cart. You will probably want to keep the varieties separated for individual pressing, fermentation, and later blending, at least until you learn what proportions of the different varieties make the most satisfying cider.

Be careful not to bruise the fruit by dropping the apples into containers. Bruised fruit will rot and can start real trouble in baskets or bins. Finally, culls and overripe fruit make an inferior cider. Cider should be made from orchard-run apples of the best quality. After all, that's why you planted the orchard.

Apple Storage

Since apples ripen at different times, the occasional cidermaker (one who puts up a single batch by blending apples before fermentation)

No windfalls should be used in making cider.

may have to store one or more varieties while awaiting the ripening of another desired cultivar. For cidermakers who choose this approach, and those who have had their almost-ripe apples harvested by the wind, storage is important.

Store only clean, sound fruit. Check the apples often for deterioration, and dispose of rotten fruit at once. It is true that one rotten apple can spoil the barrel. The storage area should be clean, well ventilated, and protected from the weather. Cooler temperatures will naturally lengthen storage and mellowing time; 70°F (21.1°C) is about the maximum, while a hot spell will make the apples deteriorate rapidly.

The fruit should not be stored in an area containing strong-smelling substances or other fruits and vegetables. Apples are very sensitive to outside aromas and will absorb them. It is better to put up some sort of temporary storage shelter than to keep them in a garage where oil, gasoline, and rubber will overpower the essence of apple. Pleasant, perfumed odors can also ruin the flavor of apples.

Nor should houseplants or potted trees to be brought inside for the winter be put in the same enclosed area with stored or ripening apples. Apples give off ethylene gas that can kill them.

DEVELOPING YOUR OWN CIDER APPLE TREES

If you enjoy the taste of English ciders — tannin-rich body and tart acidity — you may wish to perk up the cider made from your relatively bland North American apples. In some areas, nurserymen and -women can supply European bitter and bittersharp cultivars that will solve your problem. However, since this stock is now quite rare on this side of the Atlantic, you will have to try other solutions. One is to add crab apple juice from one or more of the varieties listed in the previous chapter to your cider blend. These tiny apples are high in tannin and acid. Or you can scout the countryside for wild seedling-grown trees, the apple-crabs, which grow in pastures and by the wayside, and spike the blend with their juice. But if you have an experimental turn of mind, and enjoy working with apple trees, you might like to try developing your own stock. You can produce apples that are generally more tart and puckery than dessert apples from your own "wild" seedlings, or by grafting varietal scions onto homegrown stock. These experiments are easy, fascinating, and often rewarding for the cidermaker.

Growing Your Own Seedlings

Plant the seed of any ripe hardy variety. The seeds may be planted indoors in a pot, set before a sunny window, and watered, or planted directly into your "seedling nursery," which can be a simple frame set in the ground and filled with rich soil. The pot set can be transplanted the spring after you start them. All seedlings should stay two or three years in the nursery before moving to the experimental orchard. With care they should begin to bear in six to ten years. While it's impossible to tell what the fruit is going to be like until it actually appears on the branches, crab characteristics are usually dominant in the genetic makeup of tree and fruit. The chances are great that you'll get an acidic juice with fair tannin, an excellent way to zip up juice with less character.

Top-Grafting

Both your homegrown seedlings and seedlings in the wild can be used as stock for grafting experiments. Lewis Hill, a respected northern Vermont grower, in his book *Fruits and Berries for the Home Garden,* describes such an experiment: "I once grafted a branch from a Yellow Transparent apple tree onto a seedling grown from a wild hard green apple. When the new tree began to bear fruit, instead of the soft, mushy Yellow Transparent, the apples were firm, kept longer, and had quite a zippy flavor."

If the grafting bug bites you, be prepared for an absorbing and rewarding hobby. While there are several ways of grafting apple stock, the most practical for the small cider orchard grower is the cleft, since it's done in the early spring at the same time you're pruning. Scions taken from the pruned-off branches of your orchard are grafted to seedling or wild stock during the period of dormancy. Either one or two scions can be grafted to each stock.

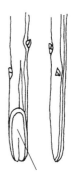

Cambium

Scions should be 4 to 5 inches long.

Step 1. Cut your scions four or five inches long from pruned growth of the previous year — the newest wood. Make sure each has several buds and is one-quarter to one-half inch in diameter, and smaller in diameter than the stock it's being fitted into. If you can't do the grafting operation the same

day you've pruned, wrap the scions gently in moist material and keep them in the refrigerator in a plastic bag until you get to the job within a few days. Do not let the scions dry.

Step 2. Using sharp pruning shears, cut off the wild or seedling stock parallel to, and four or five inches above, the ground. The size of the scion should determine which stock is chosen, and the latter must be larger than the former. Make sure the cut is level and clean, so you can see the cambium ring clearly.

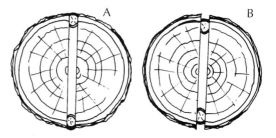

Wood and annual rings

Cambium

Inner bark

Outer bark

Cross-section of a stock or scion or limb showing the location of the important cambium layer.

Step 3. Use a sharp knife to split the stock cleanly in half to a depth of one and one-half to two inches. The split should be through the heartwood right down the middle. You may have to tap the blade to get it started. Twist the knife to open the crack, and insert a clean, freshly whittled peg to keep it open.

Step 4. Just below the lowest bud on the scion, cut a one- to one-and-one-quarter-inch two-sided taper (see drawings, page 150). Be sure you taper the right end — the buds should be pointing up. It's safest not to touch any bare wood; lay the scion on the ground, put it in your mouth, or smoke during the operation to avoid spreading bacteria.

A   B

Cross-sections, looking down on cleft grafts. In A, scions are wrongly placed since the cambiums of scion and stock are not in contact, although the outside surfaces are flush or even. The stock bark is thicker. In B, note the scions are in far enough that the cambium layer contacts the cambium of the stock.

Step 5. Slide the peg to one side of the cleft in the stock and carefully insert the graft, pressing downward until the top of the taper and

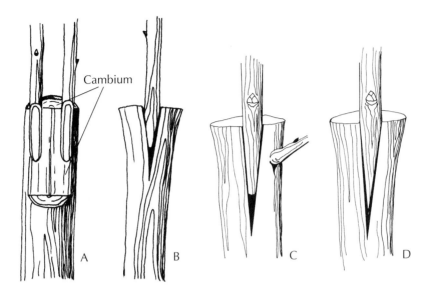

A: Cutaway to show scions in place; B: side view of scion in place;
C: scion prepared with blunt end gives better cambium contact
and stability than scion beveled to a point (D).

stock are flush. Make sure that the cambium layer of stock and scion touch. If in doubt, tilt the scion out a bit to assure a union. The cambium is the living portion of the tree that controls growth. Pale green in color, it is the layer closest to the tree's wood, which is yellow. If the cambium layers don't touch, the graft will fail.

Step 6. Remove the peg, and the natural tension of the stock's wood should grip the scion firmly. If you have split the stock too deeply and the scion is loose, coat the split with tree sealer, and then bind the split with friction tape. The tape will usually fall off or loosen during the following winter. All exposed bare wood — the cut, top of scion, stock and cleft, in fact any injured area — should be coated with sealer to protect stock and scion from bacteria.

Keep an eye on the graft during the next few weeks. The sap begins to run if the bud swells and shows signs of growth, and you've done it! Remove any root suckers and stock growth as you do on the other trees. If you grafted two scions and both grew, save the more vigorous one, and prune back the other after the first season's growth.

BEYOND CIDER:
Vinegars, Brandy, Tasting, and Cooking

The cidermaker will not stop when he or she has made excellent cider. There are further fields, and they will be explored in this chapter.

There is the making of cider vinegar — and a good cider is essential for a first step.

There is the making of apple distillates, applejack, and brandy — and be careful here about infractions of the law.

And there are other areas — learning to taste cider properly, and to judge it; and using cider in the kitchen, in a variety of drinks and dishes.

CIDER VINEGAR
"Loaf of bread," the Walrus said,
"Is what we chiefly need;
Pepper and vinegar besides
Are very good indeed —
Now if you're ready, Oysters dear,
We can begin to feed."
— Lewis Carroll, "The Walrus and the Carpenter,"
Through the Looking-Glass

The Walrus and the Carpenter, in wishing for a little vinegar to dash on their oysters, were part of a vinegar-loving tradition that goes back to the ancient origin of fermented liquors. The sharp acetic acid has been picking up bland foods and unexciting dishes for thousands of years. In

the fifth century B.C., Hippocrates prescribed vinegar doses for medical use. Legend has it that when Hannibal invaded Italy in 218 B.C., his incredible feat of crossing the Alps by an unknown route — complete with army, baggage train, and elephants — was possible only because he dissolved a pass through the mountains with copious amounts of strong, sharp vinegar.

During the Middle Ages, alchemists noticed that vinegar, with its high acid level, had a corrosive or compounding effect on minerals and metals. Vinegar became a staple commodity in every alchemist's laboratory, and many of the products turned out by these early chemists derived from combinations of vinegar with other substances. By pouring vinegar on lead, for example, the alchemist made lead acetate, better known as "sugar of lead," a deadly sweetener that proved fatal to many European cider drinkers, for sugar of lead was frequently used well into the nineteenth century to smooth and sweeten a rough, sourish cider.

$\mathcal{T}$he alchemists used the symbols:

$\overline{\underset{\cdot}{X}}$ and ⊞ for straight vinegar, while

$\mathbf{X}$ and ✚ were used to designate the distilled products.

During the Renaissance, vinegar making became big business in France, and it was flavored with such things as pepper, cloves, roses, fennel, and raspberries. By the eighteenth century some ninety-two varieties of scented vinegars and fifty-five table flavors were known in France.

The production both of household vinegar and the stronger industrial acetic acid became a booming trade and a good source of revenue in England. A 1673 Act of Parliament put a duty on "vingar-beer," but the vinegar makers had a certain reluctance to report the true number of barrels they produced to the tax authorities. Revenue suffered, so a staggering forty-shilling fine was imposed on every concealed barrel discovered by the Crown's "gagers" or "gaugers." This word for these excise men has entered the English slang lexicon as "gougers" — extortionate wretches who unfairly wring money out of people.

Whether vinegars are made from beer, wine, cider, or even sugared water, all are based on the same chemistry.

$$CH_3CH_2OH \rightarrow 2H\ CH_3CHO \rightarrow CH_3COOH$$

Ethyl alcohol, the fermentative product of yeast-converted sugar
↓
partial oxidation of the alcohol and the concurrent loss of hydrogen, forming acetaldehyde
↓
the total conversion of the acetaldehyde into acetic acid

How it all comes about is through the work of the cidermaker's worst enemy and the vinegar maker's best friend, the acetic bacteria that transform the alcohol in cider into vinegar. More than a dozen of these bacteria exist, named after such microbe sleuths as A. J. Brown, Louis Pasteur, and others who first isolated them, but for the home cider- and vinegar makers they are lumped into the single classification of *acetobacter.*

Vinegar Processes

Slow, or natural, vinegar. This traditional process, which can take several months, simply involves keeping open vats of cider or other fermented or fermenting fruit juices in a warm place. The primary fermentation converts the fruit sugars into alcohol, and the secondary fermentation in the presence of oxygen oxidizes the alcohol into acetic acid. Sometimes "mother" is added to speed the process.

Orleans process. This French development is a continuous process

---

WHAT'S IN A NAME?

The word "vinegar" is derived from the French vin aigre, *or "sour wine," since much of the vinegar on the Continent was made from wine that had gone into acetic fermentation. C. Ainsworth Mitchell, in his book on the British vinegar industry,* Vinegar: Its Manufacture and Examination, *says that beer, not wine, was the source of early British vinegar, and the product was known as ale-gar, standing in the same relationship to ale as vinegar does to wine. Following the same reasoning, perhaps cider vinegar should be called* cidergar.

---

of vinegar making, with fresh juice added from time to time to a small batch of good vinegar. As soon as the new juice "turns," a quantity is siphoned off and bottled as vinegar. The vinegar left in the barrel serves as a starter for the new juice.

Quick vinegar process. Large oak vats, pierced with bungholes for air flow and fitted with pierced false bottoms, were packed with beechwood shavings, charcoal, corncobs, or birch twigs that had been soaked for several days in strong vinegar to impregnate them with acetobacter. Cider was then allowed to trickle down through the vat, and it collected in the bottom as vinegar. This process generally took from several days to a few weeks. *Vinegar essence,* or *double vinegar,* was made this way from alcoholic spirits, and contained as much as 14 percent acetic acid, in contrast to the more usual strengths of from 3 percent to 9 percent for regularly fermented fruit juices.

Acetator process. Modern vinegar is made in an *acetator,* and the process takes only two days. The acetobacter grow very rapidly in a suspension of fermenting cider and minute air bubbles under carefully controlled conditions in modern vinegar factories lined with stainless steel vinegar vats of immense size.

While fruit and grain alcohols are the primary sources today of kitchen vinegars, acetic acid is also produced from acetylene and hardwood to become the key ingredient in such things as movie film, plastics, rayon, and dozens of acetate products.

How to Make Vinegar

Since few home cider or vinegar makers have access to beechwood shavings or modern acetators, or need a continuous flow of vinegar, they will be content to make it in the old way, either from finished cider or from pomace.

Remember that acetobacter are no friends of drinking cider. Never make vinegar in your cider room or store it in your cider cellar. The acetobacter will speedily contaminate barrels, air, utensils, and water-trap liquids, and if they don't get into your cider one year, they'll haunt you the next. Also, don't be tempted to use a vinegar barrel for cider.

Once it's been used for vinegar, keep it as a vinegar barrel, because you can scrub a vinegar barrel with a hundred pounds of soda and burn twenty sulfur candles in it, but as soon as it's filled with fresh cider the acetobacter will creep in from the pores of the staves' wood.

Vinegar from Cider

Windfall apples, not good to use for drinking cider because of the probability of acetic fermentation already working in the fallen apples, are the traditional sources of cider vinegar. Windfalls are not recommended here for making cider vinegar because of the discovery of the toxin patulin, which is often found on apples that have been lying for some time in the damp grass and on the ground. It's best to play it safe and make vinegar from good cider pressed from sound ripe apples.

When you are making and blending cider in the fall, keep your vinegar making plans in mind and set aside some cider to ferment especially for that purpose. Apples with the highest sugar content yield the most alcohol and the most acetic acid. A common mistake is thinking that very acidic, sour apples make the best vinegar — instead, apples with the most sugars make the strongest, zippiest vinegars.

Don't rely on taste to tell you which apples are high in sugar. The sugar content of apples from the same tree can vary considerably from year to year, and a high acid level in a sugar-rich apple can mask the sugar and make the fruit (and its juice) taste sour. Conversely, a low-acid apple can taste sweeter than it really is. Use a hydrometer with a Brix scale (see the section on equipment for instructions on how to read a hydrometer, pages 24–26) to measure the sugar content of the freshly expressed apple juices at cider time. A Brix reading of 10 percent sugar in the must would yield a cider of 5 percent alcohol in a complete fermentation, which in turn would produce a vinegar of 5 percent acetic acid, again, if the fermentation was complete. An agreeable table vinegar is roughly 4.8 to 5 percent acetic acid. You will want to dilute anything stronger.

Make the apple juice you have set aside for future vinegar conversion as you usually do, adding yeast and allowing it to ferment under a water trap. If the summer has been cold and rainy, or the apples you are pressing are generally low in sugar, add enough sugar or honey to bring the hydrometer reading for *potential alcohol* up to the desired level — at least 5 percent, unless you like a very mild vinegar. When the fermentation is complete, remove the water trap and pour the cider into a wide-mouthed ceramic crock or other vessel that will not react with the acid. Heavy glass, enamel, or polyethylene containers are fine. The cider needs oxygen in the acetic fermentation process, so as much of the surface as can be exposed to air should be. Cover the container with a double layer of cheesecloth that will admit the air but exclude beetles, mice, and the other foreign objects that inevitably fall into open vats. You may also simply remove the water lock and let the acetic fermentation develop in the original container, but if the air-admitting opening is small, the process will take months. Either way, the cider can be left to acetify naturally, since the acetobacter are airborne and will find their way to your infant vinegar.

You may want to hasten the vinegaring process by adding a concentration of acetobacter, known as *mother of vinegar* or, simply, *mother* — a catalyst greatly speeding up the acetification process. Cultures of mother of vinegar may be purchased at wine supply stores and in some food preparation shops catering to people who preserve or pickle home-grown produce.

Homemade Mother of Vinegar

If you have difficulty finding a local source, you can easily start your own mother. When your regular supply of cider has stopped fermenting, but before bottling-off time, siphon off enough cider to fill a pint jar. Cover the jar with cheesecloth to keep out fruit flies. These insects, *Drosophila melanogaster,* alias "pomace flies" or "vinegar flies," are attracted to the yeasts in fermenting beer, wine, and cider, and carry the acetobacter on their feet. You may welcome the acetobacter for the sake of your vinegar, but it's not necessary to provide the creatures with a heavenly bath. Put the jar in a warm, dark place far away from your cider. In two to four weeks' time — or longer in scrupulously clean places — a gelatinous mass will form on top of the liquid, and the container will smell distinctly of vinegar. The jellyfish mass is your mother of vinegar. Funnel it into a bottle and cover it with the host liquid and cap or cork it tightly. Keep it in a dark place until your set-aside vinegar cider has finished fermenting and settling. When you put the cider that is intended for vinegar into its acetic fermentation vessel, add the mother and let nature take its course. Remember that both mother and vinegar should be made in an area of subdued light, as acetic bacteria, like most microorganisms, are sapped of vitality by sunlight.

The Finished Vinegar

In a month's time, taste the vinegar. If it suits your palate, then filter it through several layers of cheesecloth into bottles and cap or cork them. If the new vinegar seems weak, wait until it's stronger before bottling. If it is too strong, dilute the vinegar by adding sterilized water either to taste or in proportions computed by titration testing.

Titration is simply the chemical process by which the unknown concentration of a substance in solution is measured against another *known* substance in solution. Finding the acid content of various liquids is a common procedure in the making of wine, cider, and vinegar. The home vinegar maker can test the acetic acid level in his or her vinegar in several ways. The most accurate method is with a direct-reading acid tester, which usually tests for tartaric acid but includes conversion tables for citric, malic, lactic, acetic, and sulfuric acid. Acid test strips and pH papers, while less accurate, will give the vinegar maker a good idea of what the finished product's strength is.

A near-perfect yield of acetic acid from alcohol is 1.0 gram of acid per 1.0 gram of alcohol. An acetic acid level of 5 percent to 7 percent is possible in vinegar made from unsweetened cider, though it will usually be less. If you have added sugar to the cider, the acetic acid can reach 10 percent or more. The acid level in vinegar used in preserving, cooking, and salads is around 5 percent.

If your vinegar is so strong that it needs considerable water to dilute it, the original brown apple cider color may fade. You can restore the rich color by adding a little caramelized sugar for coloring.

Caramel coloring. Melt one cup of sugar in a heavy enamel pan over low heat, stirring constantly until the sugar is burned black. Let the sugar cool. When it is cool, add in, almost drop by drop and very slowly, one cup of hot water. Stir over a low heat after the water is added until the mixture becomes a uniform, thin dark liquid. Stored covered, this coloring material will keep indefinitely. It will have no sweetening power after the sugar has been burned.

Vinegar from Pomace

Using pressed pomace to make apple jelly, pectin, or vinegar is a good way to realize full value for your apple dollars. Vinegar made from pomace is not cider vingar, but apple-flavored vinegar, since you must add both sugar and water. No matter what the big words on the label say, many commercial vinegars started as pomace from juice mills, or as the peels and cores from apple processing plants.

For each gallon of vinegar, boil two pounds of pomace in a gallon of water for five minutes. Strain and squeeze the pomace through cheesecloth into a jug that can take a water trap.

Since all but traces of sugar and yeast have gone with the original juice into your cider barrel, you will have to add enough sugar to the pomace squeezings to get a Brix reading on the hydrometer that corresponds to fresh apple juice. Add a wine yeast and one yeast nutrient tablet per pound of sugar to start the fermentation process. Attach a water seal and allow the squeezing-juice to ferment as you would cider. When the fermentation process has stopped and the liquid has aged a while, proceed to make vinegar just as you would with cider.

Another Way to Make Vinegar from Pomace

This traditional method of making vinegar from pomace has one drawback — you run the risk of infecting your grinder and cider press with active acetobacter. If you are fortunate enough to have a second press that you can devote solely to vinegar manufacture, or are confident you can destroy the acetobacter that collect on the cider press, you might like to try this way of making vinegar from pomace.

Heap the pomace from the apple press on a platform and allow it to ferment naturally. After several days considerable heat will be generated. Pour a few pails of warm — not boiling — water on the heap and let it stand another twenty-four hours. The pomace will absorb the water.

Now run the pomace through your grater mill, and make up cheeses as in regular cidermaking. Press the pomace. The collected liquid will be rich in acetobacter. Let it ferment in wide-mouthed crocks covered with cheesecloth in a warm place until it reaches the desired strength.

Remember that the grinder, the press, the cheesecloths, and every utensil that has come in contact with this pomace will be saturated with acetobacter.

Pasteurization and Sterilization

If you rush into vinegar making before all of the sugar in the primary fermentation has been converted to alcohol, you may have problems with mold, excessive cloudiness, and oxidation when you get ready to bottle your vinegar. The second fermentation, which converts the alcohol into acetic acid, will also be incomplete, and you will have a weak, sweet-sour cidery vinegar that will mold easily and have a short shelf life.

If you plan to use the vinegar right away in salads or preserves that are to be sealed under pressure or in a hot-water bath, a bit of unconverted sugar isn't really a problem. But if you have made a large quantity of vinegar and want to save it for future use, and you suspect that it contains unconverted sugar, it's safest to pasteurize the batch or to sterilize it.

Chemical sterilization. Adding ascorbic acid (vitamin C) or sulfur dioxide to the vinegar will preserve it. Both are available from wine supply stores. The sulfur dioxide is available as sodium metabisulfite, or Campden tablets. A single twelve-grain Campden tablet, considered one of the safe additives, is enough to destroy undesirable organisms in one gallon of vinegar. The twelve-grain tablet provides fifty parts per million of sulfur dioxide. Ascorbic acid, which is available in powdered or tablet form, should be added to the vinegar at a rate of one hundred parts per million; directions for measuring the proper quantity come with the acid.

Pasteurization. For those who watch their pennies or who favor a nonadditive approach, the familiar home-canning hot-water bath will save your vinegar.

Fill the bottles or canning jars with vinegar, leaving a two-inch headspace in bottles and a half-inch headspace in jars. Cap the bottles and put the lids on the jars; then place the containers in a canner fitted with a bottom rack. Leave one space free for a thermometer gauge. Fill the canner with water until the bottles or jars are submerged.

Thermometer gauge: Place a small, clean, empty can of the tuna-fish type upside down in the empty section of the canning rack. On it position a single, uncapped bottle filled with water. The neck of this bottle will extend above the level of the water in the canner. Drill a cork that fits the bottle neck through, using a drill bit whose diameter corresponds with that of your high-temperature thermometer. Seat the cork in the bottle. Insert the neck of the thermometer into the hole of the cork until the bulb is immersed in the water inside the bottle. The cork should hold the thermometer snugly.

Place the canning kettle over heat, and keep an eye on the thermometer until it reaches 150°F (65.5°C). Lower the heat and maintain the temperature of the bottles at 150°F (65.5°C) for three minutes, when the pasteurization will be complete.

Avoid cold drafts that might crack the bottles and rest them carefully on their sides on layers of newspaper or towels. Let the bottles cool; then store them upright in a cool, dark place. In about two weeks the sediment will settle completely, and the vinegar can be used. If you have used canning jars, remember to remove the screw-top cover, which otherwise will rust and corrode with time.

AROMATIC AND HERB VINEGARS

Once you have made good cider vinegar, it's both rewarding and fun to experiment with various flavorings and additives that create unique and delicious vinegars. One of the most exuberant vinegar recipes we've come across is that of A. A. Crumpton, printed in an old cidermaker's manual more than a hundred years ago. Mr. Crumpton described his catch-all vinegar process this way:

> As I have seen, from time to time, enquiries for making good vinegar, I will give you the way I made a half-barrel, some two years ago, which we have been using out of ever since, and it is now better than ever, and pronounced by all who have tasted it the best for strength and flavor they have ever tasted; in fact, we never dare use it full strength. In the spring, I had left several gallons of a barrel of cider, that got too sharp for drinking, to which was added nearly as much soft water, a lot of refuse molasses, the remains of a keg of beer left from the previous harvest — probably another gallon — two handfuls of dried apples, a piece of brown paper dipped in molasses, to form the mother, then added a cake of dry yeast, and let it go to work, with a piece of musquito-bar over the bunghole. Then, when fruit-canning time came, we had several kinds (raspberries and strawberries,) which, from imperfect sealing, fermented; these

went into my keg; then all the apple and peach parings were saved, put down in a stone jar, and covered with soft water, and allowed thoroughly to ferment; then strained and the liquor added to my keg, with a little molasses, from time to time, and by the end of the summer we had excellent vinegar; and we have been using, as I said, nearly two years from that same keg, saving apple parings and fermented can fruits to keep up the supply, or sometimes adding water and molasses, if it gets down much. There is a fine mother formed in the keg, which acts the same as the celebrated vinegar plant, converting every saccharine substance, into vinegar.

Herb Vinegars

Herb vinegars are easily made by adding fresh herbs to the cider vinegar, and allowing them to steep for a few hours or several weeks. Don't use more than two or three tablespoons of fresh herbs per quart of vinegar, as the preservative strength of the

Old and decorative bottles, thoroughly cleaned, make attractive containers for your homemade herb vinegars.

acid may not be able to handle large quantities of vegetable matter. A general rule is to steep the herbs in the vinegar for three to four weeks, strain the vinegar through cheesecloth, and rebottle it in sterilized containers tightly corked.

APPLEJACK AND APPLE BRANDY

Considerable confusion exists over the difference between *applejack* and *apple brandy* and whether either can be made at home. Additionally, there is a question as to the legality of making them.

The derivation of the word "applejack" is obscured in the haze of American history but the origin is undoubtedly in the colonial kitchen. Applejack can be traced back to the combination of the words "apple" and "flapjack," an apple turnover that, in addition to having a spicy fruit filling, no doubt included strong apple spirits. Depending on the climate in which it is made, this liquor can be as mild as wine or as strong as brandy, and is the end result of a process known as fractional crystallization by freezing.

Apple brandy is a product of the distiller's craft and is made by heat in simple stills and continuous stills. However, in New Jersey, traditionally the greatest apple distilling state, applejack and apple brandy are synonymous, each referring to a drink of from 50 to 75 percent alcohol made from distilled hard cider or fermented pomace sometimes blended with grain neutral spirits.

Applejack and apple brandy can be made at home but, alas, to do so in the United States without a permit is very much in violation of the Internal Revenue Service code. The penalty is staggering: For each offense the home distiller is liable to a fine of up to ten thousand dollars and five years' imprisonment, or both. (See *Cider and the Law*, page 202.)

The techniques and equipment used to manufacture applejack and apple brandy described here are not intended as practical "how-to-do-it" encouragement, but are rather a description of how it was and is done. Also, the equipment and steps parallel those for the production of nonalcoholic freeze- and heat-distilled vinegar. Unless registered, however, possession of a complete still is illegal.

Applejack

Applejack, or "cider oil," as it was once known, of varying strengths was made in the colder regions of Europe — the Isle of Jersey's product being particularly noteworthy — but it really came into its own in northern New England where severe and fluctuating winter temperatures produced a stronger drink. The usual practice was to ferment a barrel of cider to which sugar, maple syrup, raisins, or other alcohol-strengthening sweeteners were added. This barrel was then placed outside or in a barn during January and February when the temperature, dropping at night and warming during the day, caused the cider's water content to freeze, or fractionally crystallize. The ice, produced in increasingly smaller quantities, was then scooped off and discarded, or the liquid beneath was siphoned off into another container. As the weather got colder, the separation between ice and alcoholic "oil" became greater, and cold snaps, hitting lows of -30°F to -40°F (-34.5°C to -40°C), over a period of time delivered the strongest drink. A temperature of 0°F to 5°F (-17.7°C to -15°C) renders applejack of 7 to 10 percent alcohol by volume, similar to strong hard cider, while a period of -30°F (-34.5°C) weather will transform normal fermented cider into a 30 to 33 percent alcoholic "oil," somewhat like a dry cordial liqueur with a 60 to 66 proof.

In the Far North, little attention was paid to removing ice or siphoning increasingly stronger oil into other containers. The barrel was simply allowed to freeze, thaw, and refreeze until a core of unfreezable liquor formed in the center. Known as the "frozen heart," this core was tapped, by either an auger or a hot poker, and the alcohol transferred to stone jugs or bottles.

The "kick" and subsequent hangovers from imbibing applejack in somewhat less than judicious quantities are legendary, but given its alcoholic strength — less than the commonly abused 40 percent, or 80 proof, rums, vodkas, and whiskeys — it is now believed that aldehydes, esters, and fusel oils contained in the liquor were the culprits responsible for the tremulous "apple palsy." For unlike distillation by heat — in which the rich deposit of aldehydes and esters found in the "heads" and fusel oils found in the "tails" are removed by fractionation or rectification — they are concentrated in fractionally crystallized cider oil. The stronger the oil, the greater the mass of impurities by volume. In this technique it's the discarded water and not the alcohol that is purest.

Homemade Applejack

Unlike the maker of strong cider operating with an ATF ticket, the person who makes applejack without legal permission, under current law, has good reason to worry about strangers at the door. Still, regardless of revenue agent trauma, in areas of the country where the thermometer plummets and apples are grown, applejack is made. In northern Vermont, and across the Connecticut River in New Hampshire, applejack is sometimes made the old way in fifty-gallon wooden barrels. Increasingly, however, due no doubt to weight and storage requirements, immediate supply or shipping charges, and an unwillingness to gamble against the weather with fifty gallons of good drinking cider as stakes, smaller batches of 'jack are made.

Most popular are the five- and ten-gallon plastic carboys or one-gallon plastic cider mill jugs that, in addition to price, have the advantage over glass carboys: They will not shatter during extreme cold, they have handles and can be moved by someone wearing heavy gloves, and they take simple thirty-eight-millimeter screw-type water locks rather than rubber or cork stoppers. And if the weather really fails to cooperate, or the applejack maker is city-bound, the smaller jugs can be used to make a light applejack, of sorts, in a refrigerator's freezing compartment or a bit stronger 'jack in the family's deep freeze.

Two containers are used in making applejack. Fresh cider, sugar, and yeast are placed into one and allowed to foam out in primary fermentation, then are water-trapped. Applejack makers are concerned with getting the most alcohol out of the weather and the cider for their efforts, so, depending on the amount of sweetener added, they use a wine yeast capable of converting natural and added sugars to 12 to 14 percent alcohol by volume, plus nutrient tablets to assure complete fermentation. This is done during the autumn as normal cidermaking procedure, and by January the cider is completely fermented. The container is then placed outside to freeze overnight; the following morning the accumulated ice is punctured and the liquid beneath siphoned into the other container. This carboy or jug is then allowed to freeze while the first is warmed and rinsed free of ice slush. Again the oil is transferred by siphon from the frozen jug to the empty jug — back and forth, again and again the procedure is repeated until the liquid remaining won't freeze.

Sanborn C. Brown, emeritus professor of physics and former associate dean of the graduate school at Massachusetts Institute of Technology, an authority on homebrewing and cidermaking in the region, notes in his book *Wines and Beers of Old New England, A How-To-Do-It-History* that ordinary sweet cider, after its fermentation, can be made into applejack of just under 15 percent alcohol with a low temperature range of 0°F (-17.7°C), and of up to 33 percent after a run of -30°F (-34.5°C) weather.

The more alcoholic ciders will not necessarily translate into higher-alcohol applejacks. Instead, larger quantities of alcohol by volume will be produced, and it's often difficult for the fair-weather applejack maker to get them to fractionally crystallize in a refrigerator. The reason is that given the alcohol-to-water (and other freezable constituents) ratio, strong alcoholic ciders naturally contain stronger, built-in "antifreeze," while those with lesser alcohols — 4 to 7 percent — and conversely greater water content are less inhibited in the ability to fractionally crystallize. The stronger a liquid is in alcohol, the greater the temperature reduction required for separation.

APPLEJACK AFIRE

As a flambeau, no apple distillate surpasses applejack, because it contains every essence of fruit. Applejacks low in alcohol will not ignite no matter how much they are heated beforehand, so it's a wise cook who tests the spirits before anointing the golden goose with apple firewater. This is done by heating an ounce or two slowly in an enamel pan and then touching it with a match. If it doesn't burst into a rolling blue flame crowned with gold, a splash from the 100 proof (50 percent alcohol) vodka bottle comes to the rescue. If the vodka is made of grain neutral spirits and not Russian or eastern European potatoes, the addition will not conflict with the essence of apple in any way — it only guarantees colorful tabletop fireworks and the heat needed to liberate flavor.

Freezers, which for food preservation safety should be set at 0°F to -5°F (-17.7°C to -20.5°C), will make applejack of from 12 to 17 percent by volume.

Acetic ciders should not be turned into applejack, as fractional crystallization by freezing only serves to intensify the vinegar taste, unless, of course, strong vinegar is the goal. Ciders lacking flavor, aroma, and body are often made better as applejack because the removal of water leaves sense-provoking esters in great concentrations to titillate taste and nose.

Since applejack is strong, it can be bottled at the lower alcoholic end as strong cider, or, with greater alcohol content, as brandy, which has the strength to prohibit further fermentation and development of acetobacter. The drink is very flavorsome, but dry, and many prefer to sweeten it to taste before bottling.

APPLE BRANDY

Depending upon where in the world one lives, the heat-distilled product of fermented cider or pomace is known as "apple brandy," *"eau-de-vie de marc de cidre,"* "applejack," "trebern," "batzi," or, perhaps the most famous apple distillate, "Calvados." It can be identified by the name of its producer, such as "Laird's" of New Jersey, or a trade name combining the names of product, locale, and manufacturer, as "Calvabec," a Québec apple brandy. Calvabec is a product of La Cidrerie du Québec, a major cider producer with the trade name of "Cidrobec," and is made from ciders primarily of the Fameuse-McIntosh family. It contains the distinctive Mac aroma and is less expensive than Calvados imported from France.

"We use apples whose flavor and bouquet are different and possibly better than those used in France where apples are acid and not acceptable as table fruit," Alain Lecours, Cidrobec's former director of marketing, told us. *"Trou Normand"* fanciers will no doubt take issue with this observation.

There are similarities, however, in that Cidrobec's alembic, or still, is a French design and the product, by law, is aged. And more differences — the Québec still does not have a double pot, while the *Appellation Contrôlée* for the most famous Calvados region, "Calvados du pays d'Auge," mandates that all apple brandy carrying that APPELLATION seal must be distilled twice in a pot still, as is cognac, and aged for at least a year before being sold. The Québec apple brandy has a longer minimum maturation period, for at least two years in oaken barrels as required by Canadian law.

The Calvados *Appellation* further assures a product that is different from U.S. apple brandy by ruling that all fruit must be crushed in the traditional way, fermented for at least a month, distilled to a strength of 75 percent alcohol, and then placed on the market at between 40 and 50 percent. Most of the best Calvados is aged for considerably longer than a year in oak, is not normally sweetened, and may or may not be tinted with caramel coloring. In the United States, lacking appellation controls and for purposes of supply and marketing economics, apple brandy is a blend of apple and grain neutral spirits.

Harry Weiss, in his definitive work, *The History of Applejack or Apple Brandy in New Jersey from Colonial Times to the Present*, puts the reasons in a nutshell — grains return far greater alcohol volume for volume and at considerably less cost than apples. The Weiss equation holds that two bushels of sound apples are needed to make one gallon of 50 percent apple alcohol, while the same quantity of rye or other small grains will return three gallons of 50 percent, or 100 proof, and corn three and a half gallons with similar strength. Since good apples cost considerably more than grain, pure apple brandy is noncompetitive with grain spirits, and blending the costlier apple with less expensive neutral spirits lessens the disparity at the marketplace.

The Still

Apple brandy results from heating fermented cider or pomace in an enclosed container so that the alcohol contained in the liquid is isolated from the water and other ingredients. The container is a still, and the principle, which was known and practiced before 800 B.C., is based on the different boiling points of ethyl alcohol (78.4°C or 173.3°F) and water (100°C or 212°F). If fermented cider is heated above 78.4°C (173.1°F) but less than 100°C (212°F), ethyl alcohol and some lesser constituents will separate from the liquid in the form of vapor. This vapor can be made to condense by cooling and is then collected in alcoholic strengths greater than are found in the original cider.

Ethyl alcohol, the isolated intoxicant, is usually called just "alcohol," but it is also known as ethanol, industrial alcohol, fermentation alcohol, cologne spirits, fruit alcohol, methycarbinol, grain alcohol, neutral spirits, or ethyl hydroxide, depending on the fermented ingredient and the end use. During the process of heating, other alcohols and ingredients with different vaporization points are reached with each separation point or grouping known as a "fraction." Basically, three types of fractions are separated in the process of beverage distillation with two of the levels either redistilled, discarded, or used for nonconsumptive purposes.

The first fraction, with the lowest boiling point — starting at around 20.8°C (69.4°F) — is the "heads," a material rich in esters and aldehydes. In commercial distillation these fractional components may be collected for use in the manufacture of dyes, plasticizers, resins, lacquer, nail enamel, solvents, cellulose, perfumes, and synthetic rubber.

The second fraction, ethyl alcohol, boils at 78.4°C (173.1°F), melts at 112.3°C (234.1°F), has a specific gravity of 0.851 at 20°C, or 68°F, and is the key ingredient in both drinking products and medical alcohol — the latter adulterated with chemicals or "wood" (methyl) alcohol to make it exempt from alcoholic beverage taxes.

The highest-boiling fraction is the so-called "tails," the fusel oils or higher alcohols. Like the heads, they are used in the production of lacquers and enamels. Disagreeable in taste and smell and harmful if taken internally, they consist primarily of amyl and propyl alcohols. Isolating the fractions in some distilling operations is not exact, however, and traces of ethyl alcohol are contained in the tails. These may be recovered by redistillation.

Boiling Points of the Principal Volatile Cider Ingredients

HEADS	EXPRESSED IN ° CELSIUS
Acetaldehyde	21
Propionaldehyde	49
Iso-Butyraldehyde	62
Ethyl Acetate	74
Ethyl Alcohol	78.4
TAILS	
Iso-Propyl Alcohol	83
Butylaldehyde	95
Propyl Alcohol	97
Iso-Butyl Alcohol	108
Ethyl Isobutyrate	110
N. Valeraldehyde	110
Acetic Acid	117
Iso-Amyl Alcohol	128
Iso-Amyl Acetate	138
Furfural	162

Apple brandy is distilled in alembics as small as one-gallon stovetop stills found in country kitchens and as large as the gleaming copper giants of Calvados. The larger stills of simple design additionally can be fitted with heat exchangers and rectifying, or "fractioning," columns that allow for greater and purer alcoholic yields in shorter distilling time. Finally, and in most common uses, are the continuous stills. These greatly increase daily production while cutting alcohol loss during distillation to the barest minimum.

Whatever the type, a still consists of three basic parts: the heater, which can be direct flame known as "the fire," or live, or coil-contained steam; the distillation vessel (or retort, analyzer, mash-can, boiler, or cooker), in which the cider is heated; and the condenser, which consists of a neck and coiled copper, and is called the coil, worm, snake, or cooler, in which alcoholic vapors are cooled into liquid. Additionally, there are the receivers — bottles, barrels, crocks, and sometimes another still — receptacles for collecting the distillate.

Pot stills. Of all the simple stills, the "pot" is the most familiar. The pot is the heater, roundish and squat, most commonly constructed of copper but sometimes of wood like a low silo, capped with a head — a tapered funnel-like neck somewhat swanlike in shape, often called the "snout" — that connects the pot to the condenser, a water-cooled coil of copper tubing. Water surrounding the coil in the cooling tank is continuously replaced during distillation.

Pot stills are modified by placing two side by side, with the secondary unit being of the same design but smaller. In the United States this rig, now almost obsolete, is known as a "doubler," with the initial heating of cider done by direct flame or steam coils in the primary pot. From the first still, vapors of about 50 percent alcohol are straight-piped into the second, where evaporation continues. Here the intense heat of condensation within a closed container separates the alcohol further. It then rises up through the head and down through the cooling coil to condense into alcohol of about 75 percent. In a simpler version of the doubler system, vapor from the pot is allowed to pass through uncooled coils, which delivers a watery alcohol of 25 to 39 percent. This distillate, sometimes known as the "low wines," is then redistilled to double in strength.

In France, simple stills are fitted with a *chauffe-vin,* a heat-exchanging device that has the same capacity as the heater, and is placed between the snout and condenser, with the neck making a complete rifled turn as it passes through. The exchanger is filled with cider that is heated by distilling vapors traveling through the neck. After the run, the heat-exchanged, and thus warmer, cider is used to recharge the still, shortening its start-up time.

Fractioning columns. Simple stills may be fitted with heads containing disks and plates that are cooled to correspond with the sequence and boiling temperatures of undesirable volatile oils. These substances condense on the plates and then drip back into the heater while vapors heavy in ethyl alcohol are unchecked and pass through into the condenser. Advantages of rectifying are a short distilling time, as usually only one run is needed, and purity of alcohol.

Continuous stills. Since its invention in the early 1800s, the continuous still has grown in popularity to become the most used distilling device today. Operated as a single unit or combined with a pot still, the continuous still features a pair of very tall boilerlike columns, one being the counterpart of the heater, which is fired by steam and is called the "analyzer," the other a rectifier, which connects to a condenser. This is heated by live steam from the base and fed cider from the top. Pressure holds the cider on a series of perforated plates, each one acting like a mini–pot still. Depending upon the number of plates, alcohols in varying degrees of strength are obtained, rectified, and then condensed.

The Stovetop Still

There's a mistaken belief that North American "home" distillers must, by tradition, set up shop along a cool back-hollow stream or in an abandoned warehouse, utilizing ingenious hillbilly-crafted stills made of such things as discarded boilers, water heaters, and even car radiators to boil off the "lighnings" — that's "white" from corn, "Jersey" from apples. Instead, today's devotees of homemade *eau de vie* set up shop in the comfort of their own kitchens. And a highly illegal home shop avocation, and sometimes vocation, it is.

Some, particularly in counties where home or farm distilling is legal, have small five- and ten-gallon pot stills, many being family heirlooms or antiques shop finds dating from pretemperance days or illicit souvenirs of Prohibition. The majority of stills, however, are homemade.

The ordinary pressure cooker is ideally suited for a secret double identity as outlaw. The kitchen, that heart of the home with its source of convenient stovetop heat, the proximity of sink tap water for cooling the worm, and its drain, is the obvious location for such a home distillery, not the barn or cellar.

Pressure cookers all have the same basic nomenclature, be they four-quart pots with plastic handles or mammoth commercial or preserving cookers with their tops dogged down by screw-clamps. All function well as still heaters and will deliver alcohol directly proportionate to capacity, all other things (the percentage of alcohol in the cider, coil surface, and coldness and soundness of cooker) being equal.

Most important to the home distiller using a pressure cooker are:

1. **The rubber gasket that seals the cooker and cover.** If the gasket is cracked, warped, or in any way doesn't fit firmly, alcoholic vapors will escape into the air, lessening final yield.

2. Vent tube and pressure gauge. A simple pressure cooker is fitted with a small tubelike cap, like a miniature steam whistle, that is threaded into the center of the cover. This vent receives a heavy, machined cylindrical weight, which jangles or sputters while releasing steam pressure during the course of cooking. Larger cookers have both a vent and a pressure gauge, the latter a proper glass-faced degree-indicating clock positioned at the top or on one side of the cover. In still making, the vent is most often removed to accept the cooling coil. In those models where the vent is permanently affixed, the pressure gauge tap is used and the vent sealed with the weighted pressure control.

3. Safety fuse. Each cooker has a safety fuse, a guard that should never be tampered with or replaced with a solid fitting. This fuse consists of a steel, screw-type sleeve fitting that houses a core of soft metal. During household use this core will melt and drop into the cooker if the pan becomes overheated, or — and this is important to the home distiller — it will pop out if the vent becomes clogged. Because the core metal is soft, it is especially vulnerable to the corrosive action of acids in cider and will eventually break down, allowing steam and alcoholic vapors to escape.

Some home distillers advocate the use of fiberglass resin to coat the soft fuse metal, thereby making an impervious shield that, unlike a large dollop of lead solder, will not eventually corrode or add poison to the cider. However, just as a penny beneath an old, ceramic, screw electrical fuse causes fire, covering the base of a pressure cooker's screw safety fuse has caused explosions. For pressure, in all but the most minimal degree, is a sign of malfunction in simple still distillation — the heater being affixed to an open-ended coil.

If pressure builds up in normal food preparation it means particles of food have clogged the vent. In distilling it means a blockage in the neck fitting or in the coil. This is not uncommon, especially in ciders containing pieces of pomace. These solids will rise and fall during the course of heating. If the operator is careless and allows the heat to trigger a rolling boil, the fruit will ride on a crest of foam and be sucked up into the coil with the steam. Then, if the slant of just one coil isn't downward, or it's even slightly crimped, it is possible for the fruit to block the tube. Pressure might blow out the block or compact it. When this happens and there is no pressure gauge to indicate danger and the safety fuse has been replaced or sealed, the gasket can burst, sending a searing jet of steam into the room. Or, worse, extreme pressure will rupture the cooker in an explosion with scalding cider flung about like liquid shrapnel. A couple of extra safety fuses to replace those that corrode are viewed by most home distillers as a good investment.

4. Coil and cooling container. The size of the container — whether it's a two-pound coffee tin, a galvanized pail, or a cut-off milk can — will determine the length and diameter of copper tubing needed to fashion the coil. The deeper and wider the can, the greater the length or width needed to provide maximum cold surface exposure. Two-pound coffee tins, for instance, have a width of five inches and a usable cooling depth of four and a half inches. This container can accommodate nine wraps of three-eighth-inch tubing, or about fifteen feet, allowing for neck and drip-spout.

Large containers take greater lengths and/or thicknesses and are computed simply by the home distiller, who multiplies the diameter of the can by pi, or 3.14, to determine the circumference. The thickness of the coil is then divided into the depth of the can, allowing an inch at top and bottom for cold-water intake and hot-water exit vents. Then, the still maker multiplies circumference by coil total to get the length of tubing needed. An additional three or four feet is included for the neck and another four or five inches for the drip-spout. In containers such as pails, the circumference of the coils progressively diminishes because of the vessel's taper and thus requires slightly less tubing than straight-sided coolers.

The hot-water vent at the top and cold-water intake at the bottom are fashioned from several inches of metal tubing, the outside diameters of which fit firmly into hose or plastic tubing — the intake to the sink faucet while the vent hose drains by gravity into the basin. The can is drilled to take the vents and when in place, soldered with a butane torch to make them firm and watertight. On the faucet end, dishwashing machine fittings or hand shower faucet attachments are used as couplings by many.

Bending the coil. Shaping copper tubing is tricky, and still makers usually solicit a plumber's expertise in coiling cold copper, but, barring help, they can do it at home using a butane torch, a round of wood, care,

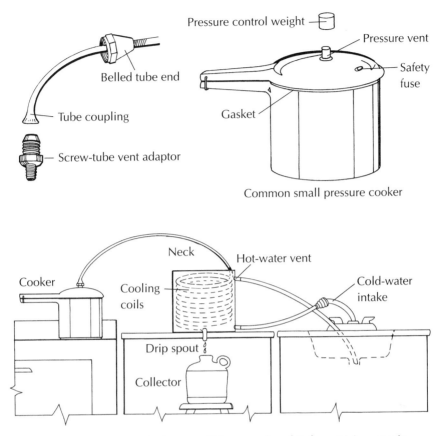

The components of a home still in a modern kitchen. Using one is dangerous, and illegal without a permit, and is not recommended.

and patience. A piece of round firewood of a size that can fit into the cooling vessel, allowing enough space between metal and wood to fit in the coil, is the first tool. This is placed on a table and one end of the tubing is stapled to its base, allowing four or five inches to protrude as the drip-spout. The home still maker then heats the tubing while turning the block slowly, wrapping the coil tightly, ever wary of kinking. This process takes time and a lot of butane. From two to four feet of tubing is left uncoiled to become the neck. The coil is then removed from the block and screwed carefully into the cooling can so the straight drip-spout exits through a hole drilled one inch from the bottom. This spout runs almost parallel with the side of the can. The still maker then heats the spout copper where it passes through the can with a torch and, using a spike inserted into the spout, carefully bends it to a near–right angle and slightly down position. Torch-fired solder is then used to seal the spout firmly to the cooler.

Neck fitting. Since the pressure cooker is primarily used for food preparation and not distilling, a standard removable brass thread-to-tube conversion fitting is employed rather than a permanent fixture. This unit, in two parts, has a double-threaded fitting that is screwed into the vent opening while the opposite end, with a larger threading, accepts a screw-cap holding the tubing. Many smaller cookers take a three-eighth-inch vent fitting while the larger threads conform to the size of the bell-shaped coupling holding the tube. The neck tubing is threaded through the coupling and a plumber's flange tool used to bell the end of the tube so it conforms to the rounded top of the vent exactly. Still makers without a flange heat the pipe and shape the bell with a dull, pliers-held wood or metal countersink, or with a spike revolved in the manner of a pestle in a mortar.

Hooking up. Preferred is the stove burner closest to the sink, as it requires less hose and allows for other uses of the range at the same time. Final stages of setting up see the cooker, complete with cover, placed onto the burner, the cooling can on a counter or nearby table positioned between cooker and sink with the drip-spout overhanging the edge so a collector can be placed beneath. Using the torch, the neck is bent into a graceful unkinked arch until the threads of tube coupling and vent fitting are perfectly aligned. Hoses for the cold-water intake and hot-water vent are measured, cut, and fitted — the cold to the bottom and hot to the top of the cooling can.

Making the Run

The cooker, filled to the manufacturer's specified capacity and not pressure cooking limits, which can be an eighth or quarter of the total, is then covered, the coil is attached, and the "mash-can" is exposed to high heat until the metal is too hot to touch. At the same time the cooling can is filled with water and the flow adjusted so intake balances the rate of flow into the sink. During the course of distilling, the cooling liquid heats, especially at the top with steam rising off the surface and top coil loop. The flow of cold water is correspondingly increased to counteract this. To prevent foaming and the danger of blocking the coil with pomace, or overrunning alcoholic vapors working through the coil with a water boil, the heat is lowered to simmer for the slow and careful recovery of spirits. Completion of the primary distillation is usually determined by taste — when the liquid dripping from the spout reaches the point where it has just a fair taste of alcohol, the cider distiller may conclude that it's done, and the container is emptied.

For the second run a high-strength or proof alcohol hydrometer, which assures greater accuracy than taste in separating the tails, is used. Standard brewing and wine hydrometers, which are common cidermaking tools, are the wrong type, as they measure "potential" and not actual alcohol. With their respective maximum ranges of 14 and 25 percent alcohols based on before-and-after-fermentation sugar readings, they are extremely useful in making the strongest cider, but their use stops there and the industrial or "alcoholometer" takes over.

The first run yields alcohol spirits of about one-sixth the quantity of cider distilled. A six-quart pressure cooker, therefore, will produce one quart of spirits if average-strength (3.4 to 4.7 percent alcohol) ciders are used. Increased cider alcoholic strengths will be reflected in greater total, but not greater strength, yields. Ordinary first-run cider distillate reads somewhere between 26 and 30 percent by weight when tested. Successive first runs are collected and stored until there is enough to charge the cooker a second time.

When the first runs collected reach the volume of the pressure cooker (such as six quarts for a six-quart cooker), the cider is ready for the second and final run. The liquid is poured into the cooker. The heat is set at low, since it's necessary to take measurements and tests right from the start. A clear kitchen measuring cup beneath the drip spout will catch the first 0.5 percent of the cooker's cider contents. (With a six-quart [192-ounce] cooker this would be 0.96 ounce, which would be rounded off to one ounce.) This is discarded. It contains the "heads," primarily aldehydes, and carries the pungent aroma of nail polish remover. No one should ever drink it.

The desired ethyl alcohol is collected next, along with several volatile components important to aroma. During the second run, the cider is tested with a hydrometer and is then collected in one container until the alcohol level falls to 40 percent, or 80 proof. This is apple distillate, ready for cutting and casking. The remainder of the run — from 15 to

Many home brandy distillers use ciders that they believe are sub-standard or downright undrinkable, believing this is the only way to salvage them. In at least two instances this is a mistake. First, the distillation of ciders that are too sweet — for reasons of stuck fermentation or an excess of added sugar — represents a loss of both potential alcohol and, as sugar was added, money. For these reasons, and the fact that the brandy bouquet is greatly enhanced when distilled from completely fermented cider that has been aged for several months, the home distiller should do everything possible to break a stuck fermentation and burn up excess sugar before distillation. Adding fresh juice, yeast, and nutrient tablets is the usual way to get fermentation started again.

Second, on the opposite end of the taste spectrum it's an error to make brandy of vinegary cider, for acetic acid is a completely distillable product of alcohol fermentation and will pass into the brandy. The absolute limit of acetic acid in cider to be distilled is 0.3 percent or less. If over that level, it is drunk as acetic cider or, if it has really turned, poured into the vinegar barrel.

40 percent alcohol — is collected separately and stored to be run through again with a fresh batch of once-distilled liquor. This fraction contains the myriad acetates and higher "tails" alcohols along with some ethyl alcohol.

Cutting the Distilled Cider

Fresh from the still, apple distillate has about as much right to be called "brandy" as moonshine does "bourbon." In fact the two are quite similar — transparent and fairly clear with gagging amounts of alcohol. A number of years ago, one of the authors attended a fresh apple-alcohol tasting where commercial moonshine, sold in a preserve jar complete with scrawled mountain-English label, New Jersy "applejack," and Calvados du Pays du Merlerault were served as test controls. The rating was as one might expect, with the French judged better than the New Jersey apple. More interesting, no one could tell the difference between the mason jar corn likker and the freshly distilled apple. Both were dreadful, real throat-scorchers, and while it's doubtful that cutting the liquids to lessen strength would have helped by itself, a thinner alcohol matured for a proper period might have.

A pressure cooker still, rudimentary in every way, can never equal the alcohol recovery of a well-run, control-laden continuous still, but it is possible to produce alcohols of from 50 to 60 percent, or 100 to 120 proof, and sometimes higher. Distillates in these ranges are cut to 40 to 45 percent alcohol, the level of popular beverages. Thinning is done by the addition of pure water in the quantity indicated by hydrometer testing. The water used is free of all vegetation, chlorine, and calcium, with distilled water, either commercial or homemade, preferred in chlorinated urban or springhouse rural areas.

Aging the Apple Distillate

Unlike cider, whose maturation can be achieved in glass as well as wood, apple distillate must be aged in wooden casks if it is to become proper brandy. Best are once-used whiskey or brandy barrels of either oak or ash, but never new barrels, as the alcohol leaches tannins from the wood during the aging process. Charred barrels, which contribute some coloring to the brandy, are a second choice. All barrels are filled, bunged tight, and then allowed to sleep in a mold-free place for one to three years. A constant temperature of around 55°F (12.7°C) is required for the longer period, while aging can be speeded up if the barrel is kept between 60° and 68°F (15.5° and 20°C). During the maturation period the strength of the alcohol decreases slightly by evaporation through stave joints and pores, but this loss is more than compensated for by less harshness and the fine flavors that develop.

Bottling Apple Brandy

Apple brandy made at home tends to be pale yellow, unless oxidized in excess or tinted with barrel char, and is quite dry. To suit sweeter tastes sugar is frequently added at the rate of a half ounce per quart bottle at bottling time. If the liquor is paler than brandy, caramel coloring is added to achieve the desired tone of amber. If ciders with poor aromatics were used in distillation and the end product is subsequently flat, richer-flavored, aromatic cider or apple juice can be simmered over a low heat until it becomes a thin syrup and then added to each bottle to suit taste.

Cider for Tasting, Drinking, and Cooking

When you have uncountable cool, golden bottles of cider neatly stacked in the cellar bins, and an additional fifty-gallon barrel or several glittering carboys maturing in a dark cellar cave, the time has come to drink it. Your liquid treasure, reminiscent of warm, hazy autumn days and the fragrance of freshly pressed apples, can be enjoyed in crystal glasses, in steaming mugs on cold winter nights, in sauces, soups, seafood dishes, to marinate game, in cider cakes or elegant chilled fruit desserts.

If you have made several different kinds of cider, or if you have cidermaking friends, an afternoon or evening of cider tasting is both fun and rewarding. This section includes some of the things to look for when you raise that first glass of homemade cider, as well as some unique recipes that call for cider or Calvados to give them a special flavor. But there is no substitute for experience and experimentation, and the amateur cidermaker worth his or her apples will soon discover new and unique ways to enjoy the golden flood in the kitchen, on the table, or in the drinks pantry.

Cider Tasting

Like wine, cider can be judged by the sensual criterion of a tasting ritual. But unlike quaffers of fermented grape juice, most fanciers of the apple do not strive for the quintessential statement by using comparative phraseology to endow their glasses with human anatomy, action, and emotion. There's no reason why crafty cider similes couldn't be used — it's just that we've never heard the contents of a cider bottle described as "a gay little dancer, pirouetting over the tongue on bubbling slippers of flavor," or, less buoyantly, "this cider is furious — just feel the bite! It should have been allowed to nap another year."

In New England, for instance, you're more likely to hear "aeehuh, might have 'nother," or, "this 'u'll do me," or even, "it'd go right good in a salad." Cider goes down very easily, and the most meaningful comment you're likely to get is a silently extended glass. There's the story about a Maine lumberjack who was treating his friends to some superior hard cider. Because he prized it so highly, he poured each of them a scant glassful and put the jug back in the cupboard. His friends tossed off their drinks, smacking their lips, and the lumberjack waited expectantly for them to start the conversation. A long silence — a heavy silence — followed until the woodsman took the hint and went to the cupboard again, remarking sheepishly, "Well, fellers, I guess a bird can't fly with only one wing."

Regardless of the commentary generated, tasting cider is a physical process in which the senses of sight, smell, taste, hearing, and touch make up the examination outline. Obviouly, before alluding to ballerinas, one should honestly see the dance. Appreciation is also due to the ballet master and the choreography, which translates in cider tasting to the maker and the manner in which the cider is served — in clean, elegant glasses, and at the right temperature.

Since cider should be transparent, use spotless, clear, untinted glasses in tastings. A tulip-shaped wine glass with a capacity of at least six ounces is perfect. The tulip glass has a round bowl that tapers slightly at the chimney to gently hold the cider bouquet at the glass's lip. A tasting glass can't really be too big, and the mammoth yet delicate burgundy snifter is the king of bouquet traps.

Avoid cut crystal, for the facets interfere with the sight of rising bubbles in effervescent ciders. Paper, waxed, or Styrofoam cups are undesirable, because they become crumpled, cider-logged, and messy, or the flavors of each kind of cider being

A replica of the Scudamore cider glass. The only known surviving glass of this type is held by the London Museum. This tall flute in thin soda glass will hold more than a pint of cider. It is engraved in diamond point with the arms of the Scudamore family. Lord Scudamore is credited with discovering the Redstreak cider apple.

tested permeate the sides and can't be cleared by rinsing. After the first sample has been tried from a Styrofoam cup, later selections poured into the same cup will pick up the preceding sample's characteristics, a serious detriment to accurate tasting. Transparent plastic cups are seldom big enough to allow for as many mouthfuls and chews as necessary for forming a solid opinion of the sample's character. Moreover, they lack finesse and heft, and, most seriously, they frequently have a light plastic odor that contaminates the bouquet.

The burgundian *tastevin*, a small silver tasting cup that reflects light through red wine like a laser, can be used to satisfy several sensual questions, but not all of them. Its shallow, light-fired brilliance passing through a fairly clear liquid makes it difficult to see fine particles in suspension and, in the case of effervescent cider, the bubbles dissipate too rapidly. Glass vessels with greater depth are the best for examining, tasting, and smelling cider.

Sweetness, more than anything else, is the characteristic to consider in selecting the right serving temperature — the sweeter the cider, the colder it should be. Drier cider may be served at room temperature — 65°F (18.3°C) — but the range of temperatures suited to cider is very great, from the 32°F (0°C)frost line for some of the light, carbonated Québec ciders to just under boiling for the potent hot mulls and cider toddies.

Chill cider by refrigerating it three to five hours, or bury the bottle up to its neck in a bucket or tub of ice for half an hour. The champagne types of cider are chilled and served at about 35°F (1.6°C); the still, sweet, semisweet, and dry ciders with an alcohol content of between 5

TRICKY DRINKING

In English cider counties a good country joke was to give an unwary stranger a draught of cider in a trick cider mug. One variety was the "frog mug," which had a ceramic frog squatting or leaping at the bottom of the mug that came into view only as the drinker took the last swallow. Another favorite design was that of a cider jug whose neck was pierced by a number of holes. In order to drink from it, the drinker had to cover the holes with his fingers or send a cascade of cider down his shirt front.

and 11 percent are at their best between 40°F and 50°F (4.4°C and 10°C). The stronger, full-bodied still ciders with an alcohol content of 12 percent higher should be cool but not ice cold — 55°F to 65°F (12.7°C to 18.3°C).

Judging Cider

The physiological processes involved in isolating and judging delicate flavors and aromas are complex, and both wine and cider tasting are acquired arts. All the thousands of flavors of food and beverages, from asparagus to Charlotte Russe to a light, slightly tart cider, are based on the four fundamental tastes — sweet, bitter, saline, and acid, blended in countless permutations to give a bewildering variety of taste sensations. When certain "taste cells" are excited on the tongue, the brain translates a particular taste for the substance that provoked the stimulation. For a substance to act on the taste cells, it must first be in a chemical solution. Taste, when associated with smell, gives "flavor."

Minute particles of a substance give the sensation of smell and these particles must be in contact with moisture. We are all familiar with the rich, luxurious aromas that come from rose gardens, lilacs, and wet grass after a rain when the air is heavy with water vapor that carries the scent-provoking particles. Since the nose is moist inside, it is the perfect chamber for the solution of volatile scent particles.

Describing scents, flavors, and tastes is a difficult job, since they are perceived differently by people, linked to obscure personal memories, and to different culturally acquired food habits. The flavors and tastes, for example, that appeal to East Asians are rarely appreciated by North Americans. One apple authority, bemoaning the lack of adjectives in the English language to describe flavors and scents, remarked:

> It is easy to recognize but difficult to describe the strong
> flavor of the Gravenstein, which arrives before the apple is
> even bitten, in virtue of an almost rose-like perfume that rushes
> up to the nose. The Cox, on the other hand, has little perfume,
> but its flavor, reminiscent of an aromatic oil, gradually stimu-
> lates the palate as if it were only set free when the apple is
> eaten, but lingers on as a delicious flavor pervading the whole
> olefactory tract.

Literary oenophiles have tried to conquer the problem of describing wines — as already noted — by giving them human personalities, but this practice has reached such an exaggerated pitch as to make teetotaling and even imbibing readers snort in disbelief. An example from the writings of the great wine connoisseur, André Simon, stretches our credulity:

> The 1905 was simply delightful; fresh, sweet, and charming; a girl of fifteen, who is already a great artist, coming on tip-toes and curtseying herself out with childish grace and laughing blue eyes. She probably never will be a Grande Dame; she may live long enough to be a sour old hag.

Cider lovers, traditionally more of a back-room group than wine aficionados, do not even have the inflated vocabulary of wine to help them describe the flavors and aromatic sensations of their favorite liquid. Professor Anthony A. Williams of the Long Ashton Research Station, University of Bristol, England, studied the aroma components of apples and ciders and their interaction with other juice constituents for several years by means of sensory assessment and gas chromatographic analyses. Part of his work involved training a cider-tasting panel and developing a special descriptive cider-tasting vocabulary. The final list of 163 words and phrases covered appearance, aroma, and taste — a highly detailed catalog of complex perception and sensations of a complex liquid. Some of Professor Williams's terms are listed here, with the omission of the more scientific comparisons.*

Evaluating Your Own Cider

When at last you pour the first glass of cider you have made yourself, all your senses will play a role in judging it. This is the time to get out your cellar book and write in the comments on bouquet, color, clarity, sparkle, and other outstanding characteristics of the finished bottle.

Sight. The colors of cider range from the palest champagne-blonde to a clear canary, from soft apricot to topaz or dark amber. Pour the cider

---

* "The Development of a Vocabulary and Profile Assessment Method for Evaluating the Flavour Contribution of Cider and Perry Aroma Constituents," *Journal of the Science of Food and Agriculture* 1975, 26, 567–582.

gently into a clear glass and hold it up to the light. Daylight is best, for artificial light can distort the true color of the liquid. The color, which will vary with the type of apples you used and the way you made the cider, should be neither too watery nor too dark, a sign of excessive oxidation. If the cider throws tints of green, red, or chalky gray, it could be suffering from a cider sickness. A naturally pink or rosé cider made by using red-fleshed crab apples, of course, is supposed to have a red tint.

Is the cider crystal clear or hazy? Many good young ciders will contain millions of microscopic spent yeast particles, pectins, and vegetable matter from the pulp, but if the bottle is well aged and is still cloudy, the cider has not been able to clear itself. This may not be a detriment to flavor, but North Americans generally prefer absolutely clear wines and ciders, and many amateur cidermakers will go to extraordinary lengths to achieve a sharp, pure clarity. A careless or accidental shake of the bottle can stir up bottom sediment and ruin the transparency of a naturally cleared cider, so pour carefully, and use only the top two-thirds to seven-eighths of the contents to avoid agitating the lees.

If you have made sparkling cider, note the extent and manner of effervescence. Naturally effervescent ciders will produce a vigorous explosion of froth as the liquid first hits the bottom of the glass, then slows, with the smaller bubbles merging to form larger silver spheres that break free from the bottom and sides to rush to the surface, where they pop. These miniature explosions send tiny particles of liquid showering over the surface and into the taster's nose, a tingle that serves to heighten the bouquet. Artificially carbonated ciders have uniform-sized bubbles that maintain their size as they rise to the surface, and while the tasting experience has a definite tingling sensation, the aroma is somewhat carbonic. Naturally carbonated ciders will maintain their fizz longer than a glass of artificially carbonated cider. Some commercial ciders contain so much CO_2 that the smell and ensuing burn of carbonic acid at the back of the throat makes for an unpleasant experience, something akin to drinking strong club soda straight.

Smell. Cider should have the fragrant aroma of the apples from which it was made. Young ciders will usually have more of the bouquet of fresh fruit than an aged cider, but the strong sensation of apple should be present in all of them. You will be able to recognize some of the more distinctive apple aromas — the highly perfumed McIntosh,

Evaluation of Hard Cider (Commercial Samples)

VARIABLE	CODE	CLARITY	SEDIMENT	COLOR	HEADSPACE	MOLD	SPARKLE
Grand Sec d'Orleans	1			light			0
Double Six	2			v. lt.			++
White Cap	3			golden			++
Golden Cider	4			dark			(+)
Selection	5			light			++
Escanciador	6			amber (med.)			+
Moussablon	7			light			+
Old Saratoga	8			v. light			0
Mayer Bros.	9			golden			0
76 HC-B ("European")	10			amber			

Notes from an informal tasting with J. Van Buren and R. Way and a study by L. Nichols and A. Proulx of freshly opened, cold hard cider. This form can be adapted to individual preferences. Odor and flavor attributes evaluated include: acetic, bland, fruity, harsh, musty, oxidized, skunky, sulfite, woody. Flavor and odor are rated on a scale of 1 to 10.

the rose-flavored Gravenstein, the Roxbury Russet, or Cox's Orange Pippin — or the lack of them. Ciders made from varieties lacking aroma, such as Cortland or Rome Beauty, will be bland unless blended with an aromatic that creates the bouquet necessary for a distinctive personality. Sniff the cider at glass lip level. The mélange of varietal perfumes will enhance the coming taste, and a deep, judicious inhalation will preview the alcohol and acid content, and warn you of the possibility of acetification. If the cider has the acetic odor of vinegar, pour it out before you contaminate your palate.

Touch. Cider is first touched by the lips, then by several sensitive areas of the mouth and throat. Push the cider with your tongue to the tender areas along the gums, chew it slightly, and then roll it along the roof of the mouth to the back of the tongue. This will reveal its

Odor	Acid	Astringent	Bitter	Other	Flavor & Odor	Remarks
		Flavor				
sulfite	+	++	++	fruity sl. sweet	7+	too much SO_2 hi alc., but bland
sulfite fruity	+	++	+	fruity sl. sweet	7	sl. acid, clean
fruity				fruity v. sweet	5	sl. ox. too sorbate! sweet
neutral		+		med. fruity	6	sl. ox.; like jc. low alc., but good
fruity McIntosh	++	++	+++	fruity (Mc)	3	v. ox., too strong v. cardboardy
sulfite fruity	+	++	++	fruity (Mc) sweet	4	rough, not pleasant, sl. cardboardy
sl. fruity	+	++	++	med. fruity med. sweet	7	sl. rough (hi alc.)
neutral		+++	+	bland (w/Mc) not v. sweet	8	more smooth; no faults
sl. fruity	+	++		v. fruity	7	woody
sl. woody neutral		++		sl. sweet v. sl. fruity	8	v. sl. acetic v. dry, clean

qualities and any faults. A cider with good body will give you a sensation of fullness and a slight heaviness in the mouth, while a thin, watery cider will give little sensation at all. The right balance of malic acid and tannin will make your mouth feel clean and perky, and you will swallow happily. After you swallow, note whether the freshness and faint aroma lingers on, or dies quickly away. A good cider, aromatic, clear, with fine body, will make you want to breathe, touch, taste, and swallow it time after time.

Taste. Another draught — hold it in your mouth. Feel the warmth of the alcohol, the caress of fruit sweetness or the bite of acid. Is the cider cloyingly sweet, does excessive acid and tannin pucker your mouth, or is it a fine mellow liquid with all its components in good balance? Open your mouth slightly and roll your tongue so the aroma will escape and rise up into your nose. Does the warmed cider continue to deliver a pleasant bouquet, has it diminished or increased? Some ciders flower within the mouth, others wither.

Sound. With sparkling and more full-bodied ciders, even the sense of sound plays a part in their appreciation. You can hear the range of effervescence in the fizzing, pinging song of bubbles, and enjoy the rich gurgle — not watery splash — of a good cider pouring out of the bottle into the glass. Just the sound of such cider will tell you about body even before you hold the glass up and note the amber liquid clinging to its sides.

The Cider Tasting

One of the most pleasant and informative ways for the amateur cidermaker to spend an afternoon or an evening is to give or go to a cider tasting, which can be as simple as several bottles and a half-dozen glasses, or as elaborate as you care to make it. Aside from the pleasant sociability of a tasting, everyone there can learn something — most especially the person who is just beginning to experiment with making his or her own cider.

The ideal tasting panel is made up of people on three distinct rungs in the cidermaking progression: Those who have never tasted cider before, those who have but who don't make their own, and the old hands, the dedicated, interested cidermakers themselves. The last can be as few as you alone, offering a few cellar selections to friends, or as many as you have cidermaking cronies eager to have their work tasted and evaluated.

First-timers. A discerning, expert palate is not necessary to enjoy a cider tasting. In fact, the willingness of people who have never tasted cider before to be frank and honest about the samples offered makes them important members of the group. They increase their own knowledge of the many-faceted world of the apple, and their untrained tastes can

The three common styles of wine glasses — for white wine, Bordeaux, and Burgundy — can be used for cider, too.

often detect imperfections that those more cider-attuned tend to gloss over. This is not to imply that those of us who make and drink cider have jaded tastes, but that people who have traveled the orchard-to-cellar trail know well its difficulties. During their own learning experiences, home cidermakers will have consumed quantities of somewhat less-than-perfect juice. So, where the home cidermaker might subconsciously be more sympathetic and forgiving of vinegary, yeasty, or oxidized bottles, the first-time taster will not, and his or her comments are useful.

Cider drinkers. While these tasters do not make their own, they have sampled commercial and probably homemade ciders and have an idea of what they like. Their experience enables them to make valid comparisons, and to offer criticism and praise and the reasons for either — valuable attributes.

The amateur cidermaker. Legally an amateur, the home cidermaker is the professional member of a tasting. He or she has acquired and utilized certain difficult skills to produce a consumable product. In a tasting the amateur cidermaker serves as an instructor to the other tasters, and just how much faith is put in his or her expertise depends on the quality of the cider from the home cellar. A successful tasting, with the proof of the exercise warm, alive, and aromatic, in mouths and minds, will very likely send your guests to the wine supply stores for carboys, plastic tubing, and packets of yeast. The makers themselves will find a tasting the best time for shop talk, comparing cellar notes and special procedures.

Cider tastings can take the form of a discussion group, with the maker pouring tastes for guests and then joining them in the tasting procedure, or a "blind tasting" where the identity of each cider and its maker is kept secret until the end, or a simple social get-together where cider is served, or, as frequently happens with tastings, a full-blown party ensues.

Deciding which ciders are to be served at a tasting is up to you, but if you're introducing people to cider for the first time, it's a good idea to offer a variety of types with the hope of serving something that will appeal to every palate. You might want to include commercial ciders with the homemade. In the order of serving, offer a well-chilled dry cider, a semisweet effervescent, and a sweet dessert cider, all three with an alcohol content of not more than 12 percent. Then offer two stronger, full-bodied ciders, one dry and the other sweeter, perhaps a cordial type. In between the two groups, serve a mild cheese and some bread or crackers so that a dry cider following a sweet will not seem more acidic than it really is.

At tastings with a larger selection the same rule applies: Taste the dry before the sweet, the young before the old, and cider with a lighter alcohol content before you sample the stronger ones. For a hearty tasting, allow at least a half bottle and a quarter pound of cheese for each person. Just a sip and a crumb of cheese will do if the tasting is in the nature of an aperitif. Depending on the seriousness of the tasting and how many glasses and accessories your household has, fresh crystal can be used for each cider, or the glasses can be rinsed between tastes. For those who are leery of saturating their taste buds with alcohol, provide a spittoon and a pitcher of water for mouth rinsing.

Cider is a flavorsome drink, and is good with the cheeses that normally go well with apples — mild cheddars, Brie, Gouda, Bel Paese, Gruyère, and Camembert. There will always be people who swear that the only way to enjoy a class of cider is to irrigate a big chunk of Limburger and a slice of Bermuda onion with it, but generally *that* cheese, the blues, strong or smoked cheddars, and other powerful cheeses will dominate the taste and bouquet of the cider. Avoid them.

A blind tasting carries the distinct mood of a party game, which isn't necessarily bad in itself, but it is also one of the fairest ways to judge a cider. The possible prejudices, for or against, commercial brands or beloved (or hated) neighborhood cidermakers are removed.

If you give a blind tasting, first cover all the labels, and then number the bottles with tags or waterproof tape. The corresponding number, with the maker's name or the brand name, should go on a hidden slip of paper.

Chill the different ciders to the proper temperatures, uncork or recap them, and place them on different tables. Then give your guests testing evaluation sheets or just a pad and pencil. The simplest scoring can be a range from one to ten — the absolute worst to the superb. At the end of the tasting, individual bottle scores are totaled, and those with the highest score are the "winners" — or at least those that please the palates of most of the people there. The differences in preference will be obvious, and the reasons, given by way of post-mortem critique, fascinating.

Flavor Evaluation/Hard Cider

Name ————————————————————————————————

Date ————————————————————

Please characterize the flavor, using the following terms —
or, if necessary, some of your own choosing:

pleasant	sparkling	fruity
unpleasant	acidic	musty
bland	acetic, vinegary	woody
harsh	chemical	sweet
clean	astringent	sulfite
spoiled, off	bitter	H_2S
still	oxidized	

v. sl. (very slight)   med. (medium or moderate)

sl. (slight)   v. (very)

Indicate degree by modifying terms:
Assign flavor rating on a scale of 1–10
(4=unpalatable or unacceptable; 7=good)

CODE	FLAVOR CHARACTERIZATION	SCORE

Usually one or two ciders will outscore the others, and their makers will have good reason to smile. However, such a test may reveal more about the flavor preferences of your guests than the innate virtues of the "winning" cider. If you happen to invite a group of people who adore bonbons, heavily frosted cakes, and sweet cocktails, it is very likely that the favorite cider will be a sweet dessert beverage. If your guests come from English cider country, the winner will most likely be a dry, somewhat acidic, full-bodied cider with a bit of haze in it.

Cider to Drink and in the Kitchen

Cider is an extraordinarily versatile beverage, which can be enjoyed straight in its many variations — dry, semisweet, sweet, sparkling, still, apple brandy, applejack, each with its own nuances of bouquet and flavor — but it is equally at home in a staggering number of hot or mulled drinks, and an uncountable variety of cocktails and aperitifs. We list here only a few of the possible ways for the ardent cider lover to enjoy this convivial liquid. Much of the delight in making cider is in trying out new combinations of flavors and other liquors to titillate your palate and give you the reputation of mixing unique and personal drinks.

The Cidermaker's Undoing

A more potent wassail bowl, which we've often thought could be the source of a good country fiddle tune.

3   quarts apple brandy, or strong "frozen-heart" applejack, or Calvados
Peel of one lemon, pared paper thin
2   cups raw (unrefined) sugar or delicate honey
2   quarts semisweet cider

Heat the apple brandy, lemon peel, and sugar in a heavy enamel pan until steaming hot, but not boiling. If true applejack is being used, it must be at least 35 percent alcohol by volume. Stir occasionally, until the sugar or honey is quite dissolved. Pour the two bottles of cider in another enamel or stainless steel pan, and heat. Warm up your punch bowl with hot water, then pour in the hot brandy mixture. Set it alight with a match. As the blue flames leap, slowly pour in the very hot cider. On a cold day the pyrotechnics and steaming gold make the spirits more spiritous. Serve in warmed mugs, after the flames die out.

Mulled Cider

Mulled cider recipes are as numerous as the apples on a mature tree in a hit year. This is an old family favorite.

2 cinnamon sticks
2 quarts dry, aromatic cider
Dash of orange bitters
½ teaspoon allspice
6 whole cloves
½ cup jasmine, clover, or orange-blossom honey
½ cup light rum

Break off a piece of cinnamon stick the length of your thumb, and put it and all the other ingredients in a heavy enamel pan. Heat the mixture over a low fire, but do not let it boil. When it's steaming hot, rinse out your best punch bowl with hot water to warm it, then strain the mulled cider into the bowl. Break the other cinnamon stick into slivered swizzle sticks, and put one in each clear glass mug. Ladle in the hot mull and serve immediately. (Do not use buckwheat or goldenrod honey, as their strong flavors overwhelm the cider.)

THE PROPER VESSEL

All cider drinks, hot or cold, should be served in fine glassware or, for hot drinks, warmed mugs. Mason jars, water pitchers, or plastic containers may hold more, but they are hardly the noble vessels that augment the fine spirits that come from the apple.

New England Butter Rum Cider

For a quiet evening à deux *when the winter
wind howls outside and snow heaps up on the windowsill, with
a cheery fire snapping in the fireplace, there are few more
comforting and soul-satisfying drinks than this.*

3–4 teaspoons raw or brown sugar, or honey
  2 wide strips lemon, orange, or lime peel
  4 ounces dark or medium-dark rum, warmed
  2 teaspoons butter
  4 whole cloves
Pinch allspice
  1 pint strong, dry cider
  1 stick cinnamon, halved

Into each eight-ounce cup or mug put 1½–2 teaspoons sugar, a strip of
orange peel, and an ounce of rum. Be sure the peel is wet with alcohol,
then fire it with a match to release the citric oils. Afer the flame dies
out, recharge each cup with a second ounce of rum, a teaspoon of butter, the cloves, and allspice. Heat the cider until piping hot, pour into
the mugs, and stir with the cinnamon sticks.

Cooking with Cider and Apple Spirits

Cider has an honorable place in the kitchen. It is the basis of the
famed Norman cuisine built on the liberal use of apple spirits, cream,
and seafood. In North America, the Québec villages where many of the
people are descended from Normans have developed regional variations
of old recipes using cider. Indeed, it is possible to browse through any
Montreal bookstore and find several cookbooks devoted entirely to
cider cookery. Two of the best are: Jehane Benoit's *Ma cuisine au cidre,* éditions du Jour, Montreal, 1973, and Angèle Landry-Day's *Le cidre á boire et
á manger,* éditions du Pélican, Québec, 1971.

Not only can cider be substituted for white wine in almost any
recipe, but it lends an incomparable and unique flavor to dishes. The
marriage of cider, cream, *fines herbes,* and *fruits de mer* should be celebrated

in every cidermaker's kitchen. Cider is an excellent companion for fish, in poaching liquids or sauces, and also blends superbly with most cheeses and meats. Like wine, cider has a tenderizing effect on the tougher cuts of meat and elderly hens, and picks up the flavor of bland meats, such as veal and chicken.

Soups

Here are two delicious soups from different regions — New England and Québec.

Massachusetts Cider Soup

    2 quarts semisweet cider
    6 slices homemade bread, cut into small croutons
    4 tablespoons butter
    Salt and pepper
    3 eggs
    4 tablespoons brown sugar or ¼ cup maple syrup
    1¾ cups medium cream
    3 tablespoons flour
    2 ounces dark Jamaican rum
    Nutmeg
    Cinnamon

Bring the cider to a gradual boil in an enamel saucepan, while browning the croutons in butter. Salt and pepper the croutons and keep them warm. Skim the cider and set it on the back of the stove to keep warm. Crack the eggs into a bowl and beat them to a froth while adding the sugar, cream, flour, and rum, a little at a time to avoid lumps. Grate in the nutmeg and add the cinnamon. Return the cider to the fire, and whisk vigorously while pouring in the cream mixture slowly. Cook for a minute or two, stirring constantly, until the soup is piping hot and creamy. Garnish with the croutons and serve immediately.

Traditional New England recipe

Québec Cold Cucumber Soup with Cider

We find that this delicious soup is best when small garden-fresh cukes are picked early in the day and chilled for a few hours.

    3 cups chilled cucumbers, coarsely chopped
    1 cup cold sour cream
    1 cup cold dry cider, still or sparkling
    ½ cup chopped shallot tails
    1 teaspoon salt
Freshly ground pepper

All the ingredients should be very cold. Put them in an electric blender and run it at the highest speed for 30 seconds. Serve the creamy, cold soup in chilled cups garnished with toasted croutons.

Angèle Landry-Day's *Le cidre á boire et à manger*

Smoked Sausages with Apples and Cider

We like this spicy treat with a well-seasoned vinaigrette dressing salad as Mme. Landry-Day recommends, with a dash of strong mustard in the dressing.

    6 large cooking apples   12 to 18 link sausages
    2 tablespoons butter   1½ cups cider

Peel the apples, core them, and cut into sections. Heat a pan and add the butter. Cook the apples, turning them gently so as not to break them. Prick the sausages, and lay them on the apple slices. Add the cider, cover, and cook for 20 minutes.

Angèle Landry-Day's *Le cidre á boire et à manger*

Baked Beans in Cider

*This is the famous Québec way of making baked beans,
a recipe that deserves to be more widely known.
Other baked beans seem to have something vital lacking after
you have tasted them slowly baked in cider.*

4 cups dried beans	1 large onion, peeled
Cold water to cover	Dry mustard
1 bottle semisweet cider	½ cup molasses
½ pound salt pork	1 tablespoon salt

Pick over, wash, and soak the beans in cold water to cover for 12 hours.

Add the cider to the drained beans, bring to a boil and boil for about half an hour. Garnish the bottom of an earthenware bean pot with pieces of salt pork, reserving some strips for the top. Turn the beans and the cider liquid into the bean pot. Roll the whole onion in dry mustard and bury it in the middle of the beans. Pour the molasses over all. Place the rest of the salt pork on top of the beans, and add enough hot water to cover. Salt, and cover the bean pot.

Bake for 4 to 6 hours in a slow oven. An hour before the beans are done, uncover the pot and add water if the beans seem too dry.

Jehane Benoit's *Ma cuisine au cidre*

Sole in Cider

Any delicate-fleshed whole fish or fish fillets can be prepared this way.

   7 tablespoons butter
   2 tablespoons chopped parsley
   2-pound sole or flounder
   ⅓ cup dry bread crumbs
   1 cup hard cider
   Salt and pepper
   4 tablespoons heavy cream

Dot a large, shallow, heatproof serving dish with half the butter and sprinkle with half the parsley. Place a well-trimmed sole in the dish. Sprinkle with the rest of the parsley and the bread crumbs and dot with the rest of the butter. Pour in the cider and season with salt and pepper.

Place the fish in a 350°F (176.6°C) oven and let it simmer (the liquid must not actually boil) for about 15 minutes or until the fish is cooked. Just before serving, add the heavy cream. Serve the fish from the dish in which it has been cooked.

Mapie, the Countess de Toulouse-Lautrec, *La Cuisine de France*

Boiled Cider

Boiled cider, which is used in many recipes, in apple butter, applesauce, and mincemeat, is nothing more than concentrated cider. This ancient and simple way of concentrating cider consists of boiling down fresh cider in an open kettle until the juice is reduced to one-fourth or one-fifth the original volume. Strong, dark, drinking ciders have been made by adding boiled cider to the fresh juice in the barrel and fermenting the lot, but modern-day cidermakers may find this concentrate more useful in the kitchen than the cidery.

For the best boiled cider, the apple pomace should be pressed as soon as it is grated, and as soon as the juice is collected from the press it should go into the evaporator, which can be as simple as a large enamel roasting pan. If the juice, or the pomace from which the juice is presssed, is allowed to stand for any length of time, the final boiled cider product will be much inferior.

Reduce five gallons of cider to one gallon over a quick, hot fire. The process should be as brief as possible. The proper consistency will be reached when a candy thermometer registers about 216°F (102.2°C). A Brix hydrometer reading will measure about 47.5°. (See pages 24–26 for information on how to use the hydrometer.) After concentration, strain the cider through a cloth, and let it stand for twenty-four hours until any sediment settles to the bottom. The clear liquid should be drawn off into a clean canning jar, and preserved by processing in boiling water for fifteen minutes.

Cider Jelly

Households that like cider apple jelly and the delicate herb-flavored apple jellies — such as thyme, marjoram, mint, sage, and summer savory — can press a run of apples especially for jelly. Apples contain natural pectin and sugar, so normally nothing need be added to the juice to make a tasty jelly.

A mixture of fully ripe apple varieties with an emphasis on crab apples or wild apple-crabs will make the best jelly. Dessert apples alone, such as McIntosh, Delicious, or Cortland, do not make good jelly and should be used only if nothing else is available. Tart, sharp apples make the most delicious jellies of all. You may press sound apples, culls, windfalls (as long as they are not bruised and fermenting), or the cores and skins left over from an apple-peeling session. If you dry apples, you will have a good supply of skins and cores for jelly making. One bushel of fruit will give about four pounds of jelly.

1. Grind the apples and press them.
2. Immediately after pressing, begin boiling down the fresh sweet cider. Old manuals advise that jelly makers never boil jelly on days when the temperature is above 66°F (18.8°C) and cite around 41°F (5°C) as the ideal temperature for jelly making. The major problem with making jelly on a warm day is that the juice begins to ferment very quickly, and fermentation can adversely affect the jelly's keeping qualities. Rapidly boil down the cider until the jelly "sheets." When the apple is concentrated to the jelling point, it will be reduced from about seven volumes of cider to one volume

of jelly. Do not boil the jelly over a low, slow heat — this makes the end product dark and gives it a caramel flavor and tough texture. The process should be rapid.

3. Strain the finished jelly through one layer of cheesecloth into clean, dry jelly jars. Screw on vacuum covers and let them cool until sealed. Or let the jelly set, pour melted paraffin on top, cover, and store.

Herb Jellies

Before removing the jelly from the heat, tie a bunch of fresh herbs — mint, basil, thyme, marjoram, lemon verbena, tarragon, sage, rose geranium, summer savory, or wild strawberry leaves — bruise the leaves, and drag the bunch through the jelly repeatedly until you get the strength of flavoring you like. A drop or two of food coloring — green for mint and sage, red for rose geranium or wild strawberry leaves — may make the jelly more attractive to you.

Large Amounts of Jelly

One of the most frustrating harvest-time chores is making small batches of jelly. Every cookbook and every commercial pectin manufacturer warns repeatedly that only small batches of jelly should be attempted, and the householder who envisions fifty jars of jelly on the pantry shelves may resent the tedious repetition of a process that yields only four or five small jars per session. The amateur cidermaker who owns a Brix-scaled hydrometer is free from these petty warnings and can make large batches of cider jelly. The Brix hydrometer is a reliable guide for the addition of sugar *if necessary* (very little sugar is needed to make apply jelly). If the jelly is to be safe from spoilage, it must achieve a Brix reading of 55° to 59°. You can often attain this reading without adding any sugar at all, depending on the amount of natural sugar in your apples. If your concentrated cider jelly falls below these Brix readings, judiciously add enough sugar to bring the level up to the desired reading. Let the cider reduce by at least three volumes before testing, and cool your test sample to 60°F (15.5°C) before taking the Brix reading, or make temperature corrections.

Cider Applesauce

An old Vermont way of making cider applesauce is to core and quarter tart apples, place them in an enamel pan, and pour in fresh sweet cider to cover. Cook until the apples are very soft, sweeten with maple syrup, and simmer until the sauce is thick and deliciously rich. Pack into clean canning jars and process in a hot-water bath for 15 minutes. In the old days, the sauce was packed directly into wooden firkins or other applesauce tubs and set out to freeze solid in cold winter weather. As the applesauce was needed, it was chopped out of the storage tub and thawed, a process that traditionally improved the flavor of the sauce.

Apple Cider Jelly

Excellent cider jelly is easily made by cooking tart apples in hard or sweet cider for 10 minutes, then straining the pulp through cheesecloth. Reserve the liquid. Add water to barely cover the apple pulp, and cook this for 15 minutes. Strain the juice into the cider liquid.

Gently boil down the combined liquids until the jelly "sheets." Pack in hot sterile jars immediately. Apple jelly needs no store-bought pectin, for the fruit is loaded with this natural jelling material. You may make jelly the same way using the pomace from the cider press instead of whole apples.

— 6 —

CIDER
AND THE LAW

$\mathcal{T}$*he home cidermaker,* like home wine- and beermakers, must be familiar with federal and state or provincial laws that affect the production and sale of cider if he or she wants to avoid the specter of revenue agents bursting through the door with axes, warrants, and the like and threatening stiff fines and possible jail sentences.

U.S. FEDERAL LAW AND REGULATIONS

"Natural" Cider. Hard cider is the noneffervescent product of the normal alcoholic fermentation of apple juice without preservative methods or materials, and when made at home or on the farm is not subject to federal excise tax. Be aware, however, that the Department of the Treasury has a broad concept of what constitutes "hard cider" (all ciders, except those under 7 percent alcohol by volume that thus fall under Food and Drug Administration regulations, and personal-use wine) and that the issue is further complicated by differences in labeling requirements from the FDA.

Cider, or hard cider, may be sold, free of any federal excise taxes, an exemption that was provided in order to allow farmers and apple growers to continue the tradition of producing cider for sale at roadside stands. Surprisingly few farmers and apple growers in the United States take advantage of this exemption, limiting themselves almost exclusively to the sale of sweet cider, or fresh apple juice. The federal law reads:

Sec. 5042. Exemption from Tax. (a) TAX-FREE PRODUCTION. —
(1) CIDER. — Subject to regulations prescribed by the Secretary, the noneffervescent product of the normal alcoholic fermentation of apple juice only, which is produced at a place other than a bonded wine cellar and without the use of preservative methods or materials, and which is sold or offered for sale as cider and not as wine or as a substitute for wine, shall not be subject to tax as wine nor to the provisions of subchapter F.

However, before you start siphoning off jugs of your cellar's best to sell to passing cider lovers, check with your state officials — either the Department of Liquor Controls or the State Attorney General's office for the laws and regulations that govern the manufacture and sale of cider in your particular state. These laws vary considerably from state to state, as the examples below in the section *State Law* indicate.

Apple "Wine." Legislation enacted in 1979 defines who may make such wine and how much. The law reads in part:

(A) EXEMPTION. — Any adult may, without payment of tax, produce wine for personal or family use and not for sale.
(B) LIMITATION. — The aggregate amount of wine exempt from tax under this paragraph with respect to any household shall not exceed —
(i) 200 gallons per calendar year if there are two or more adults in such household, or
(ii) 100 gallons per calendar year if there is only one adult in such household.
(C) ADULTS. — For purposes of this paragraph, the term 'adult' means an individual who has attained eighteen years of age, or the minimum age (if any) established by law applicable in the locality in which the household is situated at which wine may be sold to individuals, whichever is greater.

Regulations

Copies of the federal regulations covering production of alcoholic beverages may be purchased from local U.S. Government bookstores or from the following source:
U.S. Government Printing Office
Superintendent of Documents
Mail Stop: SSOP
Washington, DC 20402-9328

ATF regulations are codified as 27 CFR, and Volume 1, Parts 1 to 199, contains the most important regulations for beer and wine.

	BEER	**WINE**
Production	Part 25	Part 24
Labeling	Part 7	Part 4

Health warning statement rules for both wine and beer are in Part 16.

Technical Services Offices

By the year 2001, all Technical Services activities will be consolidated into the office in Cincinnati.

Chief, Technical Services
Bureau of Alcohol, Tobacco and Firearms
550 Main Street, Room 6525
Cincinnati, OH 45202
(513) 684-3334
Ohio, West Virginia, Kentucky, Indiana, Illinois, Michigan, Wisconsin, Minnesota, North Dakota, South Dakota, Virginia, Washington DC, Utah, Wyoming, Iowa, Missouri, Arkansas, Louisiana, Texas, Oklahoma, Kansas, Nebraska, Colorado, New Mexico, Arizona.

Chief, Technical Services
Bureau of Alcohol, Tobacco and Firearms
The Curtis Center, Suite 875
Independence Square West
Philadelphia, PA 19106
(215) 597-2246
Maine, New Hampshire, Vermont, Massachusetts, Connecticut, Rhode Island, New York, New Jersey, Pennsylvania, Delaware, Maryland.

Chief, Technical Services
Bureau of Alcohol, Tobacco and Firearms
2600 Century Parkway, NE, Suite 305
Atlanta, GA 30345
(404) 679-5080
Alabama, Florida, Georgia, Mississippi, North Carolina, South Carolina, Tennessee

Chief, Technical Services
Bureau of Alcohol, Tobacco and Firearms
221 Main Street, 11th Floor
San Francisco, CA 94105
(415) 744-7011
Montana, Idaho, Nevada, California, Oregon, Washington, Alaska, Hawaii, Guam.

Chief, Puerto Rico Operations
Carlos E. Chardon Street
Room 659
Hato Rey, PR 00918-0001
(809) 766-5584
Puerto Rico, Virgin Islands.

Cider distillates. Unfortunately for those of us who like homemade Calvados, apple marc, and applejack, *"there are no provisions in law or regulations for a period to cover the production of distilled spirits for personal consumption,"* stated Jerry Bowerman, chief, Wine, Beer, and Spirits Regulations Branch, Department of the Treasury, Bureau of Alcohol, Tobacco and Firearms. He further said:

> A person who desires to produce distilled spirit must qualify as a distilled spirit plant proprietor prior to commencing actual production. Among the requirements prescribed in Code of Federal Regulations, Title 27 CFR, Part 19, Subparts F, G, and H, qualification would entail the submission and approval of applications for registration as a distilled spirits plant and for an operating permit to cover the various activities to be conducted, the registration of all stills, preparation of a plat, plans and flow diagrams, filing of bonds and consent of surety, and installation of security devices such as walls and fences to protect the premises.

Moreover, *all* distilled spirits produced for consumption are taxed at the rate of $13.50 per proof gallon.

Home cidermakers who think they've found a way through the federal barriers to farm-made applejack by making "frozen-heart" applejack — separating the ethyl alcohol out from the chief by fractional crystallization — will be disappointed to know that

> The product derived by the drawing off of ethyl alcohol from a barrel of frozen hard cider *would be considered to be distilled spirits* as defined in 26 U.S.C. 5002(a)(80)(A). It is unlawful to produce any distilled spirits at a place other than a qualified distilled spirits plant. To do so would subject the producer to the penalties of 26 U.S.C. 5601.

The penalties are a fine of not more than $10,000 or imprisonment for not more than five years, or both, for each offense.

State Law

The following two examples of state legislation regarding cider — New York and Vermont — are given here to show the very different regulations affecting the sale of the same product. Find out the laws of your state before you start selling hard cider.

In New York, cider is defined as follows, as amended in 1977:

"Cider" means the *partially* or *fully* fermented juice of fresh whole apples, containing more than three and two-tenths per centum but not more than seven per centum alcohol by volume, when used for beverage purposes, and to which nothing has been added to increase the alcoholic content provided by natural fermentation. Nothing contained in this subdivision shall be deemed to preclude the use of such methods or materials as may be necessary to encourage a normal alcoholic fermentation and to make a product that is free of microbiological activity at the time of sale. Cider may be sweetened after fermentation with apple juice, apple juice concentrate, or sugar, separately or in combination. Cider may contain retained or added carbon dioxide.

In order to make cider for sale and to sell it wholesale, you must apply for a *cider producers and wholesalers license*, at an annual cost of $125. (Article IV-A, Section 58.) But even after you have obtained this license, if you want to sell fermented cider to the public, you need *another* certificate with another annual fee of $125 and a lot of string attached to it under Sec. 58-b of the New York State Alcoholic Beverage Control Law.

> Retail sale of cider by wholesale licenses. Notwithstanding any other law upon payment to the liquor authority of an additional annual fee of one hundred twenty-five dollars, the liquor authority may in its discretion and upon such terms and conditions as it may prescribe, issue to a licensed cider producer upon application thereof a certificate authorizing such producer to sell cider at retail in sealed containers to a householder for consumption in his home, but no sale to such householder shall be in quantities aggregating more than fifteen gallons. Revenues received by any such licensed cider producer from the sale of cider at retail to householders under such a certificate during the term thereof shall not exceed five per centum of all the revenues derived by such licensee from the sale of apples and cider during such term.

It is clear that in New York the laws regulating cider production and sales are geared to benefit large apple-grower/cidermaker businessmen and businesses holding retail licenses. The small farmer with a few acres of orchard or the amateur cidermaker who puts up a good barrel or two and envisions picking up Christmas shopping money by selling cider to the neighbors is out in left field. Here the state laws are more stringent than the federal, even subverting the reason for the federal tax exemption on cider.

In Vermont the law is somewhat more liberal regarding sales of fermented cider. Section 61 of the Vermont Statutes Annotated, Title 7, states:

> A person, partnership, association or corporation shall not furnish or sell, or expose or keep to sell, any malt or vinous beverage or spirits, or manufacture, sell, barter, transport, import, export, deliver, prescribe, furnish or possess any alcohol except as authorized by this title. However, this chapter shall not apply to the furnishing of such beverages or spirits by a person in his private dwelling, unless to an habitual drunkard, or unless such dwelling becomes a place of public resort, nor to the sale of fermented cider by the barrel or cask of not less than thirty-two liquid gallons capacity, provided the same is delivered and removed from the vendor's premises in such barrel or cask at the time of such sale.

In short, the cidermaker in Vermont can freely sell his product, without tax, license, certificate or fee, provided he sells at least thirty-two gallons per sale in a cask or barrel of at least thirty-two gallons capacity.

CANADA

Federal and provincial laws regulate the manufacture of alcoholic beverages and tobacco in Canada. The federal authorities are primarily interested in controlling distilling, strong liquor, beer, and tobacco for excise reasons, while the provinces have the most direct jurisdiction over home and commercial production of wine and cider. Federal controls are exerted in several provincial areas such as homebrewing, where in Québec and Ontario, for example, it is legal to make beer for home consumption but only after the would-be maker obtains a letter of consent from the nearest collector of federal excise. Federal controls also relate to commercial wineries and cideries via the Canada Food and Drugs Act Standards, and, on the local level through the enforcement of the *Canada Temperance Act* through which, upon petition and vote, the trafficking in intoxicating liquors in any "dry" county, town, or parish is prohibited.

For the home cidermaker it's clear squeezing, but for Canadians who want to sell their fermented apple, the laws can be liberal or rigid, depending on the province. Québec and Ontario are examples. The home cidermaker who decides to go commercial in either of these provinces must first be licensed. In Ontario the licensing provisions come under the Ontario Wine Law and require that the premises first be approved by the board before a permit is issued. Québec's industrial permits are in two categories — "strong cider" (cider containing 7 to 13 percent alcohol in volume), and "weak cider" (cider containing from 2½ to 7 percent alcohol).

However, the door is practically closed to the average home cidermaker in Québec who wants to sell a little cider at a farm stand or from his kitchen. Québec's commercial cidermaking permits are limited to apple growers, associations of apple growers, or large corporations. Moreover, Québec's commercial ciders must be made from at least 90 percent apples harvested in the province, and the law is backed up with the threat of permit revocation. Ostensibly this requirement is aimed at resolving an agricultural economic problem — what to do with the surplus apple crop — and it effectively blocks the use of the less-expensive apple concentrates by cidermakers.

Though Québec's orchard regions were once a cider bootlegger's utopia, the penalties for selling homemade alcoholic cider have just about dried up the once-lucrative market: fines of $200 to $2,000 for the first offence, and $2,000 to $10,000 for all subsequent violations.

In 1977 British Columbia enacted a law that allows the production and sale of cider from one's own orchard. Since statutes are continually undergoing revision, persons desiring to enter the alcoholic cider business would be wise to first query their respective provincial liquor control boards or other regulatory agencies.

The Excise Act (Canada) S.R. CE-12 (1972), Section 3 (1) prohibits the home manufacture of apple brandy and any other spirit by distillation or any process whatever which, as in the United States, includes fractional crystallization. Controls are effected nationally through a system of licensing, and provincially, as in Québec, by permit.

APPENDIX:

MAKING YOUR OWN EQUIPMENT

Would-be cidermakers who are short on cash but have some carpentry skills can make almost every piece of large equipment needed, either from plans, from ingenuity and imagination, or from mail-order kits.

PLANS

There are several good plans for homemade cider presses. One of the most adapted is the cider press designed in Summerland, British Columbia, for the Canada Department of Agriculture, with the assistance of C. L. Lackey. These plans can be found in the CDA publication "Home and Farm Preparation of Fruit Juices, Cider and Wines," available to Canadians from the Research Station, Summerland, British Columbia V0H 1Z0. The plans for the press have also been reprinted as Farmer's Bulletin No. 114, available from the Canada Department of Agriculture, Ottawa. Additionally, *Organic Gardening and Farming,* the American magazine now simply known as *Organic Gardening,* carried plans for a homemade cider press modeled closely on this Canadian prototype in its October 1975 issue.

The "Homemade Fruit Juice Press," which can be used either for cider- or winemaking, was designed by Donald L. Downing, retired associate professor of the Food Processing Extension Service at the New York State Agricultural Experiment Station in Geneva, New York. These plans, reproduced in part below, are available as Report No. 8, July 1972, from the station by contacting Mark McLellan or Robert Kime.

Materials

All lumber should be hardwood unless otherwise specified. All nails should be corrosion resistant or stainless steel. If the designated carriage or machine bolts are not available, the same diameter of threaded rod may be used.

Lumber

4	46″ x 4″ x 4″
7	24″ x 4″ x 4″
1	½″ x 14″ x 14″ — may be marine-grade plywood
1	¾″ x 14″ x 14″ — may be marine-grade plywood
1	¾″ x 17″ x 17″ — may be marine-grade plywood
46	¼″ x 1″ x 14″
20	¼″ x 1½″ x 14″
5	¼″ x 2″ x 20″
4	¼″ x 1½″ x 17″
4	¾″ x 2″ x 14″

Hardware

1	¾″ corrosion-resistant metal or plastic pipe
4	⅜″ x 6″ carriage
4	⅜″ x 11″ carriage
2	⅜″ x 18″ threaded rods
6	30″ x 30″ press cloths
1	1½-ton, 5–8″ lift hydraulic jack

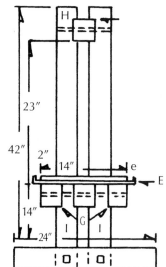

Side cross-sectional view

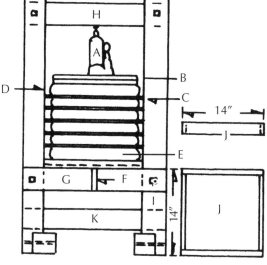

Front view of the homemade press

Cheese form

1. Notch the four upright timbers, I, in the appropriate places. Lumber should not be notched more than one-half its width.
2. Assemble uprights, I, base supports, press base supports, G and K, and press top, H, as shown, using the proper bolts. A metal plate, 3 x 3 inches, should be fastened at the point of contact of the jack.
3. Assemble the press base E by fastening the $\frac{3}{4} \times 17 \times 17$ inch board to supports G. The four $\frac{1}{4} \times 1\frac{1}{2} \times 17$ inch slats are attached to the sides of the base board E. The $\frac{1}{2} \times 14 \times 14$ inch board is centered on the larger board to channel the juice to the outlet F.
4. Assemble five 14 x 14 inch racks from $\frac{1}{4} \times 1$ inch and $\frac{1}{4} \times 1\frac{1}{2}$ inch slats. The wider slats are used at the edges. The center slat on one side may be 20 inches long and 2 inches wide so that it will serve as a guide between the uprights I.
5. The jack support, B, is made from the $\frac{3}{4} \times 14 \times 14$ inch board with six $\frac{1}{4} \times 1$ inch slats nailed across the grain on one side. A permanent jack support held by springs as in figure 4 may be used instead.
6. The cheese form J is made 14 x 14 inches with the $\frac{3}{4} \times 2 \times 14$ inch pieces.
7. The juice outlet, F, is made by drilling a suitable hole in the base plate to place a $\frac{3}{4}$-inch tube of acid-resistant metal or plastic.
8. White grain sacking or white duck cloth may be used. Specifically prepared cotton or nylon press cloths may be obtained from:

Day Equipment Corporation
1402 East Monroe
Goshen, IN 46526

OESCO, Inc.
P.O. Box 540
Conway, MA 01341

National Filter Media Corporation
1717 Dixwell Avenue
P.O. Box 4217
Hamden, CT 06514

9. All wooden parts of the press that come in direct contact with the juice should be coated with hot paraffin or painted with several coats of epoxy paint.
10. If plywood boards are used, the ends may be covered with the appropriate-sized half round.

INGENUITY

If you have an inventive turn of mind you may want to try working out your own cider-press arrangement. Successful cider presses have been rigged up by mounting an upside-down car bumper jack on a platform, and using the base plate of the jack to exert pressure on the apple pomace in the cheese racks below the jack. This simple tool can exert a thousand pounds of pressure on the pomace, and does a very credible job of extracting the juice.

Pollard and Beech, in their excellent book, *Cider-Making*, remark that anyone with the right tools can make a "simple scratcher mill" or apple grinder by using the gearing and rollers from an old hand wringer for wet laundry, and attaching an apple hopper so that the fruit feeds in the rollers. The rollers should be set with flat-headed stainless steel screws embedded in a spiral pattern, so that fruit is shredded as it passes between the rollers.

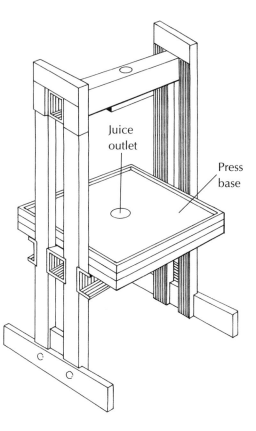

Diagram of a simple fruit press you can build.

Kits

Cider-press kits, accessories, and supplies can also be obtained from the following mail-order sources:

All Seasons Homestead Helpers
P.O. Box 99
Jeffersonville, VT 05464
Phone (802) 644-2658

Cumberland General Store
#1 Highway 68
Crossville, TN 38555
Phone (800) 334-4640

Great American Fruit Press Co.
111 Township Road 900
West Salem, OH 44287
Phone (419) 869-7541 or
(800) 285-4167

Happy Valley Manufacturing
16577 West 327th Street
Paola, KS 66071-9516
Phone (913) 849-3103
Fax (913) 849-3104

Jaffrey Manufacturing Company
Box 23527–ME
Shawnee Mission, KS 66223
Phone (913) 849-3139

Lehman's Non-Electric Catalog
1 Lehman Circle
P.O. Box 41
Kidron, OH 44636
Phone (330) 857-5757
Fax (330) 857-5785
Catalog $3.00; refunded with order over $20

Electronic Resources

Electronic resources are constantly growing and changing. Two useful sites on the Internet are:

http://www.teleport.com/~incider/ (U.S.A. source)
http://sun1.bham.ac.uk/graftong/cider/ (U.K. source)

Information on "real" cider and perry (from pears), including links to other sites, plans for presses, history of cidermaking, regulations, and other helpful data.

INDEX

Bold indicates chart material, Italics indicate illustrations

OTHER STOREY TITLES YOU WILL ENJOY

The Apple Cookbook, by Olwen Woodier. This book is an unusual collection of recipes using America's favorite fruit in beverages, appetizers, snacks, brunch, entrees, and of course, desserts. It also includes apple buying tips, taste comparisons, and instructions for preserving. 160 pages. Paperback. ISBN #0-88266-367-4.

Better Beer & How to Brew It, by M. R. Reese. With this illustrated step-by-step guide, beginners can learn how easy and inexpensive it is to brew beer at home — from choosing the equipment and ingredients, to preparing, fermenting, and aging, to bottling and serving. 128 pages. Paperback. ISBN #0-88266-257-0.

Brew Chem 101: The Basics of Homebrewing Chemistry, by Lee W. Janson, Ph.D. This book explains the basic science behind the components of beer and fermentation in an easy-to-read style. 128 pages. Paperback. ISBN #0-88266-940-0.

Brew Ware: How to Find, Adapt & Build Homebrewing Equipment, by Karl F. Lutzen and Mark Stevens. Using this fully illustrated handbook, readers can create a home brewery that is safe and makes brewing easier. 304 pages. Paperback. ISBN #0-88266-926-5.

Brewing Made Easy: From the First Batch to Creating Your Own Recipes, by Joe Fisher and Dennis Fisher. A how-to guide for brewing your own beer at home, including equipment, preparation, recipes, helpful brewing tips, and hydrometer use. 96 pages. Paperback. ISBN #0-88266-941-9.

Brewing the World's Great Beers: A Step-by-Step Guide, by Dave Miller. Easy-to-follow instructions and recipes for brewing world-class beer at home, beginning with the basic method of brewing using easy-to-use malt extracts and moving to more sophisticated methods. 160 pages. Paperback. ISBN #0-88266-775-0. Hardcover. ISBN #0-88266-776-9.

Country Wines: Making & Using Wines from Herbs, Fruits, Flowers & More, by Pattie Vargas and Rich Gulling. This book explains how to make delicious wines from fruits and berries, flowers, and herbs. 176 pages. Paperback. ISBN #0-88266-749-1.

From Vines to Wines: The Complete Guide to Growing Grapes and Making Your Own Wine, by Jeff Cox. Cox takes the home wine maker through the entire process from evaluating the site and choosing the best grape species, to vineyard care, bottling, supplies, and troubleshooting. 288 pages. Paperback. ISBN #0-88266-528-6.

Fruits and Berries for the Home Garden, by Lewis Hill. Master gardener Lewis Hill provides instructions for the absolute beginner and bushels of tips for people who've been growing fruits for years. 288 pages. Paperback. ISBN #0-88266-763-7.

Making Homemade Wine (Country Wisdom Bulletin A-75), by Robert Cluett. Step-by-step information on mastering the skill of home wine making, including equipment, troubleshooting techniques, and recipes. 32 pages. Paperback. ISBN #0-88266-289-9.

Making Liqueurs for Gifts (Country Wisdom Bulletin A-101), by Mimi Freid. Step-by-step information for making liqueurs at home, including equipment, gift presentation ideas, and fruit, specialty, and herbal liqueur recipes. 32 pages. Paperback. ISBN #0-88266-499-9.

These books and other Storey books are available at your bookstore, farm store, garden center, or directly from Storey Publishing, Schoolhouse Road, Pownal, Vermont 05261, or by calling 1-800-441-5700. www.storey.com